THE RACIAL IMAGINARY:
WRITERS ON RACE IN THE LIFE OF THE MIND

THE RACIAL IMAGINARY:

WRITERS ON RACE
IN THE LIFE OF THE MIND
EDS. CLAUDIA RANKINE, BETH LOFFREDA, AND MAX KING CAP

Book design by Douglas Kearney

Published in the United States by Fence Books
Science Library, 320
University at Albany
1400 Washington Avenue, Albany, NY 12222

www.fenceportal.org

Printed by Versa Press, Inc., East Peoria, IL, USA
and distributed by Small Press Distribution
and Consortium Book Sales and Distribution.

Cap, Max King [1963–]
Loffreda, Beth [1967–]
Rankine, Claudia [1963–]

Third Printing

Publisher's Cataloguing-in-Publication Data

The Racial imaginary : writers on race in the life
of the mind / [edited by] Claudia Rankine ;
  Beth Loffreda ; Max King Cap.
  p. cm.
  ISBN 978-1934200797

1. Race in literature. 2. Race relations in literature. 3. American literature—African American
authors—History and criticism. 4. Poetry—
Black authors—History and criticism.
5. African Americans in literature. 6. Poetics.
7. Identity politics. I. Rankine, Claudia. III.
Loffreda, Beth. III. Cap, Max King. III. Title.

PS228 .R32 R33 2015
810.9/358 —dc23

2015930807

ISBN 13: 978-1-93420-079-7

Fence Books are published in partnership with
the University at Albany and the New York State
Writers Institute, and with invaluable support
from the New York State Council on the Arts
and the National Endowment for the Arts.

"[Table of Contents] anxiety

is an affliction . . ."*

LIVES

READINGS

I wanted the point of view to

CRITIQUES

not settle in a single body.**

POETICS

Kate Clark, **Pray** (detail), 2012 *With a nod to myths that tell of gods who appeared as and/or consorted with animals, Kate Clark's sculptures cut to the taxonomic quick to claim us all as subjects in the Kingdom of Animalia.* MKC

INTRODUCTION
BETH LOFFREDA
& CLAUDIA RANKINE

The Racial Imaginary project began in March 2011, when Claudia composed an open letter about race and the creative imagination that she placed on a website[1] and invited others to respond to however they wished. If they sent a response, it was posted on the website. The notion of an open letter carried in its name a starting point for the form of these responses: personal, intimate meditations, like letters, that would nevertheless be available to an audience of more than one. Over time, Claudia invited Beth to join her in assembling the following set of compositions; and Claudia invited Max to seek out a corresponding assemblage of visual artists. This book gathers up a representative collection of what we received.

The Racial Imaginary found its start in a few intuitions. We are all, no matter how little we like it, the bearers of unwanted and often shunned memory, of a history whose infiltrations are at times so stealthy we can pretend otherwise, and at times so loud we can't hear much of anything else. We're still there—there differently than those before us, but there, otherwise known as here. And that matters for writers. That's the first intuition. The second one is that it seems a lot of us here when asked to talk about race are most comfortable, or least uncomfortable, talking about it in the language of scandal. We're all a little relieved by scandal. It's so satisfying, so clear, so easy. The wronged. The evildoers. The undeserving. The shady. The good intentions and the cynical manipulations. The righteous side taking, the head shaking. Scandal is such a help-

[1] http://www.newmediapoets.com/claudia_rankine/open/open.html

I met an other

ful, such a relieving distraction. There are times when scandal feels like the sun that race revolves around. And so it is hard to reel conversations about race back from the heavy gravitational pull of where we so often prefer them to be.

There are a few other common languages for race that we'd like to evade, too. One is the sentimental, which rather than polarize, as scandal does, smudges. The other is even simpler: the past tense. Because if we're not scandalized or sentimental about race, we're often jaded instead. This, again? Didn't we wear this out already? Hasn't enough been said, haven't enough already said it? We don't want to substitute the jaded for the shocked, nor the sentimental for the jaded. Especially when it comes to writing. This collection is founded on the idea that it's worth trying to write about race, again—in particular that something valuable happens when an individual writer reflects on race in the making of creative work. Writing could be said to rest on the faith that there is something of value in witnessing an individual mind speaking in and to its ordinary history. This never stops. And it's not that the individual expression is, because of its individuality and expressiveness, sacred, beyond questioning. We're all disagreeing in one way or another in this collection. As editors we're not seeking agreement or consensus. But we believe in the beauty and importance of an individual writer speaking in and to her history with as

much depth and seriousness as she can muster, especially when that history doesn't present it-self as an otherwise-sayable event. And since race is one of the prime ways history thrives in us, it matters that each writer says her own thing.

This collection then is best approached as a document. A moment in time, here. A series of moments in a series of individual creative lives, a collective transcript of people who were, in this time in this place, moved to respond to a question. Much can be gleaned from its incompletion, its absences, the detectable pressures on both what is here and what is not, and for those reasons too we present it to you as a document. Something to investigate, to both trust and question. We feel the absences and the pressures ourselves very much, and we at times felt some editorial impulses regarding balance, representation, that we ended up rejecting. Rather than round out the collection, whatever that might mean, we've as much as possible left it unretouched—an instance, a demonstration, of a question asked and then answered, however imperfectly or incompletely.

As we wrote this introduction, Claudia and Beth read, individually and together, writers who have deeply shaped our own view of this thing we're calling the racial imaginary, and who can be heard in what follows: Fred Moten, Lauren Berlant, Robin D. G. Kelley, Judith Butler, Toni Morrison, and most of all James Baldwin. They

and it was hard!

helped us to see more clearly the literary moment the writing in this collection partially documents, and two intertwined things about that moment in particular. One is that in our moment, writing about race has its own set of literary and intellectual conventions that we writers sometimes use and sometimes struggle to reinvent. The other is that certain assumptions about craft and aesthetics can and do warp the conversation among writers about race. These two matters typically appear in a complex, troubled embrace.

Here are a few of the tropes you would likely encounter if you started looking at writers writing about race these days. One: I met an other and it was hard! That is lightly said, but that is the essence of the trope: the anxious, entangling encounters with others that happen before anyone even makes it to the page, and that appear there primarily as an occasion for the writer to encounter her own feelings. Another: I needed to travel to see race, I went to Africa or to Asia or to the American South or to Central America—wherever I would consider not-home—to look at race, as if it now mainly can be found in a sort of wildlife preserve separate from ordinary, everyday experience. Another: race is racism. And lastly: the enduring American thing of seeing race solely as a white and black affair, of considering anti-black racism to be the scene where the real race stuff goes down. Which is accompanied by the trope of the discount: the one that fails

to extend to other people of color an authentic fullness of experience, a myopia that renders them in the terms of the "not really."

The matter of craft comes up clearly when we encounter the various tropes that white writers take recourse to repeatedly when race is on the table. These tropes are typically heartfelt; but their repetition should be taken as a sign. Here's one: "The imagination is a free space, and I have the right to imagine from the point of view of anyone I want—it is against the nature of art itself to place limits on who or what I can imagine." This language of rights is as extraordinary as it is popular, and it is striking to see how many white writers in particular conceive of race and the creative imagination as the question of whether they feel they are permitted to write a character, or a voice, or a persona, "of color." This is a decoy whose lusciousness is evident in the frequency with which it is chased. The decoy itself points to the whiteness of whiteness—that to write race would be to write "color," to write an other.

But to argue that the imagination is or can be somehow free of race—that it's the one region of self or experience that is free of race—and that I have a right to imagine whoever I want, and that it damages and deforms my art to set limits on my imagination—acts as if the imagination is not part of me, is not created by the same web of history and culture that made "me." So to say, as a white writer, that I have a right to write

. . . the scene of race taking up

about whoever I want, including writing from the point of view of characters of color—that I have a right of access and that my artistry is harmed if I am told I cannot do so—is to make a mistake. It is to begin the conversation in the wrong place. It is the wrong place because, for one, it mistakes critical response for prohibition (we've all heard the inflationary rhetoric of scandalized whiteness). But it is also a mistake because our imaginations are creatures as limited as we ourselves are. They are not some special, uninfiltrated realm that transcends the messy realities of our lives and minds. To think of creativity in terms of transcendence is itself specific and partial—a lovely dream perhaps, but an inhuman one.

It is not only white writers who make a prize of transcendence, of course. Many writers of all backgrounds see the imagination as ahistorical, as a generative place where race doesn't and shouldn't enter, a space for bodies to transcend the legislative, the economic—transcend the stuff that doesn't lend itself much poetry. In this view the imagination is postracial, a posthistorical and postpolitical utopia. Some writers of color, in the tradition of previous writers like Countee Cullen (a sly and complicated tradition, we acknowledge), don't want to have race dirtying up the primacy of the imaginative work; want the merits of the work made free by more neutral standards. To bring up race for these writers

is to inch close to the anxious space of affirmative action, the scarring qualifieds.

So everyone is here.

Transcendence is unevenly distributed and experienced, however. White writers often begin from a place where transcendence is a given—one already has access to all, one already is permitted to inhabit all, to address all. The crisis comes when one's access is questioned. For writers of color, transcendence can feel like a distant and elusive thing, because writers of color often begin from the place of being addressed, and accessed. To be a person of color in a racist culture is to be always addressable, as Judith Butler has argued, and to be addressable means one is always within stigma's reach. So one's imagination is influenced by the recognition of the need to account for this situation—even in the imagination, one feels accountable, one feels one must counter. So a writer of color may be fueled by the desire to exit that place of addressability. At the same time one may wish to write of race. And again at the same time one may wish to do any or all of these things inside a set of literary institutions that expect and even reward certain predictable performances of race. There can be a comfort, a place to hole up, a place to rest, found in that performance—that is, if that performance conforms. But even if it conforms, the performance returns the writer of color to an addressability that at any moment may become

residence in the creative act.

violent rather than safe—may become violent if the performance steps outside or beyond those comforting conformities, or even if the performance stays within them. Because the favor of largely white-run literary institutions is founded on an original, if obscured, amassment of racial power: they can always remind you you're a guest.

What we seek to detect in these examples above is the presence of a more general situation, the scene of race taking up residence in the creative act. This is what we mean by a racial imaginary, an unlyrical term, but then its lack of music is fitting. One way to know you're in the presence of—in possession of, possessed by—a racial imaginary is to see if the boundaries of one's imaginative sympathy line up, again and again, with the lines drawn by power. If the imaginative sympathy of a white writer, for example, shuts off at the edge of whiteness. This is not to say that the only solution would be to extend the imagination into other identities, that the white writer to be antiracist must write from the point of view of characters of color. It's to say that a white writer's work could also think about, expose, that racial dynamic. That what white artists might do is not imaginatively inhabit the other because that is their right as artists, but instead embody and examine the interior landscape that wishes to speak of rights, that wishes to move freely and unbounded across time, space, and lines of power, that wishes to inhabit whomever it chooses. Or that wishes to absent from view whomever it chooses.

It should also conversely not be assumed that it is easy or natural to write scenarios or characters whose race matches (whatever that might mean) one's own. This is the trap that writers of color in particular still must negotiate; it's the place where "write what you know" becomes plantational in effect.

We acknowledge that every act of imaginative sympathy inevitably has limits. Perhaps a way to expand those limits is not only to write from the perspective of a racial other but instead to inhabit, as intensely as possible, the moment in which the imagination's sympathy encounters its limit. To see what that shows you that you have not yet seen. Or: to realize one might also make strange what seems obvious, nearby, close.

Are we saying Asian writers can't write Latino characters? That white writers can't write black characters? That no one can write from a different racial other's point of view? We're saying we'd like to change the terms of that conversation, to think about creativity and the imagination without employing the language of rights and the sometimes concealing terms of craft. To ask some first-principle questions instead. So, not: can I write from another's point of view? But instead: to ask why and what for, not just if and how? What is the charisma of what I feel

She meant

estranged from, and why might I wish to enter and inhabit it. To speak not in terms of prohibition and rights, but desire. To ask what we think we know, and how we might undermine our own sense of authority. To not simply assume that the most private, interior, emotional spaces of existence—the spaces that are supposed to be the proper material of the lyric and the fictive—are most available for lyric and fictive rendering because they are somehow beyond race. To not assume that the presence of race deforms the creative act, renders the creative act sadly earthbound. We are ourselves earthbound. And race is one of the things that binds us there.

Crucial in what we're saying above is that we don't want to talk only of writing across racial divides. For we wish to also unsettle the assumption that it is easy or simple to write what one "is." Why might I assume it is easy to write what is nearest to me? How do I know what that is—and what do I miss when I keep familiar things familiar? It should be difficult to write what one knows—and if it is too easy, it is worth asking if that is because one is reproducing conventions and assumptions rewarded by the marketplaces of literature. And here again the racial preferences—the particular plots, the particular characters, the particular scenarios and personae—favored by literary institutions put special pressure on writers of color, threaten to deform what such

a writer is assumed to know and expected to produce.

The essays gathered here unveil race's operations in the act of creativity and in the institutions that support such acts. One thing they show is how race enters writing, the making of art, as a structure of feeling, as something that structures feelings in the moment of encounter, that lays down tracks of affection and repulsion, rage and hurt, desire and ache. These essays show as well that these tracks don't only occur in the making of art; they also occur (sometimes viciously, sometimes hazily) in the reception of creative work. Here we are again: we've made this thing and we've sent it out into the world for recognition—and because what we've made is in essence a field of human experience created for other humans, the field and its maker and its readers are thus subject all over again to race and its infiltrations. In that moment arise all sorts of possible hearings and mishearings, all kinds of address and redress.

For example: In that moment, writers and readers of color may feel profound and mutual anxieties that all people of color are about to be locked in, locked down, by the representation at hand, no matter who wrote it. But especially if a white writer wrote it. This anxiety is fueled by the fact that racism, in its very dailyness, in its very variety of expression, isn't fixed. It's there, and then it's not, and then it's there

well.

again. One is always doing the math: Was it there? Was it not? What just happened? Did I hear what I thought I heard? Should I let it go? Am I making too much of it? Racism often does its ugly work by not manifesting itself clearly and indisputably, and by undermining one's own ability to feel certain of exactly what forces are in play. This happens in reading as it does everywhere else. In a sense, it doubles-down the force of race—you feel it, you feel the injury, the racist address, and then you question yourself for feeling it. You wonder if you've made your own prison.

Another example: white writers can get explosively angry when asked to recognize that their racial imaginings might not be perfect—when asked to recognize that their imagination is not entirely their own—and in particular when confronted with that fact by a person of color questioning something they wrote. And the target of that anger is usually the person of color who shared with them this fact. The white writer feels injured in this moment—misunderstood and wounded—and believes it is the reader, the person of color, who has dealt the injury. This is how the white mind tends to racial "wounds"—it makes a mistake about who or what has dealt the injury. For it is not the reader of color who deals the injury. It is whiteness itself. To reconstruct the reader of color as the aggressor is one way that whiteness reasserts

its power in its moment of crisis. It has been exposed—it must now perform weakness, helplessness, it must pretend to innocence, to harmless and undefended and shocked innocence, in order to reveal the reader of color as motivated by unsavory, irrational, aggressive, political, or subjective tendencies that have lashed out at the innocent and harmed him (this is how the race card trope works to disqualify the reader bold enough to call up race where it might not be wanted: the trope enacts its dismissiveness by characterizing any mention of race as irresponsible, an injection of race "where it doesn't belong" when in fact it inheres whether it's called up or not). The white writer was taken by surprise by this attack—how could she have seen it coming? She meant well—surely this inoculates her against any charges. The attack was unfair. And so we must rally to the victim. And thus whiteness goes only briefly contested. This repositioning appears to cleanse whiteness of its power, of its aggression—for who can't hear the aggression in "I have a right of access to whomever I wish?"—and says of whiteness instead "I have been unfairly characterized and misunderstood, I have been assassinated by someone whose motivations are political and who is thus disqualified from the human endeavor that is art making." Thus the wound is paraded for all to witness, and whiteness gathers to itself again its abiding centrality, its authority, its rights. Its sanity.

It's messy, and it's

What the white writer might realize instead, in this moment of crisis, is that she may well be an injured party—but the injury was dealt long before. The injury is her whiteness. By saying "injury" we do not mean to erase from view all the benefits and privileges that whiteness endows; we do not mean to invite an unwarranted sympathy. But we do think white people in America tend to suffer an anxiety (and many have written of this, James Baldwin most powerfully of all): they know that they are white, but they must not know what they know. They know that they are white, but they cannot know that such a thing has social meaning; they know that they are white, but they must not know that their whiteness accrues power. They must not call it whiteness for to do so would be to acknowledge its force. They must instead feel themselves to be individuals upon whom nothing has acted. That's the injury, that their whiteness has veiled from them their own power to wound, has cut down their sympathy to a smaller size, has persuaded them that their imagination is uninflected, uninfiltrated. It has made them unknowing. Which is one reason why white people take recourse to innocence: I did not mean to do any harm. Or: I wanted to imagine you—isn't that good of me, haven't others said that was good of me to try? Or: I'm writing about people; they just happen to be white. Or: If I cared about politics, I would write a manifesto—what I'm trying to do is make art. Or: I

have a right to imagine whatever I want. Or: I don't see color. Or: we're all human beings.

Part of the mistake the white writer makes is that she confounds the invitation to witness her inevitable racial subjectivity with a stigmatizing charge of racism that must be rebutted at all costs. The white writer, in the moment of crisis, typically cannot tell the difference. What a white person could know instead is this: her whiteness limits *her* imagination—*not* her reader's after the fact. A deep awareness of this knowledge could indeed expand the limits—not transcend them, but expand them, make more room for the imagination. A good thing.

For one source of creativity lies in the fact that each individual is essentially strange. There is a deep strangeness, an alterity, in the individual human mind, a portion of ourselves that we never fully comprehend—and this is what writing taps, or is at least one of writing's sources, one of its engines. This might explain the enigma of writing for so many of us, that the writing so often seems to know more than we do, that we are 'behind' the writing ("behind it" in that we make it, but also "behind it" in the sense that we can't catch up with what it knows and reveals, that it is out ahead of us driven by energies in our possession but not entirely in our deliberate control). This essential strangeness, this unknowability, is a creative resource, perhaps the creative resource, the wellspring of art that shows us things we did

going to stay messy.

not know but that are somehow inevitable and true—true to a reality or a knowledge we don't yet possess, yet find in the moment of encounter possible, something we accept the fundamental being of even if its nature shocks or startles or repulses or unsettles us (Donald Barthelme's strange object covered in fur can only break your heart if you have accepted, in the instant of encounter, its essential being, even if you have not yet comprehended its strangeness, its otherness). But while it might be mystifying how creative impulses and decisions emerge from somewhere within, that doesn't mean we must make a fetish of that mysteriousness. For that unknowable portion of the human mind is also a domain of culture—a place crossed up by culture and history, where the conditions into which we were born have had their effect. Part of what is unknowable within us, at least until we investigate it, is the structuring of our very feelings and thoughts by what preceded us and is not our own, yet conditions our experience nonetheless. So the location of a writer's strangeness is also the seat of history. A writer's imagination is also the place where a racial imaginary—conceived before she came into being yet deeply lodged in her own mind—takes up its residence. And the disentangling and harnessing of these things is the writer's endless and unfinishable but not fruitless task. Another way of saying this: the writer's essential strangeness is her greatest resource, yet she must also be

in skeptical tension with her own inclinations. Because those inclinations are in part an inheritance from a racial imaginary that both is and is not hers.

We want to acknowledge that we have fallen into one of the very traps we mentioned at the start—we are having a hard time talking about race separate from racism. Indeed, we're not sure if we can or find it believable to imagine otherwise, imagine a time when or a fashion in which race outruns its birth in racism and becomes some kind of neutral, unfanged category. And we want to acknowledge too: this is a nasty business. We should not pretend that our experiences of race are otherwise. As we write, as the writers collected here write, as we read one other, the internal tumult is unavoidable. It might be soft or it might be loud, but it'll be made up of some admixture of shame, guilt, loathing, opportunism, anxiety, irritation, dismissal, self-hatred, pain, hope, affection, and other even less nameable energies. The particular chemistry may differ depending upon one's idiosyncratic mix of personal history and social location. For some it is nothing short of an assault, an assault no less painful because it is routine, an ordinary effect of negotiating a life in a world of people largely comfortable watching the assault go on, or at least willing to ignore its existence. It's messy, and it's going to stay messy. Which is the condition from which we start.

What we want to avoid at all costs is something that feels nearly impossible to evade in daily speech: an opposition between writing that accounts for race (and here we could also speak of gender, sexuality, other enmeshments of the body in time) and writing that is "universal." If we continue to think of the "universal' as better-than, as the pinnacle, we will always discount writing that doesn't look universal because it accounts for race or some other demeaned category. The universal is a fantasy. But we are captive, still, to a sensibility that champions the universal while simultaneously defining the universal, still, as white. We are captive, still, to a style of championing literature that says work by writers of color succeeds when a white person can nevertheless relate to it—that it "transcends" its category. To say this book by a writer of color is great because it transcends its particularity to say something "human" (and we've all read that review, maybe even written it ourselves) is to reveal the racist underpinning quite clearly: such a claim begins from the stance that people of color are not human, only achieve the human in certain circumstances. We don't wish to build camps. And we know there is no language that is not loaded. But we could try to say, for example, not that good writing is good because it achieves the universal, but perhaps instead that in the presence of good writing a reader is given something to know. Something is brought into being that might otherwise not be known, something is doubly witnessed.

What we mean by a racial imaginary is something we all recognize quite easily: the way our culture has imagined over and over again the narrative opportunities, the feelings and attributes and situations, the subjects and metaphors and forms and voices, available both to characters of different races and their authors. The racial imaginary changes over time, in part because artists get into tension with it, challenge it, alter its availabilities. Sometimes it changes very rapidly, as in our own lifetimes. But it has yet to disappear. Pretending it is not there—not there in imagined time and space, in lived time and space, in legislative time and space—will not hurry it out of existence. Instead our imaginings might test our inheritances, to make way for a time when such inheritances no longer ensnare us. But we are creatures of this moment, not that one.

―――――――

Beth Loffreda
Claudia Rankine

FLOATING CURRENCY

MAX KING CAP

The depiction of social and racial identity has long been attended by equivocality—a recipe of complex motivations of fetishism and degradation, exoticized beauty and reflective distancing. For the viewer these multiple readings are available when considering ethnographic portraiture such as the romanticized paintings of Native Americans by George Catlin and Karl Bodmer, the sentimental photographs by Edward Curtis, the voyeuristic Orientalism of Ingres and Delacroix, and the vulgar prurience in depictions of Saartjie Baartman—also known as *The Hottentot Venus*. What was once presented as analytically accurate now more often seems farcically corrupt, while appropriation of the image of the other has remained a common, if not entirely acceptable, practice. The compulsion to represent the other, and the drive to commandeer the other's representation of the self, remains. Unfortunately, also remaining is the comparison to the supreme exemplar, the troubling gold standard against which all racial appearance and cultural custom has been measured.

Whiteness, but not just any Whiteness, an admixture of Western and Northern European appearance, custom, and taste, remains the standard being replicated or struggled against. The tragedy of post-colonialism is that whiteness remained even in its absence to haunt the self-image of the natives, imprinting a comparative hallmark by which the savage will always know his inferiority. The greatest attributable accomplishment of this criterion is convincing the rest of the world that it wanted to be White. A subcategory within this accomplishment is a deprecation of any other metric. Thus "Black is Beautiful" becomes the Wankel engine, and "La Raza", Betamax.

That is the Quentin

This makes cultural appropriation a one-way street. When done by a member of dominant Western culture it is innovation, when done by others it is merely assimilation. Darius Rucker, the Black former frontman of the '90s band, *Hootie & the Blowfish*, has now, appropriately, embraced country music. Yet latter-day White minstrel/artist Joe Scanlan is lauded as an icon of ingenuity for masquerading as a Black woman; he has been rewarded with inclusion in the hallowed Whitney Biennial (Tyler Perry must be seething). These are acts of self-portraiture in which both artists embody another persona that contradicts their cis-race and cis-gender expectations. They seem to be equal portrayals of themselves as the other, but some selves are more equal than others.

Such antics demonstrate we are far from being a post racial, post misogynist society. On the contrary, we seem to be so entrenched in divisive tactics that we are no longer even able to consider value in contemplation and revision. We accept every new piece of information and contort it to our biases until they become bulwarks, impenetrable and permanent.

The artists included in this volume are siege engines against such intractability. They employ the varied strategies of satire, history, drama, documentary, revelation, inversion, and incongruity. They expressly do not use the demeaning tools of caricature, stereotype, fetish-ization, deprecation, aspersion, or chauvinism. The artist Liz Cohen's photography places the artist herself in unexpected roles that demand the code-switching intelligence of the viewer to decipher, while Edgar Endress examines the responses of those whose identities have long been dishonored. Race and gender identity are explored by EJ Hill, and the historicism of John Leaños reverses the *George Washington slept here* motif. Both Nery Gabriel Lemus and Charles McGill notate experiential alienage but Amis Motevalli and Dread Scott answer back with immersive revelation. Alice Shaw and Kyungmi Shin revisit genderized portraiture with chilling poise; Ian Weaver and Jay Wolke unscramble tradition, history, and exclusion.

These canny artists represent a primer on the representation of identity in art. They remember that identity is neither prescriptive nor proscriptive; it doesn't dictate or disallow, so they avoid using predictable characterizations. That is the Quentin Tarantino trap. His penchant for fetishization is formulaic, cursory, and salacious. The artists in this volume also demonstrate that while the iconography of White Westernism may be a universal language, it is not universally emulated. Its application is the artistic version of, "I believe we will be greeted as liberators." When crossing identity boundaries they remember this mnemonic: Approach with respect, come correct.

Tarantino trap.

These artists don't say that you cannot make cogent commentary on sensitive issues, just keep in mind—this is going on your permanent record. You may think you are damned clever right now but wait even just a couple of years and see how things have changed. Your poignant commentary on gender relations now just looks like rampant sexism, with a soupçon of homophobia. What you publish, exhibit, and perform is like a tattoo; you've seen the pitfalls in that practice. Use intelligence, research, and humble reflection to avoid marking yourself with humiliating regret.

Happily addicted to our multiple afflictions of inequality—uneven applications of the law, dismissive misogyny, rapacious mercantilism, gender bigotry—we as a nation can hardly expect that a more enlightened practice of identity representation in art can reform our jaundiced inclinations. We are encamped—us against them. Our relentless virtue is exhausting, while their hatred seems to invigorate. What choice do we have? These artists bring choices.

Max King Cap

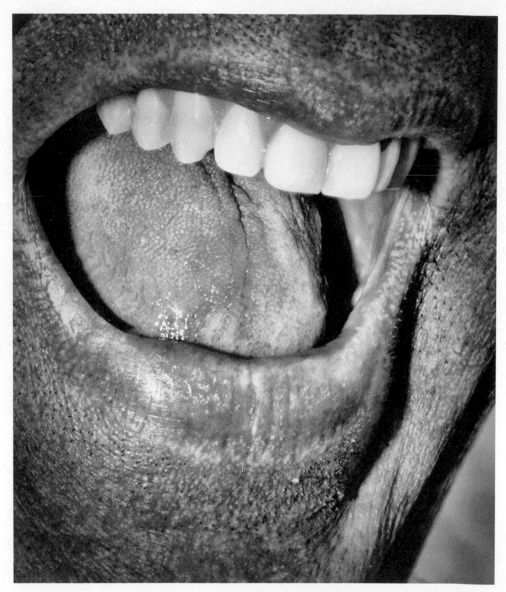

Mark Peterson,
from __Political Theatre__, 2014

Figureheads have the immediate singularity of theatrical stock characters—the fool, the miser, the boor—and these masks are what we most often see. They embody our fears, ambitions, and antipathies. MKC

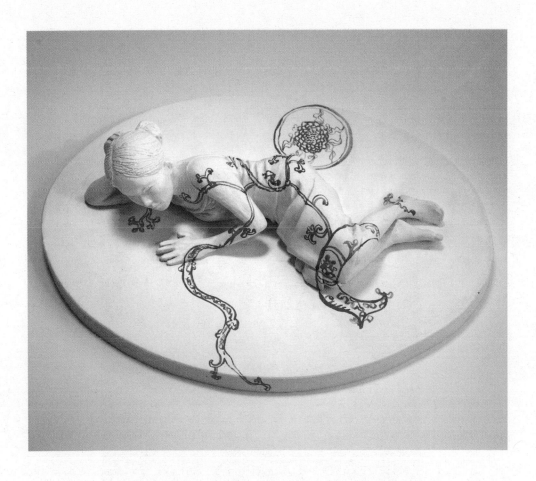

Kyungmi Shin, **<u>Chinoiserie</u>**, 2003

In this sculptural self-portrait the artist embodies the undifferentiated Asianess common in western characterizations, and the intra-Asian biases that deliver a more refined sting. MKG

(texist), **<u>The Wogs</u>**, 2014

The phrase, employed in a parliamentary debate on British citizenship for colonial subjects, was used as a rebuke to those who thought them inferior despite their exemplary war service—the jibe was aimed sarcastically at Winston Churchill. It has since become an ultra-right rallying cry for those nostalgic for "Fortress Britain." MKC

EJ Hill, **<u>This is an Imaginary Border</u>**, 2009

In taping a border dividing the city of Chicago into north and south sides, the performance artist demarcates the traditional racial partition of the city—where African American housing concentration has changed little in forty years. MKC

Photos: Jessica Hoekstra

I once saw a book on classroom management for college teachers called When Race Breaks Out. As if it's like strep throat, as if it has to be medicated, managed, healed. **Why am I so hard to distinguish, so hard to remember?** What is a work called when it punishes intimacy with paranoia? **The supposedly inclusive and forward-thinking writing culture we are part of, even at its most avant-garde, progressive, thoughtful, or friendly, is still just an unofficial white poetry club.** When you're here, you are supposed to just move through it. **Questions of race are never just about narrative or images or stereotypes, they pervade our grammars, our styles, our forms, and above all our unstated system of preferences, of aesthetic value. You say well-wrought urn, I say stunningly tedious; you say stuttering with incompetence, I say a new music for our age.** I love you. Let's not sell each other out. Especially while professing that we are here for one another.

INSTITUTIONS

FLIBBERTIGIBBET IN A WHITE ROOM/COMPETENCIES

SIMONE WHITE

I remember things I never forgot. To spend an afternoon returning to the site of some wrong committed only in my imagination against an unnamed person, a vaporous friend, is a bore and no kind of penance. What have I neglected?—has it to do with money? Probably, I've insulted someone. Even the cat, thrashing in my arms, cannot abide being touched improperly in terms of the calculus of will and affection.

Probably, it is impossible to avoid insult in the atmosphere of feint, desperation, and cluelessness that pervades this life. (Supposed to be contemplative, supposed to be romantic in the way it hearkens back, historically, materially, to an eradicated bohemia. Impossible, anyway, to forget what any previous bohemia would have been, for me, black as I am. Thank god for the enormity of my lateness.) To try is to manufacture, it is to glue, it is to piece together against every probability an evasive "we" that moves in my arms like a living animal. The more I think, the more I am estranged. What is a work called when it punishes intimacy with paranoia?

There has never been a moment when the world I lived in did not claim to be mostly white, all white, white shoe, majority white, elite white, and meanwhile the family I was in, the neighborhood I was in, the love I was in, the music I was into, the clothes, the mood, the writing were most(ly) black. If you start from that perspective, looking for the difference between claims about the whiteness of the world and its material blackness, you'll find it—the difference. I mean to be present to that difference without blowing it up into the whole point of the investigation, the mechanisms of which have got, on occasion, to be cleaned.

... the impossible whiteness

I mean, part of the investigation has to be losing track of the way of doing the work. In investigations having to do with blackness—which I'm saying are all investigations—I try never to grasp or grip with too much paranoid ferocity on blackness itself. That's a worldview and a practice: don't be gripping onto it, or you lose sight of why you are holding it in your view, or trying to hold it and get a look at it, why it is precious, why the *need* to describe it properly, in all its (still) understudied fucking massive significance. This is why there will never be a commercial, institutional, disciplinary word that describes devotional investigation of blackness. All I can do is say back to you some names and words that have led to the present proximal or provisional and insufficient understanding of how black people are in this world.

Nathaniel Mackey resorts to the term *namesake* for talking about a kind of meta-quotation that verges on the professional practice of ordinary quotation but is also a gestational gesture: I claim you and take you inside me and, so, you will come out of me. I *read* you.

By the time I roused myself from the comfort of Bedford-Stuyvesant to a poetry reading in Williamsburg in the dead of winter, over the ice, to hear Anselm Berrigan, Dana Ward, and Lauren Shufran, I had been thinking for a long time about what people mean when they say that American poetry that is not interested in reproducing the familiar (call it what you want: experimental, innovative) is a white practice, a white thing, dominated by white poets and white institutions. I'd been thinking about this as a curator at the Poetry Project, as a person who has published collections only with independent small presses with few informal or institutional connections to people of color "communities" (I use this word reluctantly not because I question the existence of these communities, but because I don't want to be understood to be saying I believe in their existence as natural; as extra-institutional, extra-economic, as ideal, in other words). I'd been thinking about it as a person who lives in, and not by accident, a thoroughly diverse intimate world that could never be described as "white." And I'd been thinking about it as a woman poet who writes poems that could never belong to any tradition but a black tradition.

I didn't know it that night, but I was just the tiniest bit pregnant. So, although I was drinking in the harmless way that I drink (maybe I had two beers), I felt inexplicably drunk and frustrated by the impossible whiteness of the room I found myself in. Let me say again: *I am used to being the only black person in the room.* It happens all the time and has happened all the time since I was a little ten-year-old pigtailed thing stuck in a tiny private girls school in Chestnut Hill. But the fact is, being used to being the only black person in the room isn't the same thing as thinking

of the room I found myself in.

that this is a tolerable or reasonable condition. Even when I was ten years old, I knew (or was told repeatedly so I had better known) that this was something to be tolerated and managed, like a nasty variety of mold. I do not enjoy it any more than I enjoy any other condition that is a scourge and ought to be eradicated.

When I say that I became *inexplicably* frustrated because I had been thinking for thirty years and now, in and out of elite educational situations, the practices of law, poetry, and teaching, about how black people in the United States *get isolated* socially, economically, and aesthetically—and how it feels to be a problem—what I'm trying to talk about is knowledge about both the fact and the wrongness of this isolation that is more solid and deeper than anything I actually know. More and more, that knowledge means refusal of "community" whose joy is in some way predicated on enjoyment of something I know good and well is wrong. It is total bullshit to enjoy being in a social or creative community that is segregated the way poetry is segregated. I'm saying that in that room, that night, I hit something like a wall or bottom or saw something that I never want to see again, which might have been my own complicity or token-ness or it might just be that I was tired and pregnant and, really, too old to be in an overcrowded white room in Williamsburg full of white people ten years younger than me, and I wanted to go home.

One reason to admire the wildness of Thomas Sayers Ellis's imagination with respect to the possible coming to pass of a map that charts Poetry crimes and misdemeanors on both historical and trivial scales, is that that map is in some ways an analogue of a smaller map (being drawn in my work) that charts the relation between black Philadelphia, its Germantown, Osage, Baltimore Avenues, to the falling-down house of John Coltrane, seeing that every day as a child, and being unable to square it, in any way, with the way grown people whispered his name (the way Baraka falls into whispers in *Black Music* ...). I cannot draw you a map, but everything that has occurred or might have occurred in any linguistic location on such a map belongs to me.

TSE's apparently two-dimensional, paranoid "A Poet's Guide to the Assassination of JFK (the Assassination of Poetry)" is, for me, a model of melancholy experimentation in and with the assumptions of Poetry competency; the demand that professional poets know their way around players, works, places, and forms, all of which contribute to an atmosphere of smugness that impedes approaching the truth of its insanely segregated reality. The wickedness of Ellis's humor is grounded, for me, in the big joke of presumed whiteness, which he is past saying because he's been doing this for a long time. I think about the ubiquitous "Kill List" and the unending commentary that surrounded its publication—as if it had provoked some genuine emergency of craft, when, for me, it just raised a lot of ethical questions that I consider to be asked and answered while leaving untouched every problem that concerns me about the operation and future of poetry as community—and I wonder: Where was the commentary on Ellis's list, aside from its having become untraceable? Its absence speaks to a broad, pressing question of how Poetry's segregation is related to what an emerging poet needs to know and the question of how to acquire that knowledge outside his immediate surroundings. We are all pressed by limited time and resources: So how and where do you spend your time? How do you come to know the lay of the land? Who are you with and how do you sound? How do you look (over your shoulder)?

The work is called poetry. Paranoia is a measure of its degree.

WHAT DO WE SEE? WHAT DO WE NOT SEE?[1]

ARI BANIAS

My reluctance to write about race and racism routinely takes the form of preemptive self-judgment—the notion that whatever I write will necessarily be overly simplistic, redundant, without impact, superficial, etc.; the conclusion being I shouldn't bother. This impulse is self-protective, yes, but it also carries inside it a troublesome idea: that race and racism don't really have to do with me, a white person—that I somehow don't "know" race or know it deeply enough. To be sure, a lot of white folks seem oblivious to the impact of our own whiteness a lot of the time, to the pain we cause, to the privileges we get—such obliviousness itself is systemic. But I want to call bullshit. The notion that race and racism somehow aren't my business gives me an unearned pass in matters that intimately involve and implicate me, and discourages me from seeing my life and its material conditions as inextricably connected to the lives of people of color. All of us live raced lives, in raced bodies; as white folks in the United States, we've been taught not to view ours as such. But they are, and deep in our guts, we know it. So what follows is my take on some of the ways I've seen systemic racism and white supremacy manifest within a larger poetry culture/community and its institutions.

Much of what's here will be all too familiar to the folks in poetry communities who are most acutely impacted by racism. So, why say what's presumably known? Because naming some of the ways systemic racism plainly appears and operates within poetry communities can help point to the places it doesn't show itself as readily, but is still very much at work. Because what's apparent about racism to some isn't apparent to everyone—and

[1] Muriel Rukeyser, 1973

There was no critical

because what's obvious to me now wasn't always. Because what I can't see yet, I hope to soon. Because the more often and more accurately the machinations of power are named, the less they are enabled, smoothed down, normalized, reinforced. Because it's probable some people will take this more seriously, or read it more carefully, coming from a white person. Because if it's read with more scrutiny or suspicion coming from a white person, that's a good thing; my perspective isn't inherently worthy of trust. Because these observations implicate me, and are also bigger than me. Because I resisted writing this, and then I resisted publishing it. Because I want to imagine that observation and acknowledgment can be precursors to dismantling systems of oppression, and to creating structures that are just.

It matters that I am writing this in the United States, a nation itself founded on colonization, slavery, and white supremacy, whose state continues to carry out policies at home and abroad that reflect these ideologies. The larger poetry landscape is necessarily shaped by these same ideologies and structural forces—ones that have made, and continue to make, navigating and thriving in it inherently difficult for people of color and easier for white people. White supremacy, being not just a matter of individual prejudice but systemic, operates—because we allow it to—with remarkable smoothness in some of the friendliest and most well-intentioned contexts;

poetry communities are no exception. Bound as this poetry landscape is to that of the United States and its economic, cultural and educational institutions, the transformation of one is not complete or possible without the transformation of the other.

Of this poetry landscape, or community, I will also say: liberal-minded, geographically fluid within the continental US, marked by regional, aesthetic, and generational affinities and differences and overlaps and pockets, but more or less connected to academia/higher ed and the MFA complex, even if not always found directly within it.

So when I think about concrete manifestations of white supremacy in this context, I first think of the plain fact of white people's gross overrepresentation in positions of authority (teaching, editing, etc.). As one typical example, the MFA program I attended had an all-white creative writing faculty, across genres, and a majority of the students in the poetry program were white/of European ancestry. Of twelve, two self-identified as of color, both of whom were mixed race and light-skinned, and routinely invisible as people of color in the context of our program. "Since we're all white here..." a professor said in class one day. "No, we're not," an Arab American student responded. The white professor didn't acknowledge having heard her. And though we were not all, in fact, white, the voices

discussion of the canon . . .

defining and controlling the terms of that conversation were. And are. As in many programs, the poetry that was presented to us as the essential work we needed to understand, the masters from whom we should learn, were overwhelmingly white Anglo poets, both contemporary and non. There was no critical discussion of the canon, or any of the ideologies or sociohistorical factors that have shaped its appearance.

The racial demographics of my program are in no way unique. They repeat throughout poetry community: in the people who own and run presses both large and small, who edit journals, who sit on editorial boards, decision-making panels for residencies, grants, fellowships, and other awards, who judge book contests, program readings and conferences, direct MFA and PhD programs, hold tenure-track teaching positions in these programs, serve as chancellors of foundations and societies, and so on. Of course, people of color do hold some of these positions, and there may be good-faith efforts to be "more diverse," but if you look at this group as a whole you gaze on a sea of white people. While numbers can be a useful place to begin, it's crucial that we know the difference between diversity and inclusion, and actually challenging a culture and structure of white supremacy in our institutions as a whole. That we support the increased inclusion of poets of color in these spaces (and notice if the same Black writer appears in every

publicity photo, and pay attention to who sits on the board of directors year after year) and don't stop there. If the sole manifestation of racial justice or change merely amounts to including a few more people of color, another fast trick of addition or subtraction can reverse such so-called progress if it becomes inconvenient or undesirable.

And what this has meant for me, is that despite being queer and transgender, I know I benefit enormously and unfairly from a structure in which my work is usually being read by white readers, who are more likely than not to identify with the racial experience (whether explicit or not) represented in my poems. The white teachers and mentors who support me, the white readers working with journals and presses, are more inclined to "get" my work, perhaps to feel addressed by it, because of their perception of our shared racial experience—a perception that's unspoken. I also know when a white judge or editor feels an affinity with my work, no one is likely to attribute that affinity to our shared racial identity. Such a connection is seen as natural, neutral, inevitable —so much so that it isn't seen at all—and no one is likely to publicly scrutinize our relationship on that basis. When the same relationship occurs, say, between a Black professor or editor and a younger Black poet, it is highly visible, and the immediate assumption would be that their connection is based on race,

So the "same position" is

a connection, in their case, that wouldn't be seen as neutral; they may fall under scrutiny, face accusations of favoritism, have the quality of their work questioned.

If a white student is knowledgeable about only the work of white poets, this is not seen as a big problem by many other white poets, for the most part. If a student of color were knowledgeable about only the work of poets of color, this would be seen by many white poets and institutions as a big gap in that student's knowledge and education. Such a student would likely have a difficult time moving forward and being taken seriously as a scholar, and would not be seen as having a well-rounded education; this student would have a difficult time securing an academic position, and might be perceived as aggressively separatist, angry, out of touch, even unstable. Whiteness is the dominant, unquestioned, unnamed, mostly invisible, presumed-to-be inevitable and neutral and universal category and perspective. Everyone, regardless of race, is expected to be fluent in it in order to participate, survive, and certainly succeed.

A whole set of cultural and aesthetic values are repeatedly brought into practice and perpetuated when white editors/critics/educators/poets decide what publishable, interesting, good poetry looks like—when they gravitate, perhaps unconsciously, perhaps not, toward work largely by other white poets, and when this work is championed again and again. When white edi-

tors don't know how to read work by indigenous poets, by Black or Middle Eastern or Asian / Pacific Islander or Latina/o poets, on its own terms; when white readers expect this work to conform to particular tropes or lexicons, expecting to see themselves in it, or to not see themselves anywhere in it at all. This impacts, on a far larger scale, over time, which poets are being perpetually published, funded, awarded residencies and fellowships, securing teaching positions, slots in graduate writing programs, and which poets are not. The magnitude and consequences of systemic racism remain, again, grossly apparent.

Although some gains have been made historically in fights for ethnic studies programs and inclusive curricula, these are always still under attack—and the traditions, histories, criticisms, experiences, and work of poets of color, when it does appear alongside the canon or in creative writing curriculum, is still overwhelmingly presented as secondary and topical. This work does not receive as much time and attention as the work of white poets, and is treated as an area of specialization or an afterthought rather than a mainstay of a seriously reimagined or dismantled canonical framework; the same goes for much poetry in translation, or poetry from outside the continental US. The work of white poets who express racist or colonialist ideas and language is still being taught as essential and valuable, with just a quick nod of acknowl-

not the same position at all.

edgment (if that) toward these white poets' "prejudices."

Because this larger poetry community tends to limit, dismiss, and silence conversations about its own racism, I know that if I want my work to be supported by more established poets, the majority of whom are white, that calling out white supremacy, the ways I see it operating in my creative and professional environs, in the written work of peers, or in the work of living established or respected poets, will likely have a negative impact on the progress of my writing career within the channels sanctioned and controlled by this community. I know that the degree to which this would impact the career of a poet of color in the same position would be far, far greater. So the "same position" is not the same position at all.

Simultaneously, poets of color face ongoing pressure, in part from a white publishing and value-determining industry, to be constant spokespeople for their racial identity and experience, to fulfill the role of addressing, writing about, and embodying "race" and the racial in their work—and these poets' work tends to be framed by white readers in a racialized context, regardless of the poet's intent. White readers can be consumers of this work and feel good about ourselves, satisfied that we have contributed somehow, or even, use our consumption of this work to signify our status as "down" or

"not-racist" among other poets. In such a framework, whiteness, again, remains invisible and unquestioned. And in the meantime, white poets experience the privilege of imaginative freedom without the expectation or obligation to write about race, without the inevitability of our work being read through the lens of race—though why shouldn't it be?

What I've named here doesn't begin to approach any sort of exhaustive documentation of structural racism within American poetry. Considering even my brief observations, it's clear who is likely to feel welcome, supported, and valued in these classrooms and publishing houses and fellowship programs and readings and conferences and informal social gatherings—and who is not. Who has the privilege of assuming their work is being considered and understood on its own terms, and who would rarely assume that. Who can speak freely, and who might want to watch their words. Much essential space has been intentionally forged by poets of color for poets of color, through anthologies, reading series, fellowships, scholarships, presses, workshops, retreats, collectives, nonprofits, informal writing groups, and so on. That institutions like Cave Canem, Kundiman, VONA, or CantoMundo are crucial in providing culturally affirming space and resources to many poets is an understatement. These organizations' existence also confirms what so many white poets in the room don't want to see: the dominant poetry culture's marginalization of people of color. In this broader landscape, poets of color are still relegated to the fringes, and white poets and poetries remain easily at the center, occupying most of the positions of power, with the loudest voices, the longest airtime, controlling the majority of existing resources, and acting as arbiters of worth in a culture of assumed and unnamed whiteness. The supposedly inclusive and forward-thinking writing culture we are part of, even at its most avant-garde, progressive, thoughtful, or friendly, is still just an unofficial white poetry club. And will remain that way until we see how we're all implicated in its function and its design, and are fed up enough to mutually imagine a radically different kind of landscape into being.

WHAT WE COULD DO WITH WRITING
CASEY LLEWELLYN

Part of why I write is to free myself. My characters are outsiders trying to place themselves in the world, and in doing this, they create a space that wasn't there before, a place where they can just be, without the limitations, assumptions, questions, and violence the external world puts on them. And the play becomes this place. This process of creating new space for existence that my characters engage in, with more or less success, is the process that drives me to write. Through writing, I create somewhere where I exist in the fullness of my identity, where I can define myself in my own terms, with my own priorities and trajectory. This process is an act in opposition to the sexism, denigration of femininity, and queerphobia that I personally experience. Through writing I explore the ways I am hurt by these aspects of society and find solutions, ways of understanding, and ways around. But I think writing could also be a place for me to address and explore the more subtle ways I am misshaped by the parts of society that I "benefit" from, like racism, capitalism, or classism—things that tear into humanness and community and yet that I have very concrete material benefits from. Writing could allow me to deconstruct and act against these things as well. I try to write myself out of the constricted space I inhabit as a queer femme woman. And I try to write myself out of my own smallness, to push through my limits of understanding, and come out somewhere new and better. I try to write myself out of the violence I experience: my own oppression and the way I oppress others; and writing about race and writing through my own racism is a big part of that.

It's hard. Just the amount of hours it has taken me to even approach this essay, finish my sentences,

. . . loudly proclaiming,

make any sense of it, proves that. I've been disappointed in the past by my efforts to write about race, and I'm disappointed now. I've written flat characters. I've written characters from too intellectual a place, so they stand for something instead of being their own agents. I've tended to make my characters victims more than I've meant or wanted them to be. I rarely feel like a good writer when I'm writing about race. But I'm not writing to feel like a good writer. I'm trying to figure something out, make something that didn't exist before.

I had the opportunity to attend some panel discussions at a convening on new play development at the Arena Stage this January. I was there working as a stage manager, but I'm also a playwright and director and was taken with the opportunity to eavesdrop on the conversations of some accomplished members of my field. One comment in particular has found me again and again in my thoughts since then and continues to ask for some resolution. In a conversation about diversity, a playwright, a black woman, expressed that since the conversation about the need for more diversity in theater had been going on for twenty years and that neither the conversation nor the field seemed to have changed significantly in that time, she was forced to question the sincerity of the expressed desire for diversity. Her comment resonated deeply with me. It seemed relevant to every institution I had ever been a part of since a

progressive day care I was in when I was two with income and race quotas to keep the sometimes inevitable-seeming white dominance of elite progressive spaces at bay. It was also a question that opened into huge other questions about how we deal with race and racism in culture and in artistic communities. In looking within myself for what to say about writing and race, I came back to the question this playwright posed about the sincerity of white artists' commitment to work against racism. If we have stated such a commitment to work toward the end of racism (or at least its power to define our existence as people, as Americans, as writers, and as artists), and some of us have, or if we feel a desire for equality, as many of us do, then why does racism continue to flourish in our artistic communities and what role does our work as white writers play in this?

I read some poetry, and I read and go to see a lot of theater, and there are some trends pertaining to race I've noticed in the work of white writers. By far the biggest trend is silence, work in which there is no mention of race or acknowledgment of racial dynamics even when casting decisions push these to the forefront. What comes forth in this scenario is a direct contradiction of theatrical logic in which what you see is what you get, instead what you get becomes increasingly irrelevant as what you see is insistently ignored. In this work, there is a sense of the artist saying softly, if pressed, this is not my issue.

see, I'm not avoiding it.

Another trend differentiates itself from this silence by loudly proclaiming, *see, I'm not avoiding it.* In this work, the white artists make clear that they are comfortable addressing race and racism through the use of self-conscious jokes poking fun at the obvious racism of the past or gauche racists of the present. The logic this work posits rests on an implied distance between the racism portrayed and the actual beliefs of the artists involved and the beliefs anticipated in the audience. This work absolves itself of any responsibility to critically address race and racism (or sexism which is often similarly dealt with by this type of piece) by placing it in the past or at a distance (attempted irony often plays a role) from the white (often male) makers. In this work, what is put forward goes both unacknowledged and unexamined, and what is left in the wake of the piece is not a critique of racism or any challenge to a racist status quo, but hundreds of years of violent racial oppression turned into laugh lines that encourage uncritical complacence in the audience. In this way, the work actively reinforces the racist status quo: the lie of a "postracial" society.

Another trend of work endeavors to call attention to itself by employing racist sentiment or imagery. The racism expressed is designed to shock. This work is often defended as importantly honest or brave for "addressing race." But perpetuating racism in one's work is hateful, immoral, and soul-killing. For all of us. Honesty and bravery have

nothing to do with it. I challenge myself like I challenge any white writer to "address race" in our work without perpetuating racist imagery and ideology.

Another widespread, age-old trend is one of work in which racist stereotypes and points of view are perpetuated presumably unintentionally simply through lack of thorough examination of the values and images being put forth in one's work. Maybe the examination of one's work through a racial lens is viewed by some white writers as unimportant or unnecessary, or maybe the critical racial lens of most white writers is just not developed enough. Either way, this trend is distressing in its persistence, as it seems critical that writers themselves be the first ones to interrogate and understand their own work and what it is putting into the world.

A recent experience of mine allowed me to reflect deeply and personally on this phenomenon. I had a workshop of a first draft of a play in which there were "magical negro"-style reverberations. Blackness in the play was supernatural and entered the scene to act on an already dominant unmarked whiteness—culturally white, class-privileged experience and language positioned as universal. It was not my intention to perpetuate racist stereotypes in my work, but I had. Often I notice my first "instincts" around race in my work betray the racist content I have ingested throughout my life in the United States, having been trained in and participating in almost exclusively, if unconsciously,

Someone is killed and we are

racist institutions (schools, jobs, professional and social communities). Often rewrites are necessary for me to work through and beyond racist constructions and representations, and I had confidence in the potential of that draft to be a force for good in the world, but I hadn't gotten there yet.

I felt very uncomfortable in that rehearsal room, not just because I was hearing a raw draft of my own work in the mouths of actors and finding it offensive, but also because I was subjecting actors of color to it. An experience I am sure was not new to them in any way as Black, Latino and Asian actors, and which I imagine took its toll. I imagine experiences like this or the anticipation (conscious or unconscious) of potential experiences like this are a constant challenge to people of color collaborating with white people and are exactly what keep a lot of white writers from addressing race as a reality in their work.

In the workshop, I experienced extreme generosity and understanding from everyone, including from the actors of color to whom I'm sure the unexamined, yet unmistakable, racism in my text was most apparent. This generosity I attribute to the fact that it was clear that I was striving for a text that does not reinscribe oppressive dynamics however far from that I was at the moment, a space created for listening and speaking honestly, and a perceived mutual respect of all parties that can, thank god, exist and persist even in the face of the racism internalized in people involved.

This experience deeply challenged me, threatened to alienate me from my writing, fearing others' judgment and hurt feelings, but the trust my collaborators put in me gave me strength. And I appreciate it as part of a process of moving toward writing liberative characterizations instead of stereotyped ones or ones that reinscribe racist ideology in the world, and understanding more closely what that looks like.

The biggest fear around race in the bottom of me, I think, is that race can really keep us from each other. Despite countless experiences in my life that prove this very wrong, it is persistent, a fear that a racist culture and society perpetuates and employs to divide us. But despite, or more concretely, because of, the obstacles a racist culture makes for us in making our work, in making our lives, we must work through them! Or we will always be living in a racist culture, making a relationship with racism at every moment of making our lives. We *can* not be racist! This is possible. But first we will have to be honest with ourselves about the ways in which we are.

Some white writers are thoughtful in addressing race and some succeed at nuanced understanding of race and racism. The work of these writers actually pushes for new ways of seeing and thinking about race, and in doing so, endeavors to create a new consciousness that enlarges the humanity of all of us.

told it's for our protection.

It is not special or new for white people in some fields to acknowledge that the work of ending racism is mostly ours, since it is our views racism stands in for and our views and actions that perpetuate it. But few white writers engage with this truth in their work, and the work is weaker because of it.

So what is up with all of this? Are we insincere when we say, yes, we want racism to end? As I have thought more about what this playwright said about sincerity, I have thought that her question is an extremely fair, challenging, and important one. I often hear the issue of diversity framed this way: Of course, diversity is something that every institution wants more of, but it's a hard problem to address, so we continue to strive for it. This seems to be an acceptable solution for the people in power in many institutions. And I agree it is a hard problem to address in that to actually address it requires deep and fundamental changes on many levels of institutional functioning, and it is almost impossible to address by way of the surface level strategies most institutions employ to address it (i.e., the minority scholarship). How do a few "invitations" to certain individuals create change in the consciousness of the institution or the way it functions?

White theater makers benefit very concretely from the dominance of the theatrical field by other white people, just as white people in general benefit from the racism in our society. We are

mostly not unjustly targeted by the police; in fact, we are passed over by them in numbers inversely proportional to the numbers black and brown people (mostly) are targeted by them; we have access proportionally to better schools, more and better jobs, and much more wealth. Our connections with other white people (we often know a ton!) have gotten us into schools, jobs, money, opportunities, connections to other powerful people and will continue to help our children (should we choose to have them). It is only with an understanding of how we benefit from racism that we can really answer the question of sincerity.

But what benefit? We feel alienated from other people. We are scared and angry. We worry if we said the right or wrong thing. We hate. The people we love get hurt. We get hurt. We lie. Are afraid, rigid. We hurt the people we love. We want justice we don't have. We want justice others don't have. We feel powerless. Someone is killed and we are told it's for our protection. No one is safe. We see difference. Manufacture it. We are far away. Are silent. Feel like bad people. Are hateful, less human. No one has justice. We rage, take it out on our loves. We can't talk. When we talk, it's violent. We speak the language of our oppressors. We are the oppressors, even our own. We hate what is inside of us. No one is treated like a person. We are treated like people when others aren't. We have no community. We see our community sick. We watch each other die.

Not listening not dreaming. Not speaking our dreams to each other. We can't write. We write narrow. Whisper mistrust into a void. Cut each other open because that's how we learned touch. Our language exploits. We exploit ourselves. We get drunk. We have addictions we can support. We have addictions we can't support. We don't have the support we need. We don't accept ourselves. We don't accept anyone else. We beat the shit out of each other. We hate ourselves. Someone says, I need you, and we build a wall. We are suspicious. We self-mutilate. We say, I need you, and someone turns away. Is suspicious. We think, I could've been close to that person. We think, what keeps me back? We think, we need to arm ourselves.

Fuck that.

I'm not gonna let racism make us all less human.

You've experienced inequality, I suspect, so you know what I mean when I say that even those of us who "benefit" from it, do and do not.

I want to live in a world in which we can all exist fully as ourselves, in which deeper love, community, thought, and creation are possible. I understand that if I don't actively work toward creating this, it will not be. I don't know what is more essential than this because everything I experience is there, my deepest self, involved. In my work outside of writing, I work toward this. In my writing, I work toward this. I have not achieved anything, but I know where I'm going—toward the fullest existence possible. The marvelous free. Love.

Our writing is part of creating the world we want to live in for our own survival. Our work outside of writing is part of it. Our lovemaking is part of it. This conversation is part of it. The society that we live in is racist. That is its logic. If we do nothing, it perpetuates itself, answers itself, yes, without asking any of us. So for those of us who answered yes, *yes, I want racism to end*, let's make ourselves part of that ending. Do that with our work. Let that be our poetics. Our writing is not separate from living, from anything. Do not let it be separate. Let us continue to do the work we do with our writing, but let's not artificially separate that work from the work of our lives, the work of ending racism, the work of engaging in the creation of the world we want to live in, actively, everyday. And let us not continue to fool ourselves with the excuse that race doesn't come up for us in our lives or is not relevant to our work or is not our issue. It is coming up all the time, and it is all of our issue. We cannot pass it off or leave it to someone else. We need only pay attention, train ourselves to see it, and work to understand it. Write honestly, consciously, responsibly, always with commitment to our deepest dreams. This fullest existence possible. This marvelous free. I love you. Let's not sell each other out. Especially while professing that we are here for one another.

RACE, FEMINISM, AND CREATIVE SPACES

MARYAM AFAQ

i.

This is not the place one should write from. It is in the middle of it all, in the murky swirl of the tree bark before it knows how many rings it will have, whether it will be chopped tomorrow or grow thick like earth. When you're here, you are supposed to just move through it.

ii.

Tonight was the second time I cried because of graduate school. I hate my MFA program. When I say I hate my MFA program, it is not a cute hate I can revel in, draw any joy from, and yes, there are those—think finding out that your best friend hates that same person you got a strange vibe from or hating the movie that everyone else loved and being right about it. It's something else that bubbles in my temples, uncomfortably, and I am counting the semesters till I will be done (one more to go).

Tonight in my class on Women Poets, we read an essay about language, power and gender. The author wrote about how her mother, a woman living without a husband in the 1960s in small-town America would fix their house, how she was a handy woman and how odd and radical it was for a woman to be doing those things at those times. A fine essay by most means except that for an essay on language, power, and feminism around the time of the civil rights era, it was odd that the author constantly referred to "women" when she really meant "white middle-class women." I noticed this when reading the essay, made a note of it in my head as "ah, yet another example of the way that whiteness is made invisible and normalized to speak for everyone," and continued with the rest of the readings.

That would be taking up

We began the discussion in our class by looking at the essay through a "feminist" perspective and questioning whether there were avenues for "radical" action left in today's world. Shortly into the conversation, it became glaringly clear to me that we were looking at this essay through a "white feminist" lens. Comments were made over and over about "women" having done this or "women" having gone through that. While I understand that for the purposes of a classroom discussion, it is reductive and impossible to incorporate all different identifications, for a graduate classroom discussion on gender, language, and power, to completely miss the way that race or class figured into the question was frankly shocking. In my small class of eight people, only two of the white women and my white woman instructor went back and forth with the white male student in charge of leading the discussion for that week.

The history being discussed in my classroom was not history that related to me in any way. It was not the history of women who've been on the margins: immigrant women, poor women, queer women, women of color, disabled women, etc. It was the history of white, mostly straight and middle-class women. In the 1960s and 70s, women poets that I identify as my foremothers, June Jordan, Audre Lorde, Lucille Clifton, Chrystos, Lorna Dee Cervantes, Gwendolyn Brooks, were working to carve a space for themselves where they did not have to compromise their experiences of being in a body that was both "non-white and woman." How is it that we still haven't made enough space for ourselves in these seemingly enlightened circles to be included in such conversations?

The discussion grazed briefly over the "first wave, second wave, third waves" of feminism here in the USA and someone commented on how sad it was that "the first wave has not even reached some places in the world." My skin began to prickle at this point and my heart and mind raced, stumbling one over the other. I wanted to jump up from my seat and run out of the classroom. I was horrified at the way this conversation was being framed and the gross assumptions that went unnoticed. Women all over the world live in varying states of deplorable situations, including very much here in the United States of America. To assume that "other places and other people" have not even made it to the "first wave of feminism" as related to United States history, and that that is someplace they need to get in order to "progress," is exactly the same as the United States government invading the sovereign states of Iraq, Afghanistan, and now, Pakistan, and killing people under the guise of "bringing democracy" and "getting rid of terrorism" as if it's the flu.

It is perhaps one of the most conflicted and ironic moments I've been in. Feeling utterly

too much space for myself.

invisible and inconsequential in a conversation that was supposedly about "women." Not to mention my distress at my own inability to speak up because I did not feel ready or comfortable to challenge a room full of white people (but for one other Asian American student) on their whiteness and privilege. That would be taking up too much space for myself. I still struggle with questioning why I am here and if I belong at this prestigious program with a cohort so unlike myself.

I am tired of the way my MFA program is structured to incorporate, nay, hold up the invisibility of whiteness, and conversations around race are never productive in the minor instances when they even exist to begin with. This program, the building it is housed in, and most of its people—do not feel like mine at all and neither do I belong to it or them, except on paper and through an identification card that lets me in at the gates. Not to forget the twenty thousand dollars of debt that I've accumulated so far to be in classrooms where over and over again, I'm either made invisible or pigeonholed as the "ethnic poet" and any history that may reflect stories of those from similar places to mine is made invisible and discounted.

This is not a personal attack on any individual or group. There are people whose friendships and presence I value in the program, even my instructor who is unable to facilitate meaningful discussions on and around race.

iii.

There are two experiences I am trying to converge here: what happened on the outside and what happened on my inside. My head is still throbbing. There is a lot more to be said for both of those.

won't you celebrate with me

won't you celebrate with me
what i have shaped into
a kind of life? i had no model.
born in babylon
both nonwhite and woman
what did i see to be except myself?
i made it up
here on this bridge between
starshine and clay,
my one hand holding tight
my other hand; come celebrate
with me that everyday
something has tried to kill me
and has failed.
—Lucille Clifton

In some ways, it was the perfect night for this to unfold. Wild rain pouring loose over Brooklyn and the same day Muslim Americans are being put on trial in hearings that will supposedly expose the threat that radicalization is to American Islam. How many ways and to how many people do I have to prove that I exist? Why does no one put young white men on trial for producing Jared Lee Loughner? Why does "radical" belong to us only when it's "bad"? Why are men not called "terrorists" when they abuse their partners and children? Why must Muslim Americans prove their "loyalty" to this country—how do we know this country is loyal to us?

I am still searching for my bridge between starshine and clay.

STATEMENT OF PURPOSE
JENNIFER CHANG

Among the many reasons I decided to study for a PhD in literature, one of the most urgent was a desire to engage in political and cultural discourses that I felt I could not engage directly enough through writing poems. This expresses more about my shortcomings as a poet than the shortcomings of the genre; however, I decided early on in my life as a scholar that for me the best media for such discourses were the essay and the classroom. Very few people will read my poems, but hundreds of people will spend a semester in my classroom, where I seek to challenge designated touchstones in the literary canon and, at the same time, open the reading of poems to questions of identity, belongingness, and how to form cultures that can accommodate difference. Teaching academic and creative writing as an adjunct in various colleges in New York and New Jersey, it struck me that the dialogic and argumentative possibilities of the classroom were exactly the materials I wanted to work with to build more inclusive communities, to cultivate voices that demanded both change and hope. I believe that reading literature attentively and collectively can make us wiser and braver.

———————

Let me be more precise. I am a Chinese American poet-scholar, born and raised in New Jersey. I've always felt American but have never felt like I fit in anywhere. My first book of poems is about anonymity because I wrote the poems during a time when I was overwhelmed by a feeling of nonexistence. (I still often feel invisible; sometimes I like it, this bleak aspiration toward dust, and sometimes I hate it.) Once, I was asked to give a reading from my book and a couple weeks before the

I was a type, not an

reading the organizer sent me the flyer she'd just distributed, which advertised a reading by Victoria Chang, a California-based poet who is my friend and who is not me. I was in Charlottesville, Virginia, where I've been living since 2006; it is a town I love and yet don't always feel welcome in. Although the organizer apologized, she became irritable and unsympathetic when I told her that I could not in good faith go through with the reading. Months later, when I saw her at a reading, where I was introduced as Jennifer Chang, she called me "Vicky." "My name is Jennifer," I said, and continued signing books. The question this anecdote triggers in me, even as I'm recounting it here, is not how do I write about this in a poem but why does this happen. The organizer was, based on my initial observation, an intelligent and sensitive person repeatedly behaving in an unintelligent and insensitive way. She made me angry, and I was surprised that she was surprised by my anger.

Why does this happen? Why am I so hard to distinguish, so hard to remember? If I did not quite exist, then my hurt and anger certainly did not exist to this woman, which means this could happen again. This was not the same as feeling invisible. For, she had seen me, and then misread me (and Victoria) by assuming an interchangeability. I was any Chang, any Asian. I was a type, not an individual. A synonym.

The History of Synonymity—

My friend Victoria was recently mistaken for me at AWP in Washington, DC. I threw a party when my book came out, and Tina, another friend and another Chang, was mistaken for me at my book party, which was in New York City. At a writers' conference in Tennessee, I was repeatedly asked if Victoria was my sister. Or was Lan Samantha Chang my sister? I tried to diffuse tension by exclaiming, "I wish!" and laughing, but I was the only one feeling any tension. Do people ask Charles Wright and C. D. Wright if they are related to each other? My partner's middle name is Wright. I have never asked him if he is related to Charles Wright or C. D. Wright, though I see that he owns books by both of them. I wonder what Jay Wright thinks.

As a scholar I write about pastoral in modernist American literature—how people belong and don't belong in a place, how the experience of double-consciousness is spatialized, how displacements based on differences of ethnicity, class, and sexual orientation change the very nature of a place. I argue that such displacements have social, cultural, and topographical consequences on American culture and identity. Where we are defines who we are, but who we are can also redefine the places we've only just arrived in. The Great Migration and im-

individual. A synonym.

migration instantiate displacements that can re-configure a neighborhood, join country to city, and remake the demographic map of the United States. If I talk to my students about how places are constituted and reconstituted by who is present, then will they pay more attention to the other people populating our campus?

We attend Mr. Jefferson's University. When I taught *Notes on the State of Virginia*, I asked my students what they thought about his assessment of racial differences, which is rooted in a motley assortment of retrograde biology and armchair anthropology. One of my African American students said that she couldn't speak because the text wasn't meant for her. But you have to speak, I told her, and to the whole class, "Everyone has to speak." That you can't speak only reinforces what he's doing so egregiously: asserting cultural authority through exclusionary practices. The intended audience of *Notes on the State of Virginia* is, presumably, surveyors, other statesmen with natural historian pretensions, founding fathers, and first Americans, but the unintended audience is inscribed into the text, absences that we see elsewhere in his writings. Or sometimes presences that cause contemporary audiences to cringe, as when he explains why Native Americans should not be enslaved.

We read it in 2011 because Thomas Jefferson drafted our nation, rehearsed and then performed some of the first scenes of American life, and is,

for better or worse, our history. That we chose this university means we insist ourselves into that audience, regardless of the author's intentions. We share a common language, the common goal of intellectual inquiry, and a common history. Whether you are black or white or Asian or Egyptian, histories of subjugation belong as much to the oppressors as the oppressed, as much to the observers as the participants. If we accept ourselves in these positions of absence—absent victims, absent perpetrators—then we reinforce historical practices that must be interrogated, redressed, and denied perpetuation. We must all be present, for we share a common responsibility.

The concept of an unintended audience frustrates me. It's not like we are reading diaries stolen from a stranger's bedside table. I forget to ask my students this, a question that might provoke further thought: is there such a thing as trespassing when we read literature?

———

I like to remind my parents that I am the first person in our family born in America. I was born on October 18, 1976, in New Brunswick, New Jersey. One of my first memories of school was World Cultures Day at the Abraham Lincoln School, PS 14, in Elizabeth, New Jersey. I arrived with a plate of potstickers my mother had made and stood in front of a construction paper map of the world, where numbers were written

"Must I be a type

into each country, as if someone were keeping score. Ireland, 16. Italy, 23. China, 1. I didn't want to share my potstickers, but I also didn't want to go home.

———

I arrived at the University of Virginia for my doctoral program in 2006. I bought a house. I was substantially older than most of my classmates, on the verge of thirty, and married, on the verge of divorce. I had graduated from the university five years earlier, from the MFA program in creative writing, and I had returned eager to apprentice myself again to a new discipline. I was literally going from one graduate students' lounge to another.

"You realize it's a different language," a professor warned me. I had run into him at a local bookstore. He was one of the professors I'd most admired and most wanted to work with now that I'd returned with a different objective, and his comment made me feel suddenly defensive and self-conscious. I knew he was only trying to be helpful, so I shrugged it off, asked him how his work was going. I tried to sound smart, less like a poet and more like a scholar. Five years later, I replay the conversation and what I should have said: "I've always been bilingual."

I should have said, "As the daughter of immigrants, I've always lived in two cultures."

The same human resources office signs the paychecks of both the poets and scholars at the university. Which is to say, all poets and scholars who work in the academy are academics. We cross Jefferson's lawn. We walk up and down the same stairs of Bryan Hall, and we take the elevator when we are tired.

"Poetry is a scholar's art," I should have said, quoting Wallace Stevens, employing a key figure in my professor's field of study, convincing him to my point of view by considering his, and thereby winning the argument, which even now is entirely in my head.

I should have said, "So what?"

———

"The wilderness rose up to it / And sprawled around, no longer wild." I can't decide if that jar in Tennessee—an object, human-made, cultural, social—intrudes on the landscape or simply refashions it. "It took dominion everywhere." Are we each a kind of jar, a kind of Adam emerging in a new place striving to rename it? Am I to read dominion with a version or covetous ambition? I never understood how I could be like nothing else in Tennessee.

———

A confession: I'm scared that if I publish this people will think I hate UVA, graduate study, writers, scholars, and white people.

(stereo-, pheno-, arche-)?"

One thing I've learned while teaching is that you have to accept the murkiness of moral ambiguity and critical inquiry and hope that your students will know what to do next. While reading J. M. Coetzee, I explained to my students that sometimes you reach the limits of rational thought and all that's left is emotion, and that becomes your burden as readers and citizens. How do you decide what the right thing to do is when reason and emotion collide? How do you respond to both what you think and what you feel in a manner that is balanced, just, and satisfactory?

I hate being wrong, but I am often wrong. I hate being asked to repeat myself.

About an unfriendly person we know, I say to my partner, "But I don't know her well enough to hate her."

If I hate myself, is it because I have absorbed the dominant prejudices of American society? Perhaps my feeling of anonymity is a sociocultural condition and describes how it feels to be a Chinese American woman in 2011. The individual in me cries out: "Must I be a type (stereo-, pheno-, arche-)?"

It is painful to be invisible. But it is also painful to be seen. Once, when I was a little girl in Elizabeth, our neighbor's son yelled from across the street, "You Jap!" His grandfather had fought in World War II. I didn't tell my parents. Weeks later, my parents invited his parents over for lunch and he wrote his name in red crayon across my chalkboard easel, so that it was no longer usable. My mother asked me why I let him do it. I told her I didn't know I could stop him.

Many things I hate are in fact things I wish were not so. I hate the weather in winter. I hate throwing out yogurt because I forgot to eat it before the expiration date. I hate how much I want to—how profoundly I feel I have to—write this.

And then one day, I am invited by e-mail to a Chinese New Year cocktail party. The hosts are new friends, fellow graduate students, and white. They suggest costumes. There will be a midnight countdown, maybe dancing, an insistence on reviving holiday cheer before February's drear overtakes us. Exclamation points abound. It will be a good time.

I read the invitation in the evening. I grow cold. I don't understand why. The hosts are white and, except for me and two other Asian students, everyone on the invitation list is white. The hosts are not bad people, so I wonder if I'm somehow not getting it. I focus on the words "cocktail party," "costumes," the inexplicable reference to "the winter solstice." I wonder if because I'm Chinese I'm not expected to show

I am preoccupied with

up in costume. I imagine what it might be like to show up at this party, a Chinese New Year cocktail party with a room full of white graduate students sipping cosmopolitans. Why can't I laugh at this? Why am I so uncomfortable? I am embarrassed by what I feel. Do I get angry more easily now that I am reading critical theory and am therefore better able to understand my subject position and the politics of aesthetics?

I think because they are new friends and read critical theory I can write to them freely. I tell them I appreciate their sense of fun, but the premise of their party is offensive. I explain that Chinese New Year is a holiday that honors the dead; it is a time for families and communities to celebrate generational continuity. When they recommend costumes, do they expect people to come dressed up like Bruce Lee or me? I reread my e-mail carefully. I know I am taking a risk; still, their words hurt me and I reason that the last thing anyone wants to do is cause hurt. I add that my message is rooted in the spirit of friendship, and then I send it.

Almost immediately, one of the hosts writes back. He is outraged that I am offended. How could I assume such malice in him? Clearly, they are not racists, though I did not use that word. Clearly, no one is asking anyone to come dressed up like "Jen Chang." He is disappointed in me. He is emphatic: they have researched Chinese New Year. What they are doing is not cul-

tural appropriation, nor is it an insult to my heritage. He accuses me of being immature and irrational. I am a careless friend and thinker. Clearly, I do not understand the discourses I'm invoking. He notes that the other host is too exasperated by my grievance to acknowledge it. He does not apologize.

How is this happening? I ask my then-husband and he says I am both too sensitive and too political. He thinks I've made a mistake; it is just a party. I ask my friends. I show them the e-mail exchange. I want to make sense of what is happening, and why. They assure me that I am not overreacting, but I do not feel assured. No one will confront the host, but how would that make any difference? I run into the other Asian woman on the invitation list. She, too, is offended but doesn't know what to say. Days later, a white woman, who was at first very sympathetic, admits that she can't understand why I won't let it go. You don't seem very Chinese, she says, trying to hurry us onto the next topic. A Korean American friend tells me that he prefers calling it Lunar New Year and that every year his family has a meal without salt to mourn their dead. He has written a poem about this. I ask him what he would do. He is applying to law school because his poems will not ensure a livelihood.

I get another e-mail and I delete it before I can read it. I want this to stop. However, I am

what to call my feeling.

preoccupied with what to call my feeling, and I am preoccupied by how hard it is to stop feeling what I feel. I close the door to my room and stare out the window. I return to researching my essay on Robert Hayden. I read J. L. Austin's *How to Do Thing with Words* and Judith Butler's *Excitable Speech*. I consider infelicitous speech acts and wonder if they offer my feeling a conceptual form. What is happening? I want an answer, but my question is too imprecise. I have lost two friends and, moreover, I have scared off many people who might have been friends. I have made a scene in the graduate students' lounge. I am not invited to many parties after this.

⸻

"That strange flower, the sun, / Is just what you say. / Have it your way. // The world is ugly, / And the people are sad." Joan Richardson reports that upon seeing a photograph of Gwendolyn Brooks, Wallace Stevens asked, "Who's the coon?" I hate this fact and I hate the empty Orientalism that makes some of his early work so sloppy and false; and yet, Stevens has written poems that I turn to again and again for comfort and meaning. Indeed, I have spent much of my life observing the nothing that is not there and the nothing that is. Which leads me to the question: how am I complicit in this—what I feel?

My feeling is a persistent sorrow and the coldest rage. It climbs my spine to reach a raw irritation in the neck, and then it turns numb like a premonition, the body's first inkling of death. My feeling has the steadiness of hours accumulating into days, and now it is many years later ... I did not expect my feeling to last, to have stayed longer than a bad habit, longer than a Whitmanian line. Do I cultivate my feeling, or does it remake me?

"The pleasures of heaven are with me and the pains of hell are with me, / The first I graft and increase upon myself, the latter I translate into a new tongue."

I write this on a Monday afternoon at my kitchen table in Charlottesville, Virginia. It is February 14, 2011, over a week into the Lunar New Year. When I began, I thought I would find consolation and thus recognize an ending to what I'm writing. I thought I would be able to articulate my feeling. I expected my feeling to resolve itself through thought and language. I expected thought and language to welcome me as if into a field of clarity.

I have thought and language. But no field, no clarity.

TO WHOM IT MAY CONCERN

JESS ROW

Years ago, when I was in graduate school, I ran into one of faculty members in my program, an African American novelist I won't name, in Borders Books just across the street from campus. He was in a hurry—going to catch a plane—and needed to buy a copy of his own new novel to bring to a friend. I hurried with him over to the Literature section, and we didn't find the book. How could this be? It had just come out. It was in every other bookstore in town.

Then a thought came into my head—I'd spent more time wandering around Borders than he had—and I took his elbow, unthinking, and led him around the corner, and popped the book out from its place in "African American Fiction."

African American fiction, where James Baldwin, Octavia E. Butler, Toni Morrison, Ralph Ellison, Andrea Lee, James Weldon Johnson, Edward P. Jones, Colson Whitehead, all resided.

He had an expression on his face that I won't try to describe.

━━━━━━━

I am a white American of English, Portuguese, French Huguenot, and Pennsylvania Dutch descent, some of whose ancestors were the Cushman family of Plymouth Colony. My wife's mother is part Bengali, part Punjabi—originally from what is now Pakistan—and her father is descended from Hungarian, Galician, and Russian Jews. Which is to say that my son and daughter, who are all these things, are descended from people who, at times, disliked or despised each other, who struggled to exclude each other from citizenship or privilege.

When I write fiction, I try to write toward my children's future—which is not to say toward some dream world where all these conflicts are resolved and forgotten. Quite the opposite. I want to write fiction in which these conflicts, historical and present, are out on the table. In which there is friction and discomfort—specifically along racial, ethnic, cultural, linguistic lines.

I've been disappointed for a long time that more writers like me (which is to say white writers) don't seem all that interested in seeking out these spaces of conflict and discomfort. But I can see why they don't.

I take it for granted that part of my background and my psychology is racist, that my psyche has been shaped by the lifelong experience of privilege in ways that I will never fully understand. But taking it for granted is only an entry point and a provocation to try to understand these things by the attentive unpacking of the mind: in my case, through writing, through Buddhist practice, and through therapy.

I think that a great deal of the psychic pain I have experienced in my life has to do with anxiety—largely unconscious anxiety—over maintaining my status as a privileged human being. I think that unconscious racial anxiety permeates our culture to a degree very few of us want to admit. And I hold a certain kind of faith, probably an absurd kind of faith, that in writing about these unconscious structures, in bringing them to my readers' attention, I will make them less powerful over my own mind.

I'm certainly not writing about them to be popular or sell books. In my experience, beyond a certain point, the American publishing industry is very uncomfortable with writers who represent characters markedly different from themselves.

Which brings me back to the point of the anecdote above.

The critic Mark McGurl, in his recent book *The Program Era*, describes much of contemporary American writing as "autopoetics," which I understand to mean at least two different things: 1) writing that is essentially autobiographical, even if it is nominally "poetry" or "fiction," and 2) writing that is *assumed to be* autobiographical or self-descriptive, authenticated by the identity of the writer.

Autopoetics is very convenient for the publishing industry, and the culture industry, because it allows marketers, salespeople, journalists, bloggers, and critics to streamline the story of the book and the story of the author into one story. It allows for niche marketing. But it does very little to promote more than a superficial sense of empathy or interrelatedness among readers or writers, and it also promotes naïve and essentialist definitions of culture, ethnicity, and race.

Autopoetics, in its default, unspoken mode, suggests that writers of color, or of some "different" ethnicity, are always writing about their own

More squirming in the

background, and that white writers who dare to mention race are doing something exciting, daring, and extraordinary. Neither of those things ought to be true. Neither of those assumptions accords with the world we live in.

―――――――――

In 2008, on his blog *Do the Math,* the jazz pianist and writer Ethan Iverson (who is white) wrote a long series of posts on the always-simmering controversy over the role of white musicians in jazz. Racially antagonistic language and attitudes are an integral part of jazz history. To choose one vivid example that has always stuck with me: the drummer Art Blakey, whose music I dearly love, was once quoted as saying that "the only way the Caucasian musician can swing is from a rope."

Iverson writes that "Racial stereotyping is best avoided in elevated dialogue, but nonetheless racial stereotyping will occur in any serious discourse about jazz eventually. At that point valuable discussion is often suddenly halted when one side or the other perceives racism or is worried about being racist. I actually don't mind racial stereotyping too much. America is the melting pot of diverse cultures, and all good American art has race 'in the mix' somehow. Hopefully my earnest and underdone phrase 'All in the Mix' doesn't shut the door to further discussion the way 'racist' does."

The literary world is not the jazz world, which is by its very nature multiracial, intermingled, and collaborative across color lines (despite the efforts of some ideologues, like Wynton Marsalis, to suppress the history and energy of such collaborations). The literary world is still, aesthetically speaking, intensely stratified. Black and white and Chinese and Filipino and Latino writers teach in the same programs, sit on the same committees, and share the same publishers, but only rarely do they read one anothers' work with any kind of serious engagement. It's possible, indeed likely, that a white poet could operate in 2011 effectively as if African American poetry doesn't exist. And, to almost the same degree, vice versa.

What this means is that discussions of race in American writing—discussions involving writers of more than one group, that is—often feel as if they're starting from square one. Oh—do we really have to go into *this* again? I once saw a book on classroom management for college teachers called *When Race Breaks Out.* As if it's like strep throat, as if it has to be medicated, managed, healed.

What often happens, in these situations, is that the "healing" involves choosing a scapegoat, someone on whom all the community's energies—its shame and anguish, its pain and frustration—can be concentrated for a short period.

Scapegoating is not healing. But it is the logical consequence of the complacency, the inertia,

audience; less sleepy applause.

and the vacuous self-satisfaction that marks so much of our literary culture.

I think what Iverson is trying to do, in proposing the phrase "All in the Mix," is to say: we can feel insulted, we can even feel attacked, or threatened, and *say* what we feel, without having to respond in kind. Of course, there are times when the aggression or insult is overwhelming and no dialogue is possible. But as Americans we are so heavily invested in shame, avoidance, and denial that most of us have never experienced authentic, face-to-face dialogue about race at all.

I would like to see us try to mix it up more. I see it happening in the work of Thomas Sayers Ellis and Junot Díaz, Danzy Senna and Susan Straight, Jonathan Lethem and Colson Whitehead, in Tony Hoagland's "The Change" and Claudia Rankine's critique of "The Change." But I'd like to see much more of it in our public arenas. More squirming in the audience; less sleepy applause.

I'm hoping, but I'm not holding my breath.

OPEN LETTER
CHARLES BERNSTEIN

Dear Claudia,

I take RACE to be the central fact for those born in the Americas. I spell it large because it comes large here. Large and without mercy.

We are all of us from somewhere else: some came running, some came screaming, some were moved from where they were at home to reservations and plantations that were, at times, akin to killing fields. Most of us just found ourselves here, with a history we never asked for, understood, or can ever fully right.

And there are all the languages: the ones lost in the prairie and on the high plains, wiped out systemically as if they were smallpox; the ones given up to start anew and the ones forbidden at pain of social or economic failure. And the ones retained, the resistant strains that bubble up through our speech like sparks of light; the voices, accents, pitches, tones, vocabulary, dialects, and ideolects that are as ineradicable as the will for freedom or the need for poetry (that is: precarious).

Language is poetry's business so it is with these resistant strains that I have been most concerned: the way that poetry resists, transforms, and remakes the standard.

The emerging poetics of the Americas transforms the US's *E pluribis unum*—out of many, one—to *E unum pluribis*—out of one, many.

Questions of race are never just about narrative or images or stereotypes, they pervade our grammars, our styles, our forms, and above all our unstated system of preferences, of aesthetic value. You say well-wrought urn, I say stunningly tedious; you say stuttering with incompetence, I say a new music for our age.

You ask for "a discussion pertinent to the more important issue of the creative imagination and race" and I agree with your insistence that this is necessary. Poetry can't be left to its own devices. We need the conversation, commentary, contention. Sometimes it hurts and sometimes it hurts too much and sometimes it's illuminating and sometimes stupefying and sometimes just silly or uninformed.

I am interested in how our projections as readers, or as citizens, taint the images we encounter. I don't think you can ever transcend that tainting, but I think it's possible to acknowledge it, or at least come to speaking terms with it.

Truly, yours,
Charles

———————

Quotation in the first paragraph adapted from Charles Olson's *Call Me Ishmael*.

In Particular: <http://jacketmagazine.com/19/bern.html> constituted itself as a Möbius strip of imaginary identity formations and actions, beginning and ending in black and white. What I wanted to create was a counter-bachelor-machine, bachelor machine being Duchamp's term for self-enclosing, non-procreative processes. Along with this poem, two of my essays provide the most detailed response I am capable of to the racial mountain in American poetry. The first is from *My Way: Speeches and Poems* and is called "Poetics of the Americas"<http://sibila.co-.br/index.php/newsibyl/1753-poetics-of-the-americas>, which I have now put online, partly in response to this forum. The second essay is from *Attack of the Difficult Poems: Essays and Inventions* (University of Chicago Press, 2011); it's called "Objectivist Blues: Scoring Speech in Second-Wave Modernist Poetry and Lyrics."

Wendy Ewald,
Queen, 2005

In her American Alphabets series, Wendy Ewald uses images as an interchange with the written word, creating a vernacular of hopes, limitations, and social stratification among her school-aged participants. MKC

I was interested in how young women, particularly white women such as myself, used language. I worked with female students at Phillips Academy in Andover, Massachusetts to create "A White Girls' Alphabet".

The girls choose words to represent letters that they thought best represented them as individuals and a group. Among these were "tearful," "sentimental," and "orgasmic." The girls were surprised at how sad a portrait of themselves they had painted with their words and how preoccupied they were with sexuality. We planned images to represent the words and I photographed them with a large format camera. Then they wrote the letter and word on the negative. WE

Dread Scott, **I Am Not a Man**, 2009

In this one-hour performance on the streets of Harlem, the artist dares to refute the civil rights claim of humanity for African Americans in view of all the evidence to the contrary; the murder by police of unarmed Black men has become unexceptional. MKC

John Lucas, **Tony & Everett**, 200?

A photographer and filmmaker of the American experience, John Lucas, has captured one of the chief peculiarities of assimilation and belonging; the longing admiration of, and the eager participation in, a club that doesn't recognize one's membership. MKC

Edgar Endress,
The Mask of the Shoeshiner, 2007

Of the many roles the mask plays in the Andes region, the mask of the shoe-shiners in La Paz, Bolivia is particularly distinctive. When a severe economic slump hit the nation, many young professionals became shoe-shiners. The shame of this lower-class occupation prompted them to cover their faces. MKO

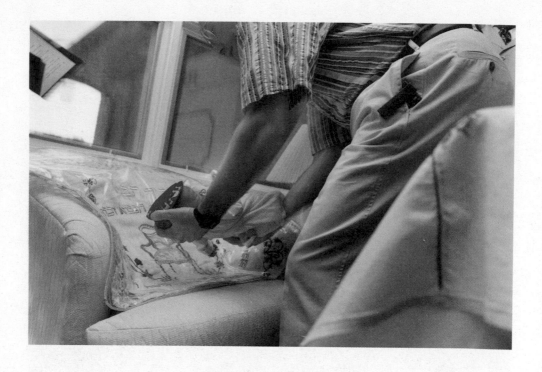

Jay Wolke, **Steve's Bris**, 1996

In his book, All Around the House (*Art Institute of Chicago*), *Jay Wolke photographs the distinct, sub-cultural communities that often express divergent interpretations of fundamental Judaism, while at the same time, negotiating the American mainstream.* MKC

Jeff Wall, **Mimic**, 1982

In restaging for the camera scenes he claims to have witnessed, Jeff Wall creates photographic costume drama. Here, a reenactment of a racist gesture performed on a Vancouver street is revived for his camera; a moment of lost anthropology. MKC

LIVES

What do I have to contribute? How could I ever do enough? Where should I start? Am I offending someone right now? I feel like a fool. You continue walking in silence. **And there, under the skin of each of them, hot and dangerous to the touch, was the story of race I had grown up with and had had little practice at revealing.** I've begun the search for these answers by merely existing. **I can see where the erasures are made in this narrative—or at least I can imagine where they begin—even if I cannot always see what they contain.** Above all, you have learned to not become crushed by having to make these adjustments in the face of a constant, sometimes blatant, sometimes quiet duress, and to remain as elegant and articulate as you are intact.

HOW DO WE INVENT LANGUAGE OF RACIAL IDENTITY— THAT IS NOT NECESSARILY CONSTRUCTING THE "SCENE OF INSTRUCTION" ABOUT RACE BUT CREATE THE LINGUISTIC MATERIAL OF RACIAL SPEECH/ THOUGHT?

RONALDO V. WILSON

The story is a familiar one. You have even found it to be repeated so often that it has become ingrained in your psyche as fact, the same old, same old, the usual, you think. Sometimes it begins with a joke over the phone, *Were you in Arizona?* Or a question,

What did they say you were doing? Or it ends in a home you made it inside of in the middle of the night: *I'm glad you're safe.* There are attempts to comfort you even more, because your friends see that, despite your escape, you're still shaking: *Do you want me to make you some tea?*

But if you are on the other side of this story, you might be saying to yourself, *not again, I did nothing wrong.* In fact, you have done everything right, so right, that when you confront what you cannot control, you must learn to relax, breathe with enough care and measure so that your body conceals its shaking—but your eyes, those are another matter. You think, *Please don't dilate—* at least not wide enough to draw any more attention to your very existence—in the wrong place at the wrong time. Of course, what's connected to the depth of this realization is that you are never where you completely belong, but you must learn to modify, to make due, to make clear your plot and push, what you read and write, map how you travel, go, go, and go. Above all, you have learned to not become crushed by having to make these adjustments in the face of a constant, sometimes blatant, sometimes quiet duress, and to remain as elegant and articulate as you are intact. Perhaps in the end, that's all that you want after the performance, after the teaching, after the ride, after the dinner, after the wine, after the dessert, after the nap, after the errand.

There is always violence, and

The night is cool, but from all the work of remaining stable, you are very, very dizzy. This dizziness is not from the wine—you drank reasonably, a bottle of a light white, split, with two of your closest friends, the shared hummus and Armenian snapper, the perfect olives and baklava. It was, after all, for your birthday, and the evening's indulgence was not what led you into the dizziness. There are other facts that have nothing to do with the dinner that edges you into the realm of being spectacle, a history of spectacle over which you have no control, things that your face, body, grooming, and circumstance cannot, at this moment, elide.

You are a visitor—the afternoon sun in Los Angeles is bright and you find yourself settling into the view of one stunning mountain range after another. At night, you are still driving the big, white rental car, trying to figure out how to maneuver the wide turns at this 2:00 AM hour, but you cannot find your way back to your friend's apartment. A pressure builds, perhaps the pressure of the self about to enjoy the late night, double dessert. You want to keep celebrating. Who knows when you will see your friends again? But you have to get back to square the bill. You have to pack. You get caught up in the struggle of trying to fill the gas tank up to match the three-fourths notch on the car's check sheet. Out to gather donuts, two chocolate glazed, a crois-sant, one old fashioned (bought a glazed cruller by mistake), one glazed bow tie, and since the woman who looks like your mother tells you the cinnamon raisin rolls are fresh and warm, you get that for yourself.

The tank's gauge never indicates the right amount, and the sky above Glendale doesn't look threatening, then you feel the approach of the slowing car of which you are also so familiar, a familiarity you anticipate by feeling, the tightening around your heart. You sigh, not out of relief, but to stay calm. You slow down your step, and then a light bursts—*Can I talk to you a minute? We've had some complaints about your driving.* I got lost. I had to fill the rental car. I'm tired, a little sleepy. *That's not good.* I'm Ronaldo Wilson, and I'm traveling. I got turned around. I'm sorry. *Are you on probation?* No, I'm a professor. I gave a talk today, and taught a class. We just gave a big performance, and soon, we have to leave and catch a red-eye home. I live in New York.

Cathy Caruth points out that "Traumatic memories are the unassimilated scraps of overwhelming experiences, which need to be integrated with existing mental schemes, and be transformed into narrative language. It appears that, in order for this to occur successfully, the traumatized person has to return to the memory often in order to complete it."[1] *Did I get away,* you

---

[1] Cathy Caruth, <u>Trauma: Explorations in Memory</u> (Baltimore: The John Hopkins University Press, 1995) 153.

someone always gets killed.

think? The event, you correctly suspect, will occur again, and though it will leave you, you continue to hope, untouched by hand, baton, bullet, or fist, what cycles is your narrative's constant repetition and spread. Your sister says she feels sad, and says something like, *You can't forget, you're a black man.*

This makes you sad, which comes from, you think, the source of her sadness. Pulled over in the middle of the day, stopped on the side of the road in Elk Grove. *You didn't do anything wrong. It's your car. You're not a bad person.* But you think this is not your story, because you understand how to talk to them. Contrite, you're wearing a black compression sweat suit, and you have finished yoga, and the last time you were pulled over, in South Hadley, you were marked, in the officers, box "B" for Black, and the time before that, in Northampton, you were marked "W" for White, and in each case, you were able to say how sorry you were for this or that, and in court, you beat the ticket by saying, *I want to apologize for taking up the court's time, and I'm not here to challenge the officer, or to deny that I drove through the turning lane. I hope you'll consider my perfect driving record, and that I simply made a mistake— if the court would just grant me leniency, this one time, I would be so very grateful.*

Sorry, Boss, yassuh, I didn't mean nothin' by it, you learn to say in the most protracted ways. Once, as a teen, you are in an old Nova, and ac-

tually think, after getting pulled over, what if I sound like a valley girl? In Sacramento, *I'm borrowing my dad's car, and I'm really late, I'm so sorry,* or, once, more recently, you are profiled in Elk Grove, in a BMW Z4, and once you are cruising in a train station in New York, carrying a red duffel bag: *Do you mind telling me where you're going?* I have done no wrong, at least not a wrong I am aware of, or I got turned around a couple of times. I pulled over to let another car pass. I am coming from a class, or simply walking down a street. There is no violence—no one gets hurt. There is always violence, and someone always gets killed. The earthquake is inevitable. The toll grows. No elbow jabs, but there is always the possibility of an elbow jab. No big black bears tazed in the night, no license is asked for. There is no report. They will not touch you, but sometimes they do touch you. One shakes your hand, another refuses, crossing his arms when you reach out to try to shake his. Where will the pieces of narrative coalesce?

As soon as I read your application, and your books, I fell in love with your work and though your writing is innovative, and exciting, and we hold you in such high esteem, you are just not the right fit here. You do not belong. Go away, run. For the listener, there are related narratives that capture the formation of the self construct ed in the moment of being pulled over, its many remnants, its cycling reminders. Caruth discusses the work of Pierre Janet, points out that he "proposed that traumatic recall remains insistent and unchanged to the precise extent that it has never, from the beginning, been fully integrated into understanding."[2] So that here, the scene of instruction in accounting for this old narrative, or the many that surround it, bleeds into what it means to be forever marked by the fact of one's existence. Building around this existence is a scene of constant interpolation, slipping in, where one slips away, examining how one escapes and begins to process the story of survival, from contrition to understanding—to engage and disengage with this story, the same old, same old, that which will always be familiar, and that which will continue to remain.

---

[2] Ibid.

RESPONSE
TO CALL FOR WRITING ABOUT WRITING ABOUT RACE
ARIELLE GREENBERG

Writing about race has been something I have become increasingly more conscious of, and invested in, since the publication of my first book of poems in 2002. I think of that book as largely apolitical, which is of course not true: every poem is informed by politics in some way, some more overtly than others, but I can't say that I was thinking much about any politics other than gender politics (which are rampant, and rather deeply explored in some ways, in that first book) as I was writing the poems therein. Those poems were mostly written in graduate school, and many of them were responses to exercises. I was playing around.

Almost ten years later, I almost never feel like playing around in that way in my poetry. There are many reasons for this, but the two most obvious are also related: motherhood and time. I don't feel a luxury of time in which to write poems these days, because of how I choose to raise my children, and when I do make time to write poems, they are the product of deeply felt, stored-up material I've been carrying around, heavily, often for weeks or months. And they are engaged in the world—and therefore in politics, and race—in ways they didn't used to be, which is also related to having children.

Writing about race—and also about class—is part of my relatively recent investment in using poetry for something other than playing around.

Which is not to say that one can't play around in a poem about race. But I'm not sure I can. Not yet, anyway. Not in poems about races other than my own.

My second book, finished on the cusp of the birth of my first child, is about my Jewish identity.

I came to realize that I'd left

It is overtly so: that was my intention in writing it, that it would be "about" this subject. I came to realize that I'd left out my Jewish identity, which is a huge part of my life (I was raised Modern Orthodox, had a parochial education, etc.) from my first book. It occurred to me that I was passing as something other than a Jewish Writer. I wanted to rectify this.

I believe that the Jewish people are and are not a race. We are certainly an ethnicity, a complex and varied ethnicity. And we have certainly sometimes been called a race, mostly by people who fear or hate us. But I also know that, as a Jewish American in 2011 who has lived most of my life in New York, or in big cities with visible Jewish populations, I am imbued with the privilege of whiteness. In terms of race, I am White. I rarely feel Other.

I think that when we talk about writing about race, we are talking about writing about power imbalances, about history, about family, about experience, about everything. But again: about power. Disempowerment. I do not feel that my ethnicity disempowers me in any substantial ways in the places and times where I live. So writing about my own ethnic/racial/religious identity is not really writing about race.

I feel it is very, very important to write about race. I encourage my students of color to write about it in ways both subtle and direct. I pay a lot of attention to good poems about race,

praising them to the heavens, because I'm so glad that these poems about something that matters are being made. And increasingly, I encourage my white students to write about whiteness. I try to talk about whiteness in poems that are "not about race," whenever this feels appropriate.

And now I notice: oh my god, I am encouraging my students of color in their writing about race. Is that racist in its own way?

Not sure. I also encourage students to write about class, to write about masculinity, to write about the identity politics, the history, the *real life*, that seems too often buried in the poem, rather than explored. So maybe it is not so terrible that I am encouraging of poems about race from students of color.

Surely it would be worse to *not* be encouraging in these situations?

Am I being a totally vile white person if I report having noticed, with pride, that a large ratio of the graduate students of color at my institution have chosen to work with me on their theses?

Does it make it any better, any worse, if I admit that maybe these students consider me a decent reader of their work, but that since we often have no faculty of color with whom they can work, I am part of the problem nonetheless?

Does it make it any better if I write about how completely pissed off I am when white poets apply for positions or fellowships specifically aimed

out my Jewish identity . . .

at poets of color? And how I have the urge to write to such white poet applicants and say "How dare you!"? No, I don't think this really makes it any better.

And do I write about whiteness myself? Or non-whiteness? Sometimes. More than I used to. Not nearly enough. Not nearly. As someone who has lived in Chicago for eight years, I feel glad to have known, taught, been friends with people of other races, and that experience has certainly entered my poems.

Chicago feels so different to me in terms of race than Boston or New York did when I lived in those cities. I have been fortunate to teach at a very racially diverse school, and so race comes up, almost without fail, in every class I teach. It spurs me to assign more readings by poets of color, to invite more poets of color to come read, and to otherwise be more conscious of race than I'd maybe be if I taught at a more typically, more white college.

(In Boston, I taught in a program at a college that was for students from underrepresented backgrounds. They were almost all African American, so in those classes, race was often a central, highly visible topic. I felt so lucky to have this be one of my earliest college teaching experiences, and I felt deeply impacted by these intense and profound opportunities to get to know students with very different backgrounds from my own. But looking back, I don't think I carried what I

learned into my other classes in the ways I could have or should have, which is to say, centrally.)

Here are some ways I've been writing about race of late: I've been trying to note, in poems, where the characters being discussed are white, even when there are no characters in the poem who are not white. I've been trying to talk a bit about whiteness. I've been also trying to write a little about how I perceive or receive blackness in others, about how I notice who is black, or how I notice blackness, or racial categories, in the world.

I am still splashing around in the shallow end of writing about race. I want to be swimming eventually. At least keeping my head afloat.

(I am aware that there are racial stereotypes about who can and cannot swim.)

Two more thoughts:

I am going to move to a place where there are very few people of color, a rural place in the North. I have thought about starting a writing project called something like "What White People in Belfast, Maine, Do." As a way of making whiteness visible. As a way of thinking about race in a place where one may rarely see someone who is not white, and could, in theory, thereby avoid thinking about race in one's daily encounters. Writing such a project seems, quite literally, the least I can do. I hope to also do far more direct activism and work on this issue, around race and around whiteness.

And finally, yes, it's embarrassing to admit in its obviousness and its utter lameness, but I feel plenty of typical white guilt about race, and I am not quite sure yet how to move past that toward something genuinely interesting and engaged. It has occurred to me that one thing I do *not* want to do is continue to be a white woman writing about whiteness and non-whiteness in isolation: that I do not want to extend the legacy of the Second Wave feminism with which I was raised, which did not adequately or sensitively consider the inherent ways in which any kind of inequality or injustice are tied up in issues of race (and class, and sexuality, for that matter, but those are issues that I do feel I'm able to address, and do address, in my writing with a lot less hang-ups than around race). The Second Wave feminists made a mistake by trying to work on single issues, often in single-race groups or organizations. I've made the same mistake in my writing, I think.

Even everything I write here feels pathetic to me. What do I have to contribute? How could I ever do enough? Where should I start? Am I offending someone right now? I feel like a fool.

It seems important, though, to even say the above. I don't feel those things about writing in general, or in writing about, say, gender. I just feel those things in writing about race. Interesting. Uninteresting. Obnoxious. Typical.

Not enough.

It seems to me the best way to move forward on this is to collaborate with writers from other races, in dialogue. I cannot and will not write about being anything other than white, because that seems really problematic and coopting to me. I don't want to speak for anyone else, raise my voice above theirs. So how can I write about race other than whiteness? By having a conversation in my work, I think. Maybe? I want to try it.

One final note: I hate writing "non-white" when I talk about this stuff, or "writers from other races" or any "non" or "other." It positions whites at the center of the language universe, of course, and at the center of the universe period. I wish there were another, more effective, less white-centric term. But I guess these phrases do point at a reality of ideology and power that describes our culture. But I want to point at them, call myself out on them.

IF I TELL THESE STORIES: NOTES ON RACISM AND THE WHITE IMAGINARY
HELEN KLONARIS

Dear Claudia,

I am grateful for your invitation. And for this gathering of poets and storytellers and scholars, thinking out loud about race and the creative imagination.

Do I think about race as a writer? All the time. I grew up in a Greek immigrant community, in a postcolonial island country where statues of Christopher Columbus loom large over the capital; where Queen Victoria still sits enthroned in the city square. Where lawmakers convene wearing the white wigs of English colonial rule. Where laws have been handed down from England and even though the country is now in the hands, more or less, of the majority, who are of African descent, old laws still work their ways into our collective dreaming, being, doing.

I grew up and spent the majority of my adult years on an island in the heartland of colonial myths of paradise: the Caribbean. I am the child of sun, sand, and sea. Of Bahama Mamas and miniature cocktail umbrellas and the ubiquitous silhouette of coconut trees at sunset. Of an island split into coastal beaches, hotels, white merchants and tourists on the north side, and on the south side, Over-the-Hill, working-class blacks whose jobs–serving customers, waiting tables, cooking, cleaning–were located on the north side. East and west were reserved for moneyed whites (and brown and black exceptions)—old money from slavery and rum running in the east, new money from investments in what the old money had built in the west. More or less. In the center were public schools populated mostly by black students, and fanning out from that center, east and west, private schools populated mostly

. . . I break the silence that

by white students and fewer brown and black. I'm a child of an English school system, and a school—twelve years from kindergarten to O-Levels—that came into existence as a response to integration in the late 1940s: Saint Andrew's was established by white parents who didn't want their white children going to school with brown and black kids.

My imagination is riddled with the stories racism built. My imagination is not a gentle place in which to play, to run and jump; it is not separate from the landscape I was schooled in. I am aware of how the island shows up there; all cut up into pieces, north, south, east, west. How plantation walls have morphed into the walls of high-end hotels and gated communities. How geography designates value. How, even while I was embarrassed by my association with a school of mostly white kids on a mostly black island, I also grew up believing in my special-ness. The landscape of my youth pulses in my imaginary. That liminal place where streams of images and thoughts flow from unconscious and conscious places and commingle. A wet-land where new stories are spawned. Stories which, if I am not careful, just repeat themselves. Repeat the bone structure and facial charac-teristics and speech patterns of the stories they come from.

I became an activist at a young age, aware and not aware that I was talking back to stories.

Talking back to Bible passages and church edicts and what my family had to say about girls and women, boys and men; these were easiest to see and resist. Hidden only slightly deeper inside silences and gestures, glances, and half-Greek, half-English phrases was the story of race; what I heard white people say and not say about our-selves; and what we said and didn't about the black people we lived next door to, the black women who came to the house to care for us, the black women and men who worked for us in our hotels and factories and retail stores all along Bay Street, and the black people who ran the country.

These are stories I am not supposed to tell. They still live in my body. I heard them spoken at dinner tables, in family talk about work, about the gov-ernment, about the country. In bars, white expats drank beer and took turns calling the government backward, and in the gaps between words and un-derneath them was the unspoken belief that "if we still ran the country, things would be better." And in the gaps between those words and underneath them was another belief: white people are natural leaders. I learned from what was said, and what wasn't.

Memory: one Sunday in church, a brown-skinned woman walks in out of the sunshine, sits in a pew on the wrong side, with the men instead of the women. She wears a simple cotton dress. Her hair is short, natural. She is in her forties, maybe. Everybody can see she is there. After the service, nobody speaks to

protects a bond of whiteness.

her. Everyone pretends we don't notice each other pretending and not speaking. I do not know why we do this. Maybe by pretending she is not there we do not have to see or hear our own thoughts about her. We do not have to acknowledge the difficulty of what it would mean to open our church doors to the black women who take care of our children. We do not have to acknowledge the ways we olive-skinned immigrants are benefiting from whiteness in a black country. Or notice the guilt we may or may not have about the visible inequities of our everyday lives. The ways light and white skin add up to better land, better schools, better food, business loans, financial progress. I learn that silence is a way of refusing to see. Of willful ignorance.

If I tell you these stories, I break the silence that protects a bond of whiteness.

What I know about you is complicated. We are friends at school, we are coworkers at work, we are even lovers at home. I am not supposed to tell you how I was also taught to fear you. O mavros erhete! The black man is coming! The clenching around words, the nervousness, the high-pitched voices. A black man walking down the street—our street—is reason for fear. My mother snatching me inside. I was six years old. The neighborhood by then was not whites only, but the story I understood in my belly and bones was that we were meant to be there; black people "coming in" were new, were exceptions to the way things were supposed to be. Never mind that people of African descent made up the majority

of the population, or that we were newly independent of colonial rule; the color of ownership in our imaginations was still white.

I am not supposed to tell you this. But it is here anyway, when I laugh with friends at lunch, say good morning when I get on the bus, or caress my lover's cheek when she comes home after a long day, the stories breathe along with us. The stories are blinking their eyes, watching me watching you. How I heard grownups complaining about the workers, the finality in their voices when they said, you know, they all steal, that's just how they are. (Never mind it was my grandfather's brother who stole a house from under him. Never mind the ways we kept our silence about the uncle who "fondled" little boys, and little girls, including my mother. The violences we were most familiar with went untold, or were quickly, aggressively shut down when they did leak out, and so our fantasies of [white] respectability, honor, goodness could remain intact ...) Stories. In tones of voice not meant to be heard by our neighbors. Secrets. The way I never said the word black because I didn't know it was ever said to mean beautiful, to mean love, to mean life. I had never heard it to mean honor, power, a person or creation of value. Of goodness. And as long as we could see blackness (the way we defined it), know where it was in relation to us, we could be comfortable in our whiteness. We could be beautiful, honorable, have the right to power, see ourselves as good. It was important to see blackness, but only in relation to our whiteness. What I mean is,

. . . we need you to be "black"

we did not want to see the culture of African people, be curious about it, understand or appreciate it in its complexity, its fullness; we needed an essentialized blackness as a reminder of what we did not want to be, who we were not. What I mean is, we need you to be "black" so we can be "white." This is what I am not supposed to tell you, and probably what you already know.

Now I am thinking about what those secrets do in unconscious places. And how they inform my imagination. And how my imagination informs what I write and the way I speak and act with other white people and how it enables and disables me from loving my black lover ...

The secrets are heavy, heaped like leather-bound storybooks one atop the other, reaching up to the sky. Teetering wildly, precariously. It is the accumulation of secrets I feel in the thick of a moment when I could speak up but don't. There is a terror, old, of the teetering tower of secrets falling down. What will happen if I open my mouth to say no? Two things are true: there is the fear of the consequences of speaking, and the privilege of knowing I will not suffer if I don't. Here in my body I know the felt sense of how racism continues: the looking away (from myself), the closing of my eyes, the clenching inside my throat. The shutting down of self-awareness, and of my voice. And with these, the shutting down of emotional intelligence, compassion, the ability to empathize

and to love. It is a lie that racism does not hurt me. And if I want to heal myself of racism, the way it inhabits me, uses me, keeps me obedient to it, I have to let the secrets fall where they may. A mess of old storybooks, splayed wide open for all to see. This is where I begin: first, dare to see what I see; second, dare to open my mouth and tell what I am not supposed to tell. Speak it, so that it isn't misleading me from the inside.

———

I had been an activist for over fourteen years when I returned to the writing of stories. I say "returned" because I had been a writer of stories in my early teenage years, but had abandoned them to essays as my activism took up more space in my life. (I remembered, though, the feeling of losing myself in a story, the way I could put myself in a character's body easily, shapeshifting, as it were, and see the world from their perspective.) I had been active in grassroots feminist movements, GLBT rights movements, and had written passionate letters against neocolonialist racist actions, but I began to feel that the activism I was part of was limited. Our arguments seemed circular, created binaries of us versus them, and the old, dominant narratives of patriarchy and colonialism persisted. Then in 2005 I traveled to the Queer Islands Conference at the University of Chicago and heard

so we can be "white."

writers like Thomas Glave and Colin Robinson and others lament the failure of the imagination to create successful queer movements in Caribbean countries. And though at first I was defensive, I had to agree that some vital element was missing.

Fearful for the imagination, I left home to study fiction in San Francisco at a little-known activist college on Valencia Street. I left home looking for a place to practice imagining. But what I found here in the Bay Area, in spite of its reputation as a progressive American community, was a more pronounced separation of people and space along color lines than had existed even in the Bahamas. And though I was an immigrant from a small place, whose identity culturally was certainly not singular, I could easily pass (if I held my tongue) into a cultural majority whose values and language and stories mattered; whose gaze mattered above all others.

When I look back now, here is what I understand: I get off the plane and walk out into the shimmering energy field of a very large story. A story that is three-dimensional. That moves when I move. A story of white supremacy that imbues everything from streets and freeways to road signs to whole neighborhoods and town centers, with itself. As I walk into the streets of the US, I am approached by this story. It offers me things. Passports. Free passes. Safe neighborhoods. Physical and mental distance from the everyday traumas of ghettos reserved for poor people of African and indigenous and Latino descent. It has the power of a black hole, to warp the structure of who I think I am.

Whatever Greekness and Africanness I brought with me, in my speech, in the movements of my lips and hands and hips when I speak; my tastes and preferences, and the ways of knowing both cultures imbued me, when I step off that plane, into these streets, all that gets rearranged and pressed quiet, and sucked out and disappeared inside this story. I will, if I am not careful, move right along with the story, and when I move along with it, because of my color and who I imagine myself to be, and who others imagine me to be, I feel no resistance. The world of shopkeepers, bank tellers, employers, my students, strangers on buses and in lines at the cinema, smile at me. I might believe, as a young woman waves at me from her bike as I cross the road in downtown Berkeley, that this is a friendly place. An easy to get along with place. Inside this story I fear no resistance. I do not even expect it. I don't expect to be followed around in clothing stores, or watched by policemen in police cars when I drive my green Honda through town, or feared and avoided as I take a walk through my neighborhood. I can take graduate critical theory classes and have it confirmed that my people—Aristotle and Socrates and Plato, for

. . . the racism of my

example—are where thought and philosophy and literature all started, and the thinking and literatures of non-European cultures, are somehow latecomers to the conversation. I can assume I am at the center, or should be, of movements and histories, and that the human story is naturally seen best through the lives of people and characters who look and sound like me.

Except that I can't. Maybe we only begin to question a story (or a system) when it fails us. My mother questioning religion and the church she grew up in when at forty she finally acknowledged the priest in whom she had confided her incest had called her the liar.

As a first-generation Greek Bahamian woman who is also queer, I don't inherit the benefits of whiteness in as substantial a measure as straight white women or men. My differences, however subtle, have provided enough friction and energy to have made walking around in the story of white supremacy complicated and uncomfortable.

Enter fiction, where what is complicated and uncomfortable in the world outside becomes a way into the unconscious stories we most need to tell.

My words, at first, were clumsy and hard to retrieve. As an activist writing nonfiction, I knew what I thought. I could use anger to fuel my words. There was clarity and conviction. And, I could draw the lines where I believed them to

be. But fiction was unruly, hard to control. What I thought had little to do with what the stories wanted to say. Robert Olen Butler says we write stories from the place where we dream. There, at the threshold of my unconscious, waiting for me to notice, was a backlog of every stereotype I had ever pushed away, resisted, suppressed. My stories were childlike, crude. Or they were long reams of lyricism with no plot in sight. Or they were sermons disguised as stories. And there, under the skin of each of them, hot and dangerous to the touch, was the story of race I had grown up with and had had little practice at revealing.

It was my return to fiction that brought me face to face with the racism of my imagination. And too, with the power to transform it.

══════════

I am a girl sitting at the dinner table. I am in love with the boy in my class who writes stories like I want to write stories. He is beautiful and runs like the wind. His eyes laugh with mine. He has a dimple in his chin that I want to touch with my fingers. And when he reads his stories in class, I stare at him with my whole self. I listen and can feel the cold marble floor, the crunch of gravel under his bare feet like it was me walking. I am in love with what he can do with words. I hear the grownups talking. One man says, My daughter came home the other day, say she has a boyfriend. She's ten, you know, so I say, what does this boyfriend look like? She says, he's

own imagination.

handsome, daddy, and his hair is curly curly. Like mine, I say. No, she say, like John's. Everyone at the table is laughing. I think it is because John is the gardener. And John is black. So the girl's boyfriend must be a black boy. My hands are sweating under the table. The boy I love writes stories like I want to write stories. I am writing a story now. My hands are itchy under the table. Everybody's face is pale, some pink, some pastry colored, some, like my father's, the color of white bread just out of the oven. When they laugh, I hear what is behind the laughter, how they are afraid when they turn out the lights at night, how they never feel safe. I see the white iron bars wrapping their windows so that no one can get in, and no one can get out. They have rifles under the bed. I wonder if Columbus and his men slept with rifles under their cots, their ships rocking, rocking underneath them, underneath them the whole of Europe, like the ocean, holding them up. I hear gunfire and the thud of feet against sand, dirt, the slapping of water, bloodied, against the sides of ships, and then silence. I feel nauseous. The men with the rifles come back, build big houses. Sleep with the rifles under their beds, because outside, they have people working for them without pay; they have people working for them who they hardly feed, who they hurt with whips and guns if they try to escape. It's these people who build the houses we're sleeping in now. Who know they built us a world for free. I can see all this behind the laughter, behind their gleaming foreheads, in the slight twitch of eyelids in between laughs. That is

when I know, in the gap between laughs, that I am not going to believe them when they will tell me do not love that boy who writes like you want to write. That is how I know to steal the gun from under my father's bed one Saturday morning and shoot the bars off the windows till my shoulder is bruised and the bars buckle and sag against the peach concrete walls, useless. The windows open wide. I am not going to believe them when they will tell me I am crazy, when they take me to a doctor who says he can make me better.

———————

In the beginning I wrote white characters who sat around talking anxiously about identity crises and disappearing out of their skin into thin air. I was uncomfortable with these stories, with the shame they seemed to be steeped in. Besides, as is the way of stories and dreams, I knew that whatever I was trying to kill, to disappear, would just come back to haunt me. I kept writing, through the shame, through the disappearances, the hauntings, till I came to a still place, a matter-of-fact place, where the character no longer tried to escape herself, to be "good," but instead showed me the uncomfortable realities she was implicated in, and in which she had agency to, at the very least, know she was implicated. In the beginning, I realized I had to write through the muck of the unconscious till I could get to something dynamic and uncluttered by shame, or fear of being seen as a racist. And something interesting began to happen. Once I could write about being implicated, I could see the story of white supremacy—of whiteness as a structure, inside the story and in my life, more clearly. Which meant, I had the power to write to interrupt that structure, dismantle it, and even begin to imagine something else. I am reminded of something a white theology professor of mine said long ago: you cannot move from a place you deny you are in. And, the writing showed me you cannot dismantle a system you choose not to see.

I don't believe the imagination is a free zone, an empty space where we are free from the stories we live out here in the world. But I do think it is a place of radical possibility. Once I found my way to that still place, to a place of seeing even when I was afraid to look, I found the imagination became a place where surprising alchemy ensued. The flow of new ideas into old ideas caused a third thing to emerge. It is that third thing I am trying to get to: the possibility of transformation in the imaginal realm, on the page, and in my body where stories live, speak, and act out here in the world.

Kensington, California

Notes on whiteness:
Whiteness isn't curious about itself or about what is doesn't know or see. You cannot know what you don't see. Whiteness is a defense ...

OPEN LETTER
ISAAC MYERS, III

Dear Open Letter,

I'm sitting at the back of a bar with four friends around two small square tables that have been pushed together between us. I'm sitting at the end of the table farthest away from the door with Lance, a White male and his girlfriend Nadine, an African American female to my left. Pat, a White male, and Carl, who I believe is one half Asian American, sits to my right.

A few hours earlier, the five of us had gathered to discuss how to raise awareness about race-related issues through a budding and in-development campaign, read poems (some our original work, some by others) about race, and get to know one another better. I read Joy Harjo's "A Map to the Next World" and feel lighter as I deliver the poem's final five lines:

> Yet, the journey we make together is
>   perfect on this earth who was
> once a star and made the same mistakes
>   as humans.
>
> We might make them again, she said.
>
> Crucial to finding the way is this: There is
>   no beginning or end.
>
> You must make your own map.

Carl reads Etheridge Knight's "A Fable" and we all let out a collective exhale of amazement and I whisper to myself "bad ... ass" upon hearing Knight's last four lines:

. . . none of us

"All we have to do is wait long enough and the bars will bend from their own inner rot. That is the *only* way." "Are all of you crazy," cried prisoner #7. "I'll get out by myself, by ratting on the rest of you to the non-colored people. That is the way, that is the *only* way!" "No-no" they all cried, "come and follow me. I have the / way, the only way to freedom." And so they argued, and to this day they are still arguing; and to this day they are still in their prison cells, their stomachs / trembling with fear.

Fast forward.

The five of us sit around the two small square tables in the middle of March at the back of a poorly lit bar in Des Moines, Iowa, with our five drinks before us. What were we talking about when he approached?

A white man in his midthirties dressed in a black button-down shirt with two or three buttons undone and open at the neck walks up to Nadine who wears her hair in an afro. Seated, she looks up at him as he stands awkwardly before our table with a beer in his hand. "Do I know you?" says the look on her face. Then it happens.

He lifts his free hand and pats Nadine's afro with the same "That's so cool" amazement that a child would graze a hand over a Chia Pet. We all know racial discrimination has reared its head again and though no one quite says it, he quickly realizes his mistake and apologizes, "I'm sorry," and raises his hands beside his chest to strike the no offense–my bad–no harm pose. Lance takes his arm from around Nadine and begins to stand, "Just go," and he apologizes again, "Seriously, I'm sorry," before he turns and retreats to his three friends who are seated at table a few feet away from us. He takes a seat with his back to us and although the incident has ended and we have attempted to return to our conversation, we're all aware that for the moment, we have been changed.

Today, as I write these words for the Open Letter project, I have just begun to realize the role and place of poetry within this cloudy and complex problem we call Race in America. Last night, when the five of us met and the poetry rang out from our voices, played upon our ears, and ran across our hearts, the possibility for something better floated about the room. We knew we could "Make our own maps" and believed we could work against "Still arguing to this day" and remaining "in our prison cells, [with our] stomachs / trembling with fear."

But two hours later, sitting in a noisy bar, we all knew that Nadine was hurt, that the four of us were hurt because we didn't speak up, and that none of us spoke up because we didn't quite know what to say. In that moment, I wish I had Harjo's poem to recite. I would have read it loud enough for the entire bar to hear. Instead, I sat as a speechless witness to racial discrimination.

spoke up . . .

Poems on race, especially those written by Black, Hispanic, Latino, Latina, Asian, and Native American poets provide people with words, thoughts, and ideas in ways that uncomfortable conversations cannot. However, having conversations that may at first be difficult is the only way to make talking about race easier. Poetry, unlike any other medium, can begin the process. This afternoon I've realized that no matter how wonderful, powerful, or beautiful a poem one writes, reads aloud, or comes across, conversations must still take place. Otherwise, who knows how long we'll remain locked in this giant prison cell.

———

As a beginning poet, I've found it difficult to always find the words that convey the lasting impression or "take home message" of my poems. Of course, the issue of how far a poet should aim to separate himself from his work always exists. Am I writing poems to share Isaac Myers's voice with readers—or should I aim to write poems that create new meaning, bring out emotions readers don't know they have, or ask readers to see or understand an occasion or topic in a new way?

Numerous times over the past few years, I've sat in workshops and listened intently to my peers interpret, peel away, and dissect the message and meaning of my poems. Often, those same peers have pointed out things that my po-ems have done well or "effectively" only for me to respond, "Oh, wow, thank you, but I didn't actually intend that."

Over time, I've come to realize that most thoughts or ideas that actually appear within my poems (as opposed to ideas that readers invent or pull away based on their individual experiences) should be written with both intent and purpose. Said otherwise, "Oh wow, I didn't actually intend that" is a sure fire sign that (1) the words on the page have come from a place that's somehow unreal, fabricated, or inauthentic and (2) I've misstated or simply missed the image or idea that I had attempted to express. So I revise as all poets must, walking the line between sharpening my intentions and "telling the truth slant" without merely re-creating a scene from my diary.

One reason I find the process of writing poetry incredibly enjoyable and rewarding is its inherent and unavoidable difficulty. Each time I am lucky enough to write a poem—on any topic—I say a small thank-you to whatever small places within my heart and mind that the words have come from. The trick to writing po-ems about race, as I see it, is a three-step process: (1) figuring out where exactly my "non-racial" po-ems come from, (2) questioning where poems based on my existence as an African American male do and should come from and (3) determining how like or unlike these two places may be.

The short and likely more accurate answer is that these two places are one and the same. How can I write a poem about the girl who sat beside me on the bus in eighth grade without remembering that she was White and I was Black? And even if the poem does not contain the lines "Devon was white / I was black," won't those two facts always shape and change the actual experience as well as affect my poem's description of that experience? The short answer is of course. Of course Devon's existence as a White girl and my own existence as a Black boy affected our relationship and as an extension, years later, my poem. Yet, the key question is how, and my only answer is that I'm still exploring.

So recently, as I've tried to write more poems that touch on race, I am sure that the poems come from the same place as all of my other pieces. However, where the question in my "non-racial" poems is how does race shape my words, the question in my poems based on race must be to what degree should, do, or must my experiences as an African American male play a role in the creation of the poem—and in addition, to what degree should my existence as an African American male affect what readers pull from the poem.

This evening, as I search for an answer to these questions, I'm confident that there's a great one out there. However, I'm nearly as certain that the answer won't come tonight, tomor-row, before the end of March, or even in the year 2011. As poets, just as people, our voices grow, mature, and develop. Sometimes this development is learning to use internal rhyme more effectively; sometimes, it's discovering, mastering, or inventing a new form. Constantly and continuously, this development is figuring out more about ourselves through both reading others' poetry and through creating our own work. Thus, I suppose only time, work, and the continual process of learning to become a more effective reader and writer of poetry will lead me to satisfactory answers. So I've begun the search for these answers by merely existing; and as a poet I continue the search through not only writing but also by holding on to the hope that over time, writing and existing become the same act.

Sincerely,
Isaac Myers, III

OF WHITENESS, OBAMA, AND THE SO-CALLED POSTRACIAL
TESS TAYLOR

Dear Claudia:

Here's an article I have been working to publish. It has to do with the way whiteness figures itself as invisible in storytelling and writing, and in lived experience. My wish as a writer about my own racial experience is to unsettle the kind of position of invisibility that whiteness so often assumes; to become uncomfortable in my own skin, to distrust what I'm told about who I am; or even to distrust what I can see. This discomfort, even a little, reminds me (even a little) not to take all the privilege I get every day from my skin for granted. It's not really a solution, but it's an exercise in keeping aware of what I'd otherwise be allowed not to think about. And it reminds me to think about my experience, always, as racial. I think before we get beyond anything we have to figure out a way to talk about what whiteness is and has been. What made it? What purpose does it serve? How and where does it work? What coercions does it offer? Toni Morrison asked us this in the mid-nineties and I don't see us answering, really, yet. Or I don't see the answers sinking in.

My current book of poems, The Forage House, attempts to excavate a history of slaveholding that was hidden in plain sight in my family, about which I was invited not to know and not to feel. I did not and do not really have full access to this history, but just to its painful marginal ghosts; to the feeling that it was there always but I don't know what that means. For generations African American writers have been telling their readers in many ways that their history is inaccessible, partial, erased. But white people have erased their own history, too—they have absented themselves equally from their own painful legacies. It is just that they have also convinced themselves that they do not need to

The postracial meant we never

remember. What might trying to remember do? What might be uncovered? How do we figure these kinds of absences and presences in poems? Anyway, this is at once too short and too long—but I hope it will be of some use to you. I admire your work and I look forward to future conversations. For what it's worth, Martha Collins and Jake York and I and some others proposed a panel on the problems of writing whiteness for AWP last year and it was turned down. Why? I keep wanting to know. I think it's time for us to try to talk about what we do when we try to understand ourselves, when we try to see what we often hide in plain sight.

Very best and good luck to you; thanks for spurring this conversation.

Yours sincerely,

Tess Taylor

Near the end of 2008, I had an exchange with a prominent New York book reviewer, one whose reviews appear in high places: *The New Yorker, The New York Times Magazine, The New York Review of Books.* We were doing the usual year-end round up, talking about books of the past year and casting predictions for the year to come. Deadlines being what they are, we were writing our "end of the year summary" in early November on the eve of the election. By the time we submitted copy, Obama had been elected. I cried as Virginia, state of my slaveholding ancestors, voted blue. In the midst of barriers broken and

power shifting, I wondered aloud how the coming era would affect the world of books. This was possibly a pundit's cheap trick: While it is silly and perhaps dangerous to link artistic expression too directly to one's president, it may also be a useful gesture. In any case, many artists I know had been depressed by eroded civil liberties, government watchdogs, and a culture that openly mocked the life of art and the mind. Would the Obama era be different?

My fellow reviewer took me up on my question, choosing to address questions of storytelling in the face of our newly emergent American identity. After all, Obama was prominently offering our national narrative a new face. The reviewer quoted a young "coffee-skinned" woman he'd heard who'd suggested that "immigrant fiction" was "past it." He quoted Bulworth, who said "The way to fix this country is for everyone to f____ everyone else for a hundred years until we're all one color." The reviewer then wondered if the novels of Díaz and Lahiri would be the last of their kind. He wrote: "will American fiction eventually leave race and background behind as a result of the blurring into unimportance the lines of ethnic and racial identity ... . if it does, as I think it will, what, if any, new kinds of fictional identities can emerge?"

It was, and is, a million-dollar question, one that predicts, and is predicated upon, both a certain hopeful transcendence, as well as a loss of

had to talk about race . . .

certain histories. It looks forward toward a time many people were predicting back in 2008—the future of the so-called postracial. Two years into the presidency, for now at least, that hope also seems like a misplaced prediction. One only has to watch the Sotomayor hearings or the Skip Gates kerfuffle or hear the chilling chants of Tea Party bigots to understand that discussions of race in this country are far from being "post" anything: they are a living, breathing lightning rod. "What's the matter with white people?" writes Joan Walsh in *Salon*, citing a study that shows that white people resent health care because they believe it helps "others." "Identity Politics leans right," write Sam Tanenhaus, noting that the people who seem to feel under attack are white people, white men especially. Perhaps "immigrant fiction" and "identity politics" may have seemed "past it," but whiteness is on the rise, and perhaps not in the way we'd wish it to be.

From this vantage, it's clear that ideas of the postracial were, if hopeful, a tad naïve. To be fair, it seemed from some vantages like the postracial itself was a way of jumping the gun, getting all of us, whoever we are, to adopt a pose of forced transcendence. If we were white, we could be absolved of uncomfortable feelings of guilt or shame about racism we saw in our present or in our past. The postracial meant we never had to talk about race—It was finished! In this, the current amnesia resembled the old amnesia, where we didn't acknowledge race at all. If we were of color, well, hey, we could put down whatever ax we'd been grinding. In fact it was damn well near our responsibility to do so. After all, Obama was in the White House. Identity politics could be over: Forget those difficult years of discussing quotas or affirmative action. Forget glaring inequities in infant mortality or poverty or college graduation. Forget what our parents or their parents or their parents went through. We were "post": The blended nation was on the rise.

Don't get me wrong here. Statistics and cultural fantasies do align, and we are becoming a more blended nation yearly: Any trip to the East Village or San Francisco will show layers on layers, the fabled beauty of the multiracial Benetton ad, the elaborate hybrid mixings that made the *Onion* recently joke that bigots were behind in "racial slur development" for our new mixed-race selves. We are increasingly mixing with one another—but only 2 percent of the population in 2006 called themselves "mixed race," which is hardly a sign that we feel ourselves as blended. (I am eagerly watching for the results of the 2010 census.) For what it's worth, countries that are melting pots *do* melt: The Anglo-Saxons and the Franco-Normans were pretty separate—and full of elaborate class and caste distinctions—for about four hundred years until they became, legally, linguistically, genetically, etc. indistinguishable from one another. Their postracial happened because they slowly

It's a tempting myth,

became one race: the English. In fact, races are blending all the time, cultures are, and always have been. Racial purity is about the stupidest myth out there. "Whiteness" doesn't exist biologically and never has. Socially it's in flux. I only point out that the Anglo-Normans took four hundred years to sleep with each other to the point of cultural amnesia because we're only barely one generation into an era when the former crime of miscegenation is even legal. We may have come a long way, baby, but baby, we also have a long way to go. Oddly, this relates to another bizarro double standard in the way we've talked about race in America. Attending a liberal arts college or a fine arts university, we may get into conversations about the social construction of race, the biological non-existence of race. Reviewing Nell Painter's recent book *The History of White People* in the *New York Times*, Linda Gordon flippantly remarks, "'Whiteness Studies' have so proliferated in the last two decades that historians might be forgiven a yawn in response to being told that racial divisions are fundamentally arbitrary ... " It's great that Painter, who is African American, can point out to us that whiteness has a history, and that Gordon can yawn. And it's lovely that in the academic world the idea that race has no biological basis is so familiar as to seem passé. It seems to be an idea, however, that's missing from the same segment of the population that denies the existence of evolution, which is to say, a lot of people out there. And what's passé amid academics for the last

two decades seems not to be having much effect on the tenor of discourse outside the academy.

What exists outside the academy are a series of entrenched social patterns that our new understandings of biology don't yet seem poised to change. Here's another example: In January 2009, still feeling good about the new hopefulness of the Obama era, the *Oxford American*, which refers to itself as "The Southern Magazine of Good Writing" devoted an issue to *RACE: Past Present and Future*. Its cover had a mid-1970s picture of Angela Davis, the super-fro version with the big hair. Its contributors—who included such wonderful writers as Jericho Brown, Ai, and Rita Dove—were nearly all black. The *Oxford American* is a great literary magazine, and this was a great issue, so in a way I feel mean to point out its blind spot, especially since there are so many worse offenders out there. Still, its oddly monochromatic contributors' list took part in another crucial myth, one stickily mixed with the hope for the postracial. The myth goes like this: Race is something that people of color "have." Race is black people. Race is "other" people. The combined message is clear: If race is something to get beyond; to get "post," it's up to people of color to get beyond it. This feeds into the feeling of forced transcendence. Written this way, the transcendence is not collective. Since white people have no race, they have nothing to get beyond, nothing to transcend. Since we white people are "raceless" we've been "post" all along.

a fine fog to wander into . . .

Really? It's a tempting myth, a fine fog to wander into, and perhaps one in which we white people are already stuck. We can stay here in it, looking out at our picket fences. But suppose we try to creep out and ask ourselves who we are, we normal white people, we vast field of nothingness, we raceless normative majority? Are we really as nothing as all that? Do we not experience race? Do we not have narratives of that experience? Hath we not, like Shylock, eyes? The questions of what stories of identity we believe we belong to and which stories we believe we can access are not mere idle chatter. They are a place where are lived geographies and our literary imaginations lie across one another, where the stories we tell ourselves and are told about who we are forge the matrix out of which we judge the world. And we are perhaps most dangerous, we white people, when we impute to ourselves a position of standing nowhere, of being nothing. During the Sonia Sotomayor hearings, we saw, as a country, how delicate the problem of Sotomayor's perceived otherness was. Justice Alito (a conservative supported by conservatives) told a story of disappearing from some mild Italianness into whiteness. He had done the right thing: He had shed ethnicity to become normal. Sotomayor's assertion that the body in which she lived might affect either the story of her life or the nature of her wisdom or outlook was seen as suspect. She was asked to disembody her justice, to renege

her own history of social and gendered and racial experience. She was asked to make herself invisible to these categories. In the process, she was asked to step into a space of normativity that is so strong that it doesn't even acknowledge its own existence. She was asked to assume neutrality, but the clear message was this: Neutrality means impartiality, but only whiteness is neutral. However, what is missing from this normal is what has been missing from racial and surely from postracial discourse all along. In the history of articulating multiple othernesses, the very center from which those othernesses deviated has stayed oddly unexamined. Perhaps one reason that it is premature to even try to have any so-called postracial discourse is that we have never really discussed the racial experience so many of us inhabit daily—the space of whiteness. We don't even seem to acknowledge we exist, so it's obvious that we don't know how to look critically at the myths and formations of our country's apparently central ethnic group—white, normal; white, WASPy or not WASPy; white, the great normalizing zone of whiteness in America. We have treated it as a norm from which other things deviate, rather than as a force that could be explained or analyzed, rather than a group that has rules and identity, that is, even now, undergoing a distinct history of racialization. One has only to look at the state of Texas, which has just erased Thomas Jefferson from the textbooks,

The document exists but it

as well as any mention of people of color in favor of other narratives, to see how whiteness can be actively rewritten and purified. I do not mean to suggest that white people are actually a uniform group at all. I don't mean to assert that we exist biologically. In fact, we don't "exist" per se, and perhaps that is what is most unsettling about us. We exert privilege, we have culture, we hog history, but we have been constructed socially, and we like to retell the myths of ourselves with new constellations of erasures. Culturally we're a motley crew, of course: As the descendant of Massachusetts Puritans on one side and Virginia Royalists—with some fancy ancestors and some nameless Scotch and Irish laborers mixed in— I can tell you that whiteness, even WASPy, English-descended whiteness, has its distinct microclimates. Some whitenesses are better than others, even within families. Some whitenesses are erased or are contested. Nevertheless, the general experience of whiteness, as lived and acted upon in public life, feels so strong and so neutral that it feels like a safe place from which to hide from the experience of experiencing race. I see this often: In my freshman English class when I ask my students to write about their experiences of race, and invariably one white student raises her hand and says, "but I don't have any experiences of race." I have known students of color to argue that they have never experienced racism or to wonder what it means to have a different-

colored skin. I have known students of color who don't feel comfortable merely recanting premade stories that relate to images of their racial experience. However, I have never known a student of color to argue that they have "no race."

But back to white people, who do feel raceless. Is it merely that we feel left out? We want to be both normal and normative, and when we are not, some of us seem to want to get dangerous. The group of people who now feel under attack are the very people who alternately write their own un-self-critical histories, and then get violent when anyone challenges them. White people in the Tea Party and in the Supreme Court commentaries and in the state of Texas are showing us that they, or many of them, are not postracial. They assert, suddenly, their own presence. They craft new and exclusionary stories of identity. They refortify the mythologies that make them most comfortable. They create an increasingly fundamentalist sense of themselves. They entrench themselves in newly sanitized versions of their own history: In short, they feel threatened.

In their feelings of threat these people craft new stories of identity, ones that talk about their whiteness as patriotic, their whiteness as self-sufficient, their whiteness as Christian, their whiteness as the sole cultural force that founded this country. Because these people feel so threatened by having their space of normativity threatened,

relies on fields of absence . . .

they retrench themselves in false histories of their own—and this country's—racial purity.

Oddly, on one level, and one level only, I agree with these people. I would propose that before we get to the postracial, and after we read the 2009 issue of *Oxford American*, we begin to acknowledge whiteness, and talk about what it is. I think we must talk about whiteness the way we must also talk about Christianity in this country—it's no good if we give up the discussion of what it is or could be to people intent on using it for violent motives. Here's the rub: To begin to talk about whiteness or white experience seems immediately to link one to supremacists, to racists, to white nationalism. The problems of approaching whiteness can often preclude our allowing a different kind of identity story to emerge and be explored—the story of how we became so normal at all, and what we have left out or do not see in order to become so. Of course whiteness in America has its own rich and troubled and complex history, a history built on excluding other histories. One of my ancestors, William Randolph, arrived in 1674. His pedigree in England, while probably of some status—he had an uncle who was a court poet, trained by Ben Jonson—was uncertain. He was ambitious, a man on the make. He was good at networking. His first move when he was in America was to court favor with the Berkeley family ("westward the course of Empire"), get himself a land grant, and to involve himself in the triangle trade, and become one of the most prominent, and propertied, landowners—and slaveholders—in Virginia. The next thing he did, almost immediately, was to invent and buttress his family tree, to write a version of it that connected him back not merely to his uncle in court but to some battle in Scotland generations before, one that identified him as a long supporter of the Royalist line. He got the best out of two American myths: In the first he arrived as a second son with very little money in his pocket; in the second, he got himself a very distinguished and possibly false genealogy. He was, in both senses, a self-made man, but in both cases, that self-making relied upon omissions, re-creation, convenient exploitation. So much for bootstraps. When I read this story now something becomes clear to me: William Randolph's first act in America was one of anxiety. He actually poses for his portrait hanging onto his papers, his claim, his family line. The document exists but it relies on fields of absence: He has both erased others, actively deracinating hundreds of Africans, at the same time as he has reinvented himself in order to climb. Here in fact is one narrative of whiteness.

If you are white and reading this article, you may actually think that your family history is nothing like William Randolph's, that your family never enslaved people, that this erasure was only of your past, of the country your grand-

Does whiteness have a feeling,

parents or their grandparents came from. William Randolph might seem like a central power; his children might seem to hold the cultural capital that makes the whole system feel screwed up, and William Randolph might just be the best bad guy around. But at the center of William Randolph's story is a haunting and familiar enough story about being ready to climb. Randolph is, of course, only the first of so many eager people who would do the same thing, whether as English indentured servants or as people who changed their name because it was convenient or because they were told to—who had the idea to go west, the idea to become free, white, and twenty-one, whose hope was to arrive in what Emerson called "this new and unapproachable America." In her remarkable 1993 book *Playing in the Dark*, writing about this experience of self invention, Toni Morrison has described the arrival in America as a chance for immigrants to lose identity, to shed their old nationality, to enter a space of radical equality (available only to white men.) In short, Morrison puts it, this was a chance for rebirth, a chance to be "born again."

In a deft move, Morrison's word choice links whiteness to evangelism, to the kind of Christianity whose promise of salvation offers to erase past, personal history, transgressive action—anything beyond its margins. Being born again offers a chance to remake the self, but it also has meant forgetting, meant entering a space of

radical amnesia. William Randolph may have more in common with basic white experience than we might be comfortable with. Perhaps arriving at this "new yet unapproachable America" has always offered certain of us who can and are willing to shift and lose and hide our racial markers—as a price of entry, as a cost of belonging in certain quarters, so that we might, like William Randolph, be ready to approach. I can think of the friend who was told that her jewelry was "too big" to be at a corporate law firm; the blank stare of a cousin when I brought home the man I married, whose last name is Schreiner. "Schreiner," she said, "what kind of name is that?" It was a hundred years after the first Schreiner came from Germany and put up a sod hut on the plains out in the harsh Dakotas, to settle where the Sioux were still being sacrificed in treaty after treaty—the question seemed, at least to this cousin of mine, to have purchase. That name, she seemed to say, was other. I have another ancestor that people often think of when they think of slaveholders: Thomas Jefferson. Thomas Jefferson, the enlightenment thinker who is now apparently too secular for the Texas State Board of Education. I wonder if it's not merely his secularism that prompted them to edit him away, but also his uneasy racial legacy, the haunting story of the hidden-in-plain-sight family whose children were freed and whose families lived on without access to his legacy. In a way, it is most

or spectrum of feelings?

easy and necessary for me to talk about the making of this particular whiteness; it haunts and shapes my and my family's experience today. It is a history which, if full of absences, has been written, and I can see it as a line from which I come. I can see where the erasures are made in this narrative—or at least I can imagine where they begin—even if I cannot always see what they contain. I can't always make out what was erased, what happened in the margins, but I see very clearly that the margins have been made, that certain things and people and chapters have been left out on whom my sense of whiteness now relies. I offer myself up as a strong example of what stories that look at whiteness might yield. I am a person about whom other people could say "oh, well you are the people who held slaves," "you are the rich white people who were the bad guys," as if by not being descended from slaveholders but from bondsmen or Norwegian immigrants I might not have a reckoning to do. Perhaps this is true, and perhaps I do have more stories at my disposal that begin to make some of this reckoning possible. But because I have such an obviously violent whiteness in my past I feel certain that whiteness has more often than not relied on violence to police itself, to come into being. Because I have an obvious story of erasure in my past, it simply happens to be more obvious to me that the whiteness that I have inherited has relied, across time and space, on violence and ex-

clusion. And I think much, if not all, of whiteness in America has that same violence and exclusion at its root, and perhaps before we are "past it" it will be time to understand what "it" was in the first place. As Morrison wisely puts it, it's not just that we need to think about the history of racism in this country in term of its victims, or in terms of the reasons whiteness has been fabricated in the first place. She writes that "(these) well-established stud(ies) should be joined with another, equally important one: the impact of racism on those who perpetuate it."

Does whiteness have a feeling, or spectrum of feelings? To acknowledge what Morrison is suggesting, to really allow it in, we would have to figure out what it means to "perpetuate racism," to try to figure out where racism exists and what it feels like to live in its presence. Is that a feeling of whiteness? Is it something we live with—our own internal debates about how to live near, and whether to acknowledge, and how to feel racisms that exist around, and perhaps inside ourselves?

Another bit of my family were Scots, and their name means only that: Scottish. Their name wends back into the hills of North Carolina, deep into a history that did not give them a name. They merely came from Scotland. They may have come indentured (I don't know), but they got beyond the Virginia plantation system and headed for the Blue Ridge. Once there, they disappear into their namelessness, claim-

I wonder too, about the

ing instead a whole hilly country for origin, and ending in another hilly country where they kept a dialect to themselves for centuries. There's no question that part of the story of whiteness is the ambivalent struggle of arrival, the ambivalence of joining other white people, of assimilating—which, even among, say, the descendants of the English and Scottish themselves has not always been a straightforward task. "We've all come to look for America," sing Simon and Garfunkel. This is the story of the Godfather, or of the *Sopranos*, of all mafia stories in which the goal of the mobster generation is to secure a place at Columbia for their kids. The dream of the postracial seems to hover there, in an ivy space in which one finally, at long last, approaches America, and begins to be able to harvest the riches of having arrived.

Could this be why, upon reaching such a place, a college, the proverbial New Jerusalem, that City on a Hill, everyone gathered in the classroom, especially the white kids, are so eager to claim that they have no race, no ethnicity? A professor at the liberal arts college I attended once told me that the purpose of the freshman year writing class was to shake the Cleveland off the students. That it was to denude them, to strip them of—who knows—the banal, the possibly ethnic, the suburban ... but nonetheless the markers of where they came from. In college, students are in some small way expected to be "born again." I

have no problem shaking the Shaker Heights out of my students if it means broadening their horizons, but I do wonder about the wider metaphor there; is indeed the writing class a place to aim for the "postracial" or a place designed to make my students feel as if they did not know where they came from? I wonder too, about the goal of the postracial, about what has to be forgotten, and by whom, in order to achieve it. I wish I did not feel that such forgettings would necessarily be political, slanted toward some peoples' forgettings at the expense of others.

I suppose that I then favor a narrative strategy of alert discomfort to one that is based on selective amnesia—one that might continue at least until we become as blended as the Anglo-Normans and really can't tell who we are any more. Then again, all narratives are based on forgetting. So the questions I'd ask are what are we forgetting and why? For now, even if it has no biological basis, I can't forget about whiteness: I'd argue that whiteness has a prevalent social reality, one that we can see reflected in the statistics about poverty and drop-out rates, and one we hear in the strident, defensive tones of the Tea Party. It's a social force that maps our lives both as we live and as we inherit them.

So, yes, I would like to talk about whiteness. The discussions I want to have about whiteness are the ones that we could keep learning from.

goal of the postracial . . .

I want to ask how was it made, whether we want it, what purposes it serves, what it would take to undo, what parts of it do we like, what parts of it are we ashamed of. At least we could acknowledge more what is hidden in plain sight. And yet it's precisely this that most haunts whiteness. We do not know where it comes from. We are encouraged to hide, to ignore, to erase, to forget, to hope that we come from nowhere except the present tense. We are invited to participate in a space of our own normalcy, in which we have no racial experience, exert no force, claim without claiming. During my childhood I remember being encouraged not to ask too many questions about slavery or slaveholding as it had affected my family. I was told that it was complicated; or that Thomas Jefferson had been a good man and so had the family been. These were things I talked about only with my father in California; I felt actively disinvited from asking such questions in Virginia. I have eventually broached these topics with some of my family, but not with out much kind of shame. *That was what happened*, or *It wasn't as bad as they said it was*; or even that *Black people should have figured out by now how to live*. These were all words and sentiments I heard expressed behind closed doors. And more than that I had a sense that I was not supposed to ask for a more complete version of the story, or even to suppose there was a story there at all. And to look at the records of that slavery, even one as well documented as the one Jefferson crafted in his farm book, is to gaze into enormous fields of omission, absences that can't be filled in.

In time, I didn't ask those kinds of questions anymore: In fact, my amnesia on this topic was so great that when the DNA evidence came out ten years ago about Thomas Jefferson and Sally Hemings, I remember being shocked not because of the imputed children, but because I had actually forgotten, little by little, subliminally over the years, not quite that I was related to Jefferson, but that Jefferson held slaves, that I was related to slavery, that slavery was related to me. Perhaps in a way, I was postracial. I also think I was deliberately invited to forget and to be forgetful, not to know, not to consider. I admit that I did not actively consider or know, but I also felt uninvited from the project of considering.

I thought of myself that I had no history, that I had no race. And yet that history was there, of course, so obviously informing so much of the life that I had inherited that I wondered how I had missed it. How had I missed it? What was hidden in plain sight? My whiteness was hidden in plain sight.

INTRODUCTION
ZHOU XIAOJING

These vignettes of everyday encounters with racism have been selected from among students' responses to one of the assignments in my course, Introduction to Ethnic Studies. While this course is required only for those who minor in Ethnic Studies, it attracts students from a wide range of disciplines and of various racial and ethnic backgrounds. I believe the fact that its enrollment is full every semester it is offered indicates students perceive a need to learn about race and ethnicity, a subject that affects them or matters to them.

This course is a challenging one for most students, who have not previously been exposed to the kinds of critical theories used in the assigned readings, much less applied these in their own writing. Nevertheless they stay, and generally rise to the challenge. The diversity of their backgrounds enriches the learning that takes place in the class. We all take risks in various ways as we investigate issues that are both personal and political. One of the risks I take is using an excerpt from the documentary *The Color of Fear* (1994), directed by Lee Mun Wah, in which a group of American men of African, Asian, European, and Latino descent engage in an extended conversation about racism. When I first used this film, in an American Studies course some years ago, I was surprised by some students' response that "all the men of color are ganging up on the white man." The fact that the white man, David, talks down to the black man, Victor, and denies the existence of racial inequality by claiming that people like Victor are responsible for creating their own obstacles to their upward mobility, seemed to elude those students.

A similar blind spot was evident in the perspectives of some of these same students when I showed another documentary, *Who Killed Vincent Chin* (1987), directed by Christine Choy and Renee Tajima-Pena. It is about the murder of a Chinese American engineer, Vincent Chin, by two white men who smashed his skull with a baseball bat. For this crime, the sentence imposed on each of them was three years' probation and a fine of $3,780. Some students in the class said the killing had nothing to do with race, maintaining that it was Chin's own fault that he got killed because he "should have remained quiet" when he was called racist names by one of his attackers. Encountering this blind spot in my students' perspective, and its resultant denial of racial injustice, compelled me to rethink my pedagogy, and to expand my own lexicon and conceptual framework for the study of race and ethnicity in particular social, historical, and cultural environments. When I later began using both documentaries again in my Introduction to Ethnic Studies course, I made it my practice to first familiarize students with critical race theories and expose them to abundant past and present evidence of the mutually constitutive structural and ideological process of racial formation in the United States. Now students find David's claims laughable, and consider the sentence given to Vincent Chin's murderers outrageous. When one of my colleagues also used *The*

Color of Fear in one of her classes, but without first equipping her students with the theory and evidence necessary to interpret it, and she told me she was brought to tears by her students' outraged response to how David is "treated" by the men of color in the film, this reconfirmed for me the value of showing this documentary only at the end of the semester.

At the same time, however, it seemed to me that a valuable part of the learning experience was lost when the apparently "unintentional" racism in both documentaries becomes too obvious to the students to demand in-depth examination. To allow the learning process to be more challenging, more provocative, and more emotionally charged, I now show excerpts from *The Color of Fear* on the first day of class. I call students' attention to both the implications of David's remarks and his manner of address to Victor and other men of color in their group. One of the threads of critical inquiry we identify and follow throughout the course is the privileged position from which David makes his "color-blind" claims, as well as the implications and consequences of such claims. The reduction of racial discrimination to a matter of individual opinion, accompanied by the denial of institutionalized racial inequality, which underlies David's remarks, serves as a starting point for the class to explore the structural and ideological dimensions of the social construction of race. As our exploration

"It therefore

moves through the history to the contemporary nation-state and an increasingly globalized world, the starting point of our investigation remains relevant and exigent.

At the same time, our understanding of racism and its impact is broadened by theoretical perspectives such as those articulated by Étienne Balibar. In his essay "Is There a 'Neo-Racism'?", Balibar defines racism as "a true 'total social phenomenon'" which "inscribes itself in practices (forms of violence, contempt, intolerance, humiliation and exploitation), in discourses and representations [...] and which are articulated around stigmata of otherness (name, skin color, religious practices). It therefore organizes affects [...]."[1] This capacious perspective provides us with a useful conceptual framework for better understanding our everyday encounters in which various forms of racism can be either overly aggressive or subtly humiliating.

Informed of those theoretical perspectives, each student in my Introduction to Ethnic Studies class was asked to write a brief depiction of their personal experience of different forms of racism. These vignettes capture the ways in which racial positioning underlies our everyday encounters.

[1] Étienne Balibar, "Is There a 'Neo-Racism'?" Race, Nation, Class: Ambiguous Identities, edited by Étienne Balibar and Immanuel Wallerstein, translated by Chris Turner (London: Verso, 1991), 17–18.

At Soccer Practice

You arrive early at soccer practice so you can talk with your teammates and relax. You end up speaking with a parent. "How are you today?" "Good," you respond. "Still in school?" he asks.

At the Car Dealer's

As we walk around looking at cars,
A car salesman approaches us.
"Can I help you?" says he, making eye contact
    with my partner.
"Are you looking for a car?"
"Yes," I reply though the salesman still ignores me.
"Whatcha looking for?" he asks my partner again.
"A medium-sized SUV," I speak again.
  He turns and looks at me, "huh?"
"So you want a mid-size car, where do you work?"
  He looks at my partner.
"I work at Pacific, you know, the university" I say.
"Really, what do you do there? Are you a
    custodian?"
"No, in the admissions office. I process
    applications."
"Where do you live?"
"The east side, off of Waterloo."
"Hmmm ... you must have worked really hard to
  get that good job."

organizes affects . . . "

On My Way Home

Walking home at night you begin to realize
    you are not alone.
A man walks behind you calmly at your
    own pace,
But you do not feel calm.
You turn to see his face,
Your heart begins to race,
You begin to walk faster
Then faster
Until you are running in fear,
From the man still walking calmly.

In Kentucky

A cold winter morning,
You walk into a café to buy black coffee.
The employee hands you a cup
Pointing you in the direction,
You fill your cup until your hands are warm.
The aroma and warmth ease your tiredness.
You look out at the snowstorm and decide
    to refill the cup.
The manager smiles at you,
While the employee comes to confront you,
Demanding to see a receipt of the purchase.

Case Number 12-34353

You head to the Stockton-Is-Magnificent street
fair that celebrates what the city has to offer. You
park on N Commerce Street, parallel to Miracle
Mile where all the shops, people, booths, and
festivities are.
As you get out of your car you look around
    and notice strangers with familiar faces.
You feel safe knowing people are around if
    anything happens ...
Suddenly, you are attacked. They push you
    backwards.
Your back hits a fence. Threatened with a knife,
    you cuss and strike out.
You fight back, yell, scream, and run down
    the street toward the fair.
As you come across women walking toward
the event, they stop when they hear you calling
for help, but they only stare at you. They seem
frightened of YOU.
You hear the officer making a call, "A woman,"
    he says, "age nineteen."
The officer asks for a description of the attackers
You say they were one male and two females,
about your height or a little taller; they were between fourteen and twenty years old.
    You add, their skin tone resembled yours,
light caramel.

"Why a basketball player?

At a Gas Station

We stop to get gas. A stranger approaches.

"That's a handsome boy you've got there. What are
you going to be when you grow up, young man?
A basketball player?"

"No ... I want to be a doctor."

"Good choice."

As you leave the gas station,
You wonder, "Why a basketball player?"
Why not a doctor!

Sitting in traffic
On the way home, you keep thinking "Why a
basketball player?"
Why not a doctor.

When you get home, you find yourself still
questioning:

"Why a basketball player? Why not a doctor?"

"Why a basketball player! Why not a doctor!"

"Why a basketball player. Why not a doctor."

Why ask?

At the Art Supply Store

You and your friend walk into the art supply store,
Syllabus of the art class in hand,
With just enough money for the list of materials
you need.

As you walk past the checkout counter,
they whisper,

"Look at them ... "

You try not to mind and continue walking.

Then you hear a voice sharp and clear,

"Can we get a security scan on sections A and B."

You feel the security camera slowly turn,
lens staring at you.

You feel judged because of

The clothes you wear, the hair on your face,

The muscle on your body, the color of your skin.

You try to ignore, you walk to the back of the store,

Thinking you can find your supplies there.

But what you find is the manager of the store
chasing you down the aisle.

She corners you in the back like a wolf stalking
two sheep.

Eyeing you from top to bottom, she says loudly
and impatiently,

"Excuse me, boys, how may I help you?"

Enraged, but you calmly say, "Where are
your sketch pads?"

"Oh! Right this way, sir. Follow me."

ZHOU XIAOJING

Why not a doctor?"

On the Playground

You're playing with the other kids when your mom
   comes to pick you up.
No one knows who this woman is.
She does not look like the others.
She does not talk like the others.
She utters a few words.
The kids laugh, they do not understand what
   she is saying.
Her voice, no, her accent is weird and funny to them.
Who is this lady, she can't be your mom.
She's soooo different!

On the Volleyball Court

You sit and laugh with your volleyball team
Glad to be among them.
But when they begin a game, you wish you
   were elsewhere.

The girls go around holding out their arms to match
   against other arms:
Chocolate
Coca
Ochre
Mahogany
When it's your turn and you hold your arm up
There is a silent pause, then you hear cloud
   and clear:
"You're yellow!" The game is over.
You are black like them.
They don't see you, only the you who isn't you.

Prepackaged Meat at Walmart

You are unpackaging meat. You line it up on
white trays and you stack the trays onto silver
shelves. Behind you two of your coworkers discuss
one of the coworker's marital problems.
You hear one of them say, "Because, I mean, I
have no family." You turn around, a stack of silver
shelves filled, ready for you in your white lab coat
to push it out onto the sales floor.
In a raised voice with a hint of anger, the other
coworker turns to you. "That's the problem. Your
family supports you, feeds you, lets you live at
home. We don't have nice families."
You didn't expect that anger. "You're right," you say.
She levels out. "We're on our own."
"I know people like that," the first coworker says.
"At least he works."
You steer your silver shelves of white trays filled
with prepackaged meat out the double door and
toward the sales floor. Stock the walls. Arrange the
product neatly. Make it look the same and clean.
A customer asks you, "Do you have any chicken
breasts with the bones and the skins still there?"
You point to one package that has skin.
"That's it?"
You scan the shelf. Out of nearly ten varieties of
chicken breast products nine are skinless and one
has skin.
"Yeah," she tells you. You'd never really noticed
   the difference.

They move away

In Seattle

I am waiting, searching for a parking space.
Not far away a car is backing out.
I turn on the blinker, move closer,
   waiting patiently.

The driver, upon leaving the spot,
looks at me, the passenger looks at me.

Our eyes meet.
The car stops, and they stay there patiently.
No movement.

I leave and start searching again.
In my rearview mirror
I see them leaving.

In My Neighborhood

You walk down the street of a mostly white
   neighborhood, humming a tune stuck in
   your head.
They walk toward you laughing and joking
   till they see you.
They move away as you walk by them.
You hear them whisper when you are finally
   past them.
You continue walking in silence.

A Small Town in Texas

It's the second period Spanish class. The bell rings and you take your seat. Not too close to the front, or the middle, but next to the door where you can easily escape when an hour has passed.

The TV is turned on for the seemingly same mundane daily announcements. The whole class stands up for the Pledge of Allegiance. You carefully get out of your seat and place your hand over your heart. You recite the same words, emphasizing each syllable, meaning every word wholeheartedly.

The brief moment of silence is interrupted by the blond-haired boy on the other side of the class, as he blurts calmly, "Kill the Muslims."

No one speaks, no one laughs. Instead they turn their heads toward you and you, not knowing what to do, what to say, look down at the desk, at the floor, hoping that the ground would open up and swallow you whole away from the prying eyes.

A sudden realization comes to you as you say to yourself, *but I'm not even Muslim.*

as you walk by them.

Authors of the Vignettes

Anise Abraham, African American, is an English major with a concentration in Film Studies, and an Ethnic Studies minor at the University of the Pacific.

Zachery Artozqui, a nineteen-year-old white male of European decent, is a freshman and first-generation college student, majoring in Environmental Science with double minors in Geology and Biology at the University of the Pacific.

Alicia Calhoun, a forty-four-year-old African American female, is a Sociology major and Ethnic Studies minor at the University of the Pacific.

Lorena Campos, Chicana, is a Stockton, California, native, a Political Science major, and an Ethnic Studies minor at the University of the Pacific.

Adnan Hashtam, Pakistani American, is a junior with double majors in English and Philosophy, and double minors in Ethnic Studies and Gender Studies at the University of the Pacific.

Jackie Johnson, half-Persian, half-Caucasian, is a Psychology major at the University of the Pacific.

Emilia Briceño López, Mexican American, is a nontraditional student majoring in Spanish with a concentration in Culture and Civilization at the University of the Pacific.

Flora On, Chinese American, is an Environmental Studies major with a concentration in Environmental Policy, and a Sustainability minor at the University of the Pacific.

Sandra Padilla, Mexican American, is a Math major, a soccer player, and freshman at the University of the Pacific.

John Steiner, white, is an English major, Ethnic Studies minor, and honors student at the University of the Pacific.

Sukhman Sandhu, Indian American, is an English major and Ethnic Studies minor at the University of the Pacific.

Sarah Unger, half-German and half–Native American, is an English major, Ethnic Studies minor, and honors student at the University of the Pacific.

Jillian Yelinek, half-Czechoslovakian and half–Blackfoot Native American, but often identified as white, is a freshman with double majors in Psychology and English at the University of the Pacific.

Alice Shaw, **Opposite 3 (Left)** and **Opposite 2 (Right)**, 2007

In her examination of gender roles and gender identity, self-proclaimed tomboy Alice Shaw creates a pair of portraits with her ostensible opposite. In revising prescribed masculine and feminine categorization, Shaw reveals the porous border. MKC

Nery Gabriel Lemus, **<u>Fade Away</u>**, 2007

In this incisive parallel, the artist reveals the peculiarity of the rancor often witnessed in encounters between Latino and African American men. The identical haircuts, along with shared fashion and musical tastes, hide the simmering contempt members of each group may hold for the other. MKC

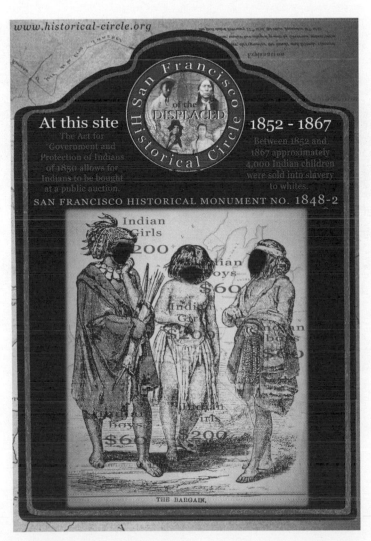

John Jota Leaños, **San Francisco Historical Monument 1848–2**, 2003

In a series of information kiosks on the streets of San Francisco, Leaños recounts a catalog of colonialist crimes against indigenous Californians. This work, that references legislation that allows for the trade in Indian slaves, was one of a group that was approved, denied, then reapproved by the San Francisco Arts Commission. MKC

Mark Peterson,
from **Acts of Charity**, 2014

The clubby merrymaking of the wealthy portrayed in Mark Peterson's series, Acts of Charity, illustrates not only Fitzgerald's line from The Great Gatsby, "…wherever people played polo and were rich together," but also conveys the vague malevolence of wealth and power, and its clannish consumers. MKC

Jay Wolke, <u>Torah Reading-B'nai Zaken Ethiopian Congregation</u>, 1994

In this, another of the images from his series, All Around the House, Jay Wolke photographs the diversity of description and practice among Jewish life in America, encompassing its broad spectrum—Orthodox, Reform, Humanistic. MKC

So blindness is the necessary condition for openness? **Where, in all her love for classification, did she want them to reside?** I can't take him up into my archive of heroes, I can't make him my flag. **I vowed to stop censoring myself, to be willing to write about race even if it made me look bad, to be more willing to make mistakes, to blunder.**

READINGS

There were stretches of time when I grew weary of it. **The bones, like vines, reach up and out and grasp our ankles, winding around them and locking all of us together whether we like it or not.** I failed in that way I don't wholly know how to describe—in some secret way, some helpless way; I perpetuated some arrogance I'd meant to dismantle. **This is the difference between epiphany and critique, gaining power and losing it.** Why did you try to say this in a poem if you weren't going to take it higher?

"THERE ARE NO RATS": SOME FIGURING ON RACE

JOSHUA WEINER

The Adventures of Huckleberry Finn (1885) is a great novel, and a better novel than *Uncle Tom's Cabin* (1852) in just about every way that matters for a work of literature, but it's also a better novel *about* race in America. Better because richly confused. Its confusion is its failure, and its failure is its meaning. *Uncle Tom's Cabin* knows what it's about, knows what it wants to do, and goes about doing it very effectively. It understands something real about racism, its psychology and institutionalization. It helped end slavery. And its failure as art is not important. The failure of Mark Twain's novel is.

———

What do I mean by that? Stowe's novel appears to fulfill her intentions. It may be melodramatic & sentimental, but it also makes the reader feel something; and the feeling was transformed into social protest. Twain's novel appears confused in its final episode, confused about the issue of race and the problem of slavery. What Tom Sawyer does to Jim at the end, how he leads Jim to play a dehumanizing role in a twisted fantasy: it's as if Twain doesn't understand his own novel. As if the character of Jim, its essential human nobility and emotional honesty, was traded in for a two-bit episode.

———

A race fantasy. A boy's adventure story. Twain's entertainment? Or a grim parody of Tom Sawyer? The book's confusion, and the confusion it's created in the minds of its readers, seems analogous to the confusion around the issue of race and representation in American culture & society.

...intentional racism in art

Miles Davis claimed he could tell whether a musician was black or white by virtue of the playing itself. An essential black sound. The absence of a black sound.

I find much of my wavering dis-ease as a reader of *Huck Finn* located not in racist epithet but in the vernacular sound of nineteenth-century Southern American black speech, Jim's dialect and the representational vocal score for expressing both the fugitive slave's humanity and his degradation through a kind of rigged minstrelsy.

I want to say, intentional racism in art doesn't make great art. That when we find racism in great art, it is of the unconscious, a shade of consciousness; in the weave, the wave, the story. Thread, particle, tone. The pigment of sound. But when it comes to racism, the unconscious seems itself a kind of privileged presumption, one that sees the world according to a dominant structure founded to advance certain interests, without seeing the structure itself.

One function of art is to disrupt the structure, so that we can see it. One way for art to reveal the working of the structure is to disrupt the domi-

nant paradigm of a particular art form, to expose the working of the medium, in the medium. The symbolic role of such revelation ripples outward to the society in which the artwork resides. This is what Bertolt Brecht taught us. This is what it means to be a critical artist.

"I am not a racist." Or: "I am a racist, like everyone else." What kind of claims can we make for ourselves when we're peeling back the poly-ply tissue of a psychosocial pathology? Caught in a tautology, one's claims of not being racist are precisely the indication of one's racism.

I am a product of my time, my nation. Essentially? Contingently? Anthropology says yes. Yet some Christian Germans in Hitler's fatherland tried to save some Jewish Germans. How did that happen?

Imagining a frightening time, not so long ago, when one could say, "I am a racist," without stigma, as in "I am a venture capitalist," "I am a federalist," "I am a psychiatrist," "I am a ventriloquist."

If we are all racist, consciously/unconsciously— in that we are never not aware of racial identities

doesn't make great art.

around us; and if we all inherit deeply planted seeds of racial prejudice; still, that does not make us all equally racist. We know this. The civil rights movement in this country, and before that, abolitionism, the antislavery movement, born out of moral outrage and a political progressive ambition to improve the conditions of humankind (and of individual souls to grow ethically): the historic will to freedom gives the lie. Conservatism always wants to shore up the status quo because it's good for conservatism. But the Constitution's constitution depends on the notion of social justice, and justice requires the possibility of change. The great insight into the mind of racism (and brilliant rhetorical move) in Frederick Douglass's *Narrative of the Life* (1845) comes when Douglass dramatically renders precisely how slavery oppresses both slave and slave master. It makes each less than human, distorts the personality, and poisons the soul. To end slavery, in other words, is to liberate the slave master as well as the slave.

In Chang-rae Lee's first novel, *Native Speaker* (1995), a Korean American councilman, John Kwang, is building a campaign to run for mayor of New York. Henry Park, also Korean, is a kind of corporate spy, gathering information about individuals that clients then use to destroy them. Park is working on the campaign undercover

against this man of his own race, who hopes to achieve a kind of racial breakthrough in New York City politics, to become a new minority who can best represent the best interests of the most people. "Everyone can see the landscape is changing," says Kwang at one point to Park, "Soon there will be more brown and yellow than black and white. And yet the politics, especially minority politics, remain cast in terms that barely acknowledge us. It's an old syntax... . And if I don't receive the blessing of African Americans, am I still a *minority* politician? Who is the heavy now? ... You should know, how there must be a way to speak truthfully and not be demonized or made a traitor."

"Very softly," I [Park] said to him, offering the steady answer of my life. "And to yourself."

The issue in the novel, of speaking about racial identity—of speaking *as* a racially identified subject—truthfully, to oneself or to others, involves an ethical confusion heightened by a kind of internal complex audible in the voice itself, Henry Park's indelible *foreignness*. (Elsewhere, his correct use of "healthful" for the idiomatic but incorrect "healthy" is subtly expressive, much like his inability to speak Korean with native fluency.) A painful state of self-alienation. Lelia, his estranged spouse, a white woman (and a speech therapist), names his condition on her way out the door, *"False speaker of language."*

Wright appears to

At a conference in Orono, in 1996, I heard Robert von Hallberg disagree with Ann Charters about Langston Hughes's poems, arguing that Hughes's poetic achievement may be overstated. Her response: "The poems weren't written for you." In other words, the audience Hughes imagined did not include white literature professors, but a largely uneducated urban black one. In other words, poems written for such an audience can't be compared to those written for an audience imagined by, say, T. S. Eliot, according to the same critical criteria. Von Hallberg was right to counter: "That's not a defensible intellectual position." In other words, you can't promote the aesthetic value of one work over another based on *exceptional* reasoning; for one thing, it's condescending to the poet and the poems. Yet she wasn't wrong: people value the poems, regardless. The poems make their impact outside the arena of responsible evaluative criticism.

Some recent white poems that think about race. In C. K. Williams's "The Singing" (2003), the young black man walking on a city street in the same direction as the poet is "speaking black." "It didn't matter," writes Williams, "I could tell he was making his / song up which pleased me / he was nice-looking / Husky dressed in some style of big pants obviously / full of himself / hence

his lyrical overflowing ..." The scene of instruction is one of implied identification, inscribed in Williams's own lyrical full-of-himself overflowing; but there are limits, errors of perception, dull presumptions that Williams comically deflates ("I thought how droll / to have my height / incorporated into his song"). The poet's presumption—liberal, egotistical, & well intended: his big poetry pants—inspire the youth to change his song—less as threat, more as correction—from the mono-verbum "Big" to "I'm not a nice person, I'm not a nice person." "It occurred to me to sing back 'I'm not a nice / person either' but I couldn't come up with a tune // Besides I wouldn't have meant it nor he have believed / it both of us / knew just where we were / In the duet we composed the equation we made / the conventions to / which we were condemned."

The representation of personal speech responsive to the drama of race in the public sphere, the poem balances with acute sensitivity what one can and cannot say in the imaginary space of the American democratic vista posited by Whitman.

Another example. Robert Pinsky's "Window" (1991), in which the poet relates how "My mother Mary Beamish who came from Cork / Held me to see the snowfall out the window— /

have been mistaken.

Windhold she sometimes said, as if in Irish / It held wind out, or showed us that wind was old. / *Wind-hole* in Anglo-Saxon: faces like brick, / They worshipped Eastre's rabbit, and mistletoe / That was Thor's jissom where thunder struck the oak. / We took their language in our mouth and chewed / (Some of the consonants drove us nearly crazy / Because we were Chinese—or was that just the food / My father brought from the restaurant downstairs?) / In the fells, by the falls, the Old Ghetto or New Jersey, / Little Havana or Little Russia—I forget, / because the baby wasn't me, the way / These words are not."

We are reminded in the poet's word-consciousness that language itself involves us in the processes of history that include the processes of racial identification—warring tribes, colonial domination, immigrant survival. We find identities inscribed in language, so do we all dip into the language stream unconsciously, even as we are made in the convergence of family, nation, and race.

I am reviewing a book by Matthew Hart, *Nations of Nothing but Poetry: Modernism, Transnationalism, and Synthetic Vernacular Writing* (2010). A good, interesting, well-conceived book. In the introduction, Hart turns to Gertrude Stein's "Melanctha" from *Three Lives* (1909), her experiment in naturalistic fiction, in which she performs a vocal, vernacular impression of a mulatta. When Richard Wright first encountered this literary performance, Hart reminds us, "he celebrated ... the way it opened his ears to 'the magic of the spoken word,' evoking 'the speech of my grandmother, who spoke a deep, pure Negro dialect.'" But Hart agrees with another scholar, Michael North, that "texts such as 'Melanctha' inhere less in their mimesis of black language than in how they provide evidence for the way the Anglo-American avant-garde conducted its formal experiments 'over a third figure, a black one.'" That Stein's impression of a black voice in 'Melanctha' might be a prismatic reflection of queerness does not mitigate, according to this view, an act of appropriation. The real vulgarity, "from our twenty-first-century perspective" is in "Stein's engagement with blackness."

Hearing the white writer's vernacular blackface, the black writer's recognition of something profoundly his own; his sense of family, place of origin, the sound of a people; a black sound; in other words, *himself.* Wright appears to have been mistaken. How is that possible?

. . . through the <u>angry</u> streets

"I saw the best minds of my generation destroyed by madness, starving hysterical naked, / dragging themselves through the negro streets at dawn looking for an angry fix, / angelheaded hipsters burning for the ancient heavenly connection to the starry dynamo in the machinery of night... ." So read the famous opening lines of Allen Ginsberg's *Howl* (1956). Ten nouns (counting the phrase "machinery of night" as one), ten adjectives. Six sets of adjective/noun "pairs": Best minds, negro streets, angry fix, angelheaded hipsters, ancient heavenly connection, starry dynamo. How careful are his pairings of adjective and noun?

An early draft of *Howl* reads a little differently. The best minds of Ginsberg's generation are found dragging themselves through the *angry streets* at dawn looking for a *negro fix*.

Is it possible to read Ginsberg's process in this revision? First thought, best thought? Jack Kerouac's letters to Ginsberg during the composition of the poem plead with the poet that he not change anything (no "secondary emendations made in time's reconsidering backstep"). But Ginsberg's resolve to make the best poem possible is greater than his interest in adhering dog-

matically to any zen jazz spontaneous blow poetics. *First thought, best thought* doesn't mean you don't change the poem; the need to recognize the need to change is, after all, one of the noble truths. To revise in the spirit of the first impulse, to change while staying connected to the energy and purpose of the original occasion. Such is the middle way of Ginsberg's ethos. In his first compositional moves, Ginsberg discovers an unconscious racist association between being black and using, or pushing. An urban racist cliché. By transposing the adjectives he exercises higher awareness and saves the poem. He implies a political, psychological, and spiritual condition behind the reaching for drugs (*angry fix*); and, with *negro streets,* he grounds the suggestion of a racial space, an urban geography defined by race (e.g., Harlem) in a literal fact, *the tarmac is black.*

In 1936, Knopf publishes a new book by Wallace Stevens, *Ideas of Order,* in a dust jacket with a statement by the poet that includes these words: "The book is essentially a book of pure poetry. I believe that, in my society, the poet should be an exponent of the imagination in that society. *Ideas of Order* attempts to illustrate the role of the imagination in life, and particularly in life at the present. The more realistic life may be, the more it needs the stimulus of the imagination."

...looking for a <u>negro</u> fix.

The book includes the poem "Like Decorations in a Nigger Cemetery."

Submitting the poem to *Poetry* in 1934, Stevens wrote to the editor, Morton Zabel, that "the title refers to the litter one usually finds in a nigger cemetery and is a phrase used by Judge Powell last winter in Key West."

'We were walking in Key West,' the Judge recalled [in *Parts of a World: Wallace Stevens Remembered*], 'when I stopped to look through a fence. I explained that I thought it enclosed a graveyard, as some of the rubbish looked 'like decorations in a nigger cemetery.' He was interested when I explained the custom of negroes to decorate graves with broken pieces of glass, old pots, broken pieces of furniture, dolls' heads and what not. The poem itself is an olio, and the title is fitting.'"

Olio. A heavily spiced stew; a mixture, hodge-podge; a medley of musical pieces. Vaudeville or musical entertainment presented between acts of a minstrel show.

The American Heritage Dictionary.

One *usually* finds? A habit of Stevens, to peruse such cemeteries? One adopts the language and points of view of influential friends, bosses, lovers, patrons.

"For Arthur Powell."

Pure poetry? The stimulus of the imagination? If our residence in the real requires such stimulus, for Stevens the poetic imagination requires the stimulus of the vulgate, verbal & material debris, the world; what Stevens perceives as vulgar.

"The leaden pigeon on the entrance gate."

"How easily the feelings flow this afternoon / Over the simplest words: / It is too cold, for work, now, in the fields."

The aphoristic tercets that make up Stevens's poem lay scattered in disarray, resisting (*almost successfully*) not only the intelligence, but also meaningful ideas of order.

No exchange

"Like Decorations in a Nigger Cemetery." A master of apophasis, Stevens (again) indicates *the nothing that is* there, hovering ghost in the verbal blank before the poem's title: What, *what IS like* these decorations?

"Consider the odd morphology of regret."

That derivation, unstated.

One of the most radical movies in American film is a double-barrelled satiric blast at militant black power rhetoric and American consumer capitalism, Robert Downey Sr.'s *Putney Swope* (1969). After the chairman of the board at a Madison Avenue ad agency keels over, the board holds an election. Each member of the executive committee believes he should be the new chairman, but all must follow the company by-law of refraining from casting a vote for himself. Each member therefore defensively votes for the one black man on the board, Putney Swope, thinking no one else will vote for him. Swope wins. As the new chairman, Swope turns the agency upside down, firing white employees, renaming the company Truth and Soul, Inc., and refusing to work with manufacturers of war toys, alcohol,

and tobacco. The film is shot in black & white, but the outrageous ads that send up American racial stereotypes are shot in color. The agency is so successful under its new leadership that the US government identifies it as a viable threat. The film goes where the absurdist logic takes it, to a final image that subverts the whole system: a bonfire of cash.

"Money is a kind of poetry." —Wallace Stevens.

What is the *exchange value* of the race signifier?

Yusef Komunyakaa's poem, "Facing It" (1988). How the speaker's "black face fades / hiding inside the black granite" of the Vietnam Veteran's Memorial in Washington, DC. The material granite, brought to a smooth shiny black surface, seems to absorb the black poet's physical reflection. "I turn / this way—the stone lets me go. / I turn that way—I'm inside / the Vietnam Memorial / again, depending on the light / to make a difference." The plain style conveys a terribly complex situation. The activity of light on polished stone reflects and erases the poet's identity, even as the wound of the war itself is felt to reflect and erase the poet's identity. One is either "let go" or entrapped. The conditions are mutual-

is possible.

ly exclusive, and have undesirable consequences. If let go, the poet cannot know himself, for some fundamental aspect of himself has been forged in the war; when reflected, the poet comprehends the contingency of self, and the terrible details of that contingency. The contingency is the war, and it is also his race, in America—its history, which is also his history, our history.

———————————

But it is not only himself that he sees reflected in the stone, which is the war, which is the death that war brings, which is the memory of the death that war brings. As he walks down into the lower plane of the memorial, into the grave out of which the memorial rises, he scans the fifty-eight thousand names, "half-expecting to find / my own in letters like smoke." He touches an engraved name and sees the explosion that killed the man signified by that name. He sees the names "shimmer on a woman's blouse / but when she walks away / the names stay on the wall." This is one reason we need memorials, for otherwise the names will not stay with us, on us, who have not been directly wounded. For those who have, the stone reflects and holds them. Peering into it, they see their ghost image.

———————————

When "a white vet's image floats / closer to" the poet, the man's "pale eyes / look through mine.

I'm a window. / He's lost his right / arm inside the stone. In the black mirror / a woman's trying to erase names: / No, she's brushing a boy's hair." The names won't be erased, they are carved in the stone. But the double wounding of the war—to be a vet, to be a black vet—creates the state of uncertainty in which the black poet feels the threat of an existential erasure: locked in the stone of our tragic history, black identity is transparent; we look through it, and see only what society has engraved on the surface: in the social life the black poet returns to once the war is over, he is an incarnation of Ralph Ellison's Invisible Man. No exchange is possible.

———————————

Maya Lin, a Chinese American, who was four years old when the war began in 1955, created the Vietnam Veterans Memorial. Upon her winning the open design competition, Lin's plan for the memorial was criticized based on racist objections. Ross Perot is reported to have called her an "egg roll" after her Asian heritage was revealed. (Fortunately, it was a "blind" competition. So, blindness is the necessary condition for openness?)

———————————

Others objected to the memorial's abstraction, an objection to which Congress responded by placing off to one side near the monument a

"Why should we

figurative bronze statue of a band of soldiers and an American flag. Where Lin's abstraction draws enormous power from its placement below ground surface, its listing of the tens of thousands of dead, its dark reflective cut stone, and the way it draws a suggestive clean line between the Washington and Lincoln memorials, so the bronze statue of the soldiers appears trite. *Exchange* value is depreciated as representational value is made explicit.

⸻

In Percival Everett's novel *Erasure* (2001), Thelonious "Monk" Ellison, a black academic and novelist, writes allusive, metaphysical novels more indebted to a European literary tradition than an African American "folk" tradition. By writing against the grain of accepted racial literary expectations, he is thereby criticized for work that appears "irrelevant" to the black experience in America, as if that were the only conceivable artistic objective of an African American writer. When another novel that exploits black stereotypes is chosen by a television book club, Monk, in a fit of rage, writes a satire, *My Pafology,* that brings together everything he hates about novels such as Richard Wright's *Native Son* (1940) and Sapphire's *Push* (1996)—the way they play into both black and white needs to represent black experience in terms so constrained they distort what is possible to feel and understand about

racial existence. When the book goes to auction and sells for an enormous sum, Monk retitles the book, *Fuck*. But nothing can dissuade a panel of novelists from choosing his put-on, a brutal caricature of urban black experience, for a high-profile award. He's caught in a self-enfolding web spun from a psychosocial pathology we've all created. In a final fictive move that completes the Möbius band of twisted reality, with no distinction between inside and out, Monk finds himself on television, saying the words that belong to the debased protagonist of his own story, who, at the end of Monk's narrative, finds himself on television. Everett's novel ends with Newton's declaration, *"hypotheses non fingo,"* "I contrive no hypotheses."

⸻

What Monk infers, what he discovers by induction, is what cannot otherwise be proven. There is no escape from racial binding. It is the kind of discovery that the form of fictive experiment is best suited to reveal and explore.

⸻

Spring 1989. I'm working in a grocery store and moonlighting as an assistant for a large lecture course at Berkeley on contemporary American fiction. We're reading Saul Bellows's *Mr. Sammler's Planet* (1970). In it, Sammler, a complex, conflicted character, a highly intelligent Euro-

have to read this?"

pean Jew twisted by historical violence (having experienced the Holocaust firsthand) holds some mean ideas, his perception limited in part by his uncertainty facing a quickly changing America of the 1960s. In conveying Sammler's point of view, Bellow writes this sentence: "Millions of civilized people wanted oceanic, boundless, primitive, neckfree nobility, experienced a strange release of galloping impulses, and acquired the peculiar aim of sexual niggerhood for everyone." Sammler's vulnerability is colored by his racism, his condition in part forged and determined by the racism of others. Bellow captures something of his character's state of mind with a limited omniscience. Later, when Sammler observes a black pickpocket in action on the bus, the man turns to Sammler threateningly, and, in a shocking scene, whips out his cock, which Bellow describes in terms dramatically grotesque, a moment of vivid ugly human reduction.

———

At the end of the first lecture about Bellow's novel, a woman raises her hand, and, called on, stands up in the lecture hall. "Why should we have to read this?"

———

At the next lecture, the professor, Alex Zwerdling, gives a spirited well-reasoned defense of reading as a way of imaginatively entering other points of view, even ones that we find odious; of not settling only for views of the world we find comforting, or enlightened, or even decent.

———

But the scene with the pickpocket is not a character's point of view. It's an authorial set-up. It's meant to stage an event that has later unforeseen implications for the pickpocket and Sammler, his own understanding of the world, his place in it, his involvement in it, his connection to others who seem different and threatening. The scene belongs to Bellow's point of view, not Sammler's. It is not meaningless, but troubling, both in the way Bellow intends, and in some ways perhaps that he does not.

———

After the lecture, I head out to Sproul Plaza to buy a baked potato. Sitting with my steaming buttery carbs on the long steps in front of the administration building, where, twenty-five years earlier, the Free Speech Movement kicked off. I'm enjoying the midday sun, the warm lapping feeling of spring air. If there is such a thing as a comfort zone, I'm in it, and it feels great.

"Are you a Jew?" What? I look over. An old crone is sitting near me, looking at my profile.

"'Americans! Americans!'

"What?"

"Are you a Jew?"

"I'm an American, like you."

"No, you're not. You're a Jew, you *fucking Jew.*"

In *Berkeley.* It was funny; but the curdling accusation—that I heard it as *an accusation*—startled me, even scared me a little, which surprised me because I was in no danger. The stability I felt moments earlier vanished, and I found myself in a vertiginous free fall, the state of ironic consciousness one hears frequently in Baudelaire's poems, and that I would have been happy in that moment to have kept there.

I was not under interrogation by Gestapo; she was not an official of the Holy Tribunal, nor a US Senator. What power did she have over me at that moment? Such is the immediate complex of the one called out: the protective privilege of class ripped away, for a traumatic instant I am more vulnerable than even one of the most marginal, the most vulnerable, a bedraggled old crone, living on the street.

Why didn't I say, "Yes, I am." Why did I internally cross the wires of race and nation?

A deep racial instinct, transmitted across thousands of years, survival by blending in, triggered in that instant of denial. A denial of difference.

Was it possible I wasn't *really* American? Since that day, I have never felt myself entirely to be one.

Crossing on the Staten Island Ferry, Henry Park's wife shouts into the wind, "I never understood that word ... *Gook.*" Henry Park, whose father fought in the Korean War, responds:

"when the American GIs came to a place they'd be met by all the Korean villagers, who'd be hungry and excited, all shouting and screaming. The villagers would be yelling, *Mee-gook! Mee-gook!* and so that's what they were to the GIs, just gooks, that's what they seemed to be calling themselves, but that wasn't it at all."

"What were they saying?"

"'Americans! Americans!' *Mee-gook* means America."

(I write "old crone" in revenge.)

JOSHUA WEINER

<u>Mee-gook</u> means America."

In Henry Roth's *Call It Sleep* (1934), six-year-old protagonist David Schearl negotiates the streets of New York, the anti-Semitism and rough life of its tenement slums, all the while trying to avoid his father's violent rages. When David begins his religious education, he remains wary of the rabbi, described as "short and bulbous," with "large hairy fingers" he runs through a "glossy crinkled" beard. He is untidy in ill-fitting clothes that are stained and baggy; his tie hangs crooked around a soiled collar; his whole figure gives off an "oily gleam." Who, when angered, "rasped" with a "wheedling venomous tone."

A great American novel, neglected on publication, championed decades later, that brought a modernist style of rendering the speed and intensity of consciousness to urban immigrant (ethnic) experience, and the sound of Jews on the Lower East Side in the first decades of the last century. How ungrateful, then, do I feel in my uneasiness over the stereotype of the oily and rough-mannered Reb Yidel, the anti-Semitic epithet tucked into his very name (though, as heard in the world of its characters, it probably rhymes with *deed* more than *did*.)

After a time, Reb Yidel perceives David as potentially gifted with an intuitive feel for Hebrew; and when he hears Reb Yidel translate a passage from Isaiah, David, despite the rabbi's corporal discipline, feels himself drawn deeper into the language of the Bible, and its implications for his own experience.

"'But just when Isaiah let out this cry—I am unclean—one of the angels flew to the altar and with tongs drew out a fiery coal. Understand? With tongs. And with that coal, down he flew to Isaiah and with that coal touched his lips— Here!' The rabbi's fingers stabbed the air. 'You are clean! And the instant that coal touched Isaiah's lips, then he heard God's own voice say, Whom shall I send? Who will go for us? And Isaiah spoke and—'"

The rabbi is interrupted by a blast of laughing boisterous boys, a riotous tumble of youthful Lower East Side Jewish dialect.

The import of this lesson for David will be central to later events, as he searches for the voice of God in his world. For the novel itself, the lesson probes into a deep mystery about language and

Good art is subversive, and

identity. The biblical story in the rabbi's idiom—especially its comic dramatic emphasis of the literal (*Understand? With tongs.*)—is no King James Version—a kind of pure poetry—but indelibly unclean. Vulgar. Beyond, even, the vulgate. The presence of a Jewish sound. And for Roth, no cemetery decoration, but a living sign.

———

There can be no burning cleansing coal for imaginative writing about race in America.

———

Imaginative writing that polices itself from making "politically incorrect" statements; or from dramatizing difficult conflicts and disturbing states of consciousness; or from using language disapproved of by today's liberal mores; such writing is useless. (Henry Roth knew all about such self-censorship, and stopped writing for many decades out of the internal conflicts created by his sense of social responsibility). One of the social functions of literary art—especially the novel, which concerns itself with the individual & society in a way less commonly found in poetry—is to expose moral hypocrisy where it hides from view, in our best intentions. That hypocrisy is often embedded in language itself. But because language itself has a social function, excavation requires first the establishment of dialogical multiplicity. Prose fiction is often

better suited for this work, because the worlds it constructs are more immediately understood by readers to be fictive, and the social reality rendered therein is complex and more variously contingent than what we often find in poetry. (Robert Browning's dramatic monologues went a long way in restoring to poetry the dramatic irony that the modern novel had monopolized in the wake of a degraded romanticism.) Living works of fiction are contradictory, toe no party line; even when they reify established orders, they do not do so without also challenging them. They do not make nice. If they make beautiful, they also make ugly. The issue is often where to locate the author's point of view, as if that were stable. Readers so strongly feel that need for stability that it stands in for perceptions of coherence. (This may be one reason why we still read the Victorian novel.)

———

Good art is subversive, and its subversions can be subtle. It may rock foundations, invert formulaic thinking, send up received ideas (e.g., what constitutes racism; or, what constitutes a principled antiracism), thwart generic expectations, question authority (including its own), break ground, invent new forms, renew existing forms, and join a tradition of doing just that, but not necessarily with the clarion call of revolution. Its secret worming into the mind and the culture is

its subversions can be subtle.

an aspect of its motion, its value. The perfection it realizes disturbs the status quo, often by virtue of its deepest flaws. The only failure its not allowed is a failure of the imagination.

———

The idea recently floating around the internet, that the reason for such immediate silence on the subject of racism in imaginative writing is due to a prevailing unspoken feeling that to enter the debate is, ipso facto, to publicly acknowledge that one is a racist; such notions entertain a fallacious, pernicious, zero-sum logic, a weird version of the logic underlying the game of representation & identity politics (weird in itself) that, without a priori possession of authenticating experience or *being*, one can't imagine another identity.

———

(Could this be one reason we're presently buried in memoir?)

———

Anne Winters's "A Grade School History." A great poem *about* race, from a wonderful book, *The Key to the City* (1986), that deserves widespread recognition. Great, formally, because it unfolds with the kind of lyric compression we expect from poetry *and* the social complexity we expect from both fictive and historical narrative. Great,

ethically, because the story of individual awareness, perception, and conscience (the poet's) is defined by its limits as well as its capacities. In 110 or so lines of knotty, musical, rhythmically idiosyncratic and fictively detailed free verse, Winters joins race consciousness to a drama of class consciousness, and the politics of urban geography. "It's only at night now I cross the Line / where once I crossed to school each morning: / our paradigm of difference, Broadway." Opening lines that define the Line—customary, accepted, understood, between city neighborhoods—open further to indicate birthlines, lines of music, and other kinds that can't or shan't be crossed. The consciousness of the poet-as-child is informed by histories of race from her "fifthgrade United States / history—out of focus, and weird"— weird as the Dutch word *Haarlem,* a weirdness that enfolds her horrifying dreams of "the Middle Passage: the slaves crouched too close on their grid / to sit or lie down; tongues swollen, extruded; their eyes in the placid whorls of a period engraving staring / up from the page... . Half-waking, I grasp / my forgotten color..."

———

When a black boy in the school hangs himself in the bathroom, the poem rehearses the kind of empty facile reasoning offered by bureaucrats— "'The child is troubled,' / one teacher said. 'No attention.' 'Troublemaker, and so on.' / Though

To listen closely,

lately he'd been quieter, 'a disturb / influence,' his mother, having died. And filling up with that / and too much other difference, at last / became entirely him … That was all." The inadequacy of imagination, of empathy, of action, is painfully rendered in the illiterate non-adjective, "disturb." Equally disturbing to the poet child is her awareness that his death begins another kind of injustice, in which "He had no story now. / He'd turned into part / of mine, or the school's," and beyond the school, or the speaker, to "the Haitian slavetrade in somebody's / memoirs: 'Les Ibo se pendent,' the Ibo hang themselves—unsuitable / for grade school histories. (It was/a tie that he used, though, a man's tie. I saw it / later on in the office.)"

═══════════════

The calls come in. In response to the tragedy, there must be change. Smaller classes? A school psychologist? "The Mayor / would speak the boy's eulogy. A strung-up black teacher slapped me / for slapping a roach off my black friend Rachel's/shoulder—'A likely story!'"

═══════════════

One hears a way of thinking in these lines that eludes even the awareness of the speaker (but not the poet). The poet plants it with a cunning both subtle and shocking, to create a dramatic irony that collapses the stability of the knowing consciousness of the speaker herself. The tension of the suicide's aftermath may lead a black teacher to overreact to the child's brushing an insect off a friend's shoulder—a misperception of racial aggression. But the aggression is displaced into language itself. "A strung-up black teacher." What the speaker means is that the teacher's nerves are "high-strung," as we commonly say. What she actually says reveals the embedded history of racism, lurking in the idiom we speak.

═══════════════

"Perhaps it is the role of art to put us in complicity with things as they happen."
—Lyn Hejinian

═══════════════

"As for my dreams, I ought to / have lost, as a luxury, my freedom of the black / capitol within our capitol," Winters writes, "But I went on / crossing there nightly."

═══════════════

Action of mind, that records, imagines, blends, and cognitively superimposes; that creates the space of racial consciousness in the poet, no less powerfully than the airstreams playing the Aeolian harp in a Romantic poem, the force of Nature forming the imagination that will, in turn, create the poem that forms and contains emblems of the same force; such actions drive the poem

with sympathy.

and constitute its form. In Winters, Society, not Nature, is the Nurse, often a cruel one (no coincidence that the poet child works a "Merit job" at school, in the nurses' office).

———

The mayor never comes. Three years later, though, he does show up at the school, "my father read it out / from the *Times*." "And no / connection, no eulogy, but it seems a rat / ran across the stage while he was talking and this / is what he said: There are no rats. Somebody / must have caught this one and let it loose on me / just to make trouble."

———

One of the great last lines in contemporary poetry of ethical conscience (by definition a poetry of the *impure*). The callous neglect, political expediency, and well-suited-up bureaucratic cluelessness finds final expression in the Mayor's unconscious spontaneous dissembling denial, a big lie in which the urgent issues of race, class, and urban geography tangle in a single knot of unaddressed need.

———

A poetry of connection, of dramatic social imagination, of personal exigent inquiry. Its ambitions are to achieve, with the formal force of poetry, the kind of ethical social consciousness we expect to find in the novel, history, and investigative journalism.

———

There are no rats. Remember that next time you hear fantasies about "postracial" America.

———

To be a poem, first of all, and, first of all, to be more than a poem.

———

"For *outness* is but the feeling of *otherness* (alterity) rendered intuitive, or alterity visually represented."
   —Coleridge.

———

To listen closely, with sympathy. "Big ears," as they say in jazz. Benny Goodman listening to Thelonious Monk for the first time, "I don't understand it, but I can hear he has a sense of humor."

FROM CIRCUMSTANCE TO CONSTELLATION: RICHARD PRYOR, RESISTANCE, AND THE RACIAL IMAGINARY'S ARCHIVE

FARID MATUK

Sometime in 1960 two white boys bicycling to a fishing hole in McDuffie County, Georgia encountered the body of a lynched man. The photograph of the body taken by the officials the boys called in is one of the most recent in Without Sanctuary, the online and print archive of lynching photographs. The site reports that the photograph was snapped shortly after "the Georgia Bureau of Investigation's chief looked briefly at the scene and declared, 'Suicide.'" On June 7, 1998, Shawn Berry, Lawrence Russell Brewer, and John King dragged James Byrd, Jr. for three miles behind a pick-up truck along an asphalt road. Byrd was killed when his body hit the edge of a culvert, severing his right arm and head. The murderers drove on for another mile before dumping his torso in front of an African American cemetery in Jasper, Texas. Roughly in the middle of the timespan between these two horror stories, Richard Pryor gave an interview which was intended to be used to promote the film *Stir Crazy* to television audiences but would, by virtue of his great effort to foreground the banality of racial terror, be destined for the future Internet's private screens. Pryor's deferred arrival before our eyes is a sort of triumph; at least he was dangerous for twenty or so years.

Exploring the field of "docupoetry," poet and scholar Joseph Harrington writes,

"For Derrida, archive fever denotes the mania to define what's in and what's out. 'But where does the outside commence? This,' Derrida asserts, 'is the question of the archive. There are undoubtedly no others.' The job of the archivist is not only to prevent documents from leaving the archive, but, perhaps more importantly, to keep out those that don't belong there. This is, of course, a political decision that involves repression and destruction, even as it involves preservation."

In resisting such repression, in hauling the obscenity of US race relations onto the stage of his interview, Pryor managed, at least temporarily, to destroy whatever place the archive of race might have reserved for him in its register of exceptional representatives. But before we try to meet Pryor at his limit point, let cannibal Jeffrey Dahmer help us to consider the stakes of Pryor's performance by crystalizing at least some of the discursive mechanisms of white supremacy.

On May 27, 1991, Konerak Sinthasomphone became Dahmer's thirteenth victim. Konerak, a Laotian teenager, lived in Dahmer's neighborhood and was the older brother of a boy Dahmer had been convicted of molesting in 1988. After finding Konerak walking in the street—bloody, confused, and naked—Sandra Smith and her cousin, Nicole Childress, both eighteen years old and black, called 9-1-1. Dahmer had drilled a hole into the back of the boy's cranium and injected hydrochloric acid into his brain to make of Sinthasomphone something over which Dahmer might enjoy complete mastery. Officers Gabrish and Balcerzak arrived on the scene and saw that Smith and Childress were arguing with Dahmer over the boy's fate. Dahmer convinced the officers that

the boy was his nineteen-year-old lover and was, unfortunately, drunk. The cops led the boy back to Dahmer's apartment over the girls' protests. The two policemen did not attempt to verify Sinthasomphone's age, and failed to run a background check that would have revealed that Dahmer was a convicted child molester still under probation. Thirty minutes after the officers left the apartment, Dahmer strangled the fourteen-year-old boy, had sex with his corpse, photographed its dismemberment and decapitation, and boiled the head. Police transcripts of the officers' exchange with their dispatcher show that they joked and laughed about the encounter: "Intoxicated Asian, naked male was returned to his sober boyfriend," one officer reported, adding, [his partner] "is going to get deloused." Glenda Cleveland, whose daughter and niece had reported Sinthasomphone's condition to the police, later called police headquarters asking repeatedly what had happened to the "child," to which an officer from the scene responded, "It wasn't a child, it was an adult ... It is all taken care of ... It's a boyfriend-boyfriend thing."

The ways in which Konerak Sinthasomphone's story troubles are many and profound. Though we cannot know exactly how race figured into Dahmer's desire, we know the vast majority of his victims were African American men. Dahmer's compulsion to inhabit, control, and ultimately consume bodies of color materializes any theorizing one might do about a white gaze. Moreover,

. . . Americans today live

Sinthasomphone was a child, his naked body testifying from the bleeding hole in his skull, with the exposure of his genitals, with the disorientation of his person. Dahmer used the authority of his own white masculinity, the dominant culture's perceived indeterminacy of Asian age, its anxiety about gay sexuality, and its disdain for poor black women to invalidate the various "speaking subjects" and their testimonies that attempted to represent a version of that moment that might have saved the boy.

It is easy enough to cut short one's thinking about this story by appealing to Dahmer's pathology. Doing so conceals the ways Sinthasompone's death is painfully emblematic of racism's mechanics, a move that serves the current discourse of postracial, post–identity politics America in which commentators, literary critics, and conceptual poets remind us that embodied identities are fictions that conceal something (class struggle, the materiality of words) more important.[1] Certainly it is true that identity categories are collective fictions. But critiques of multiculturalism's investment in categories do not attend to the ways in which othered bodies do not get to choose their own performances. They ignore the ways in which marginalized people are blamed as the authors of the projections their bodies are made to bear, projections that serve to keep power hidden, operative, and pervasive.

In the United States there are more black people in correctional control today than were enslaved ten years prior to the start of the Civil War, according to legal scholar Michelle Alexander. Her book *The New Jim Crow* argues that the gains of the civil rights movement are actually quite minimal and that Americans today live in a racial caste system. Alexander argues that systems of racial control never went away; they only took on new forms, new articulations, and new names. President Reagan's "War on Drugs" made it easier for local law enforcement to charge drug offenders with felony crimes. Felons are the only group that can be discriminated against in terms of housing, employment, access to education, and voting, all with full consent of the law. Against the notion that black crime rates match black incarceration rates, Alexander argues this "war has been waged almost exclusively in poor communities of color, even though studies consistently show that people of all colors use and sell illegal drugs at remarkably similar rates." She continues, "The drug war was part of a grand and highly successful Republican Party strategy of using racially coded political appeals on issues of crime and welfare to attract poor and working class white voters who were resentful of, and threatened by, desegregation, busing, and affirmative action." To add some stark figures to Alexander's vision of a new Jim Crow: one in every fifteen black men is incarcerated, according to the

---

[1] See Walter Benn Michaels, see Vanessa Place.

in a racial caste system.

Pew Center Charitable Trusts, and when a 2008 study looked at black men ages twenty to thirty-four, the incarceration rate jumped forty percent to one in every nine, compared to one in every one hundred and six white men. The Pew report also found "especially startling" incarceration rates among black and white women, noting that one in every three hundred and fifty-five white women ages thirty-five to thirty-nine is incarcerated, compared with one in every one hundred black women.

Those of us left outside the jail, those of us left inside the country, those of us protected by the police, can choose to craft poetics as various as we are and that attend to the indeterminacy of authorship, language, and categories, while also attending to a social order that projects the manners and shapes of its dominance onto our bodies. Poet Robert Duncan called his dear friend Denise Levertov to a similar attention: "as workers in words, it *is* our business to keep alive in the language definitions as well as forces, to create crises in meaning, yes—but this is to create meaning in which we are the more aware of the crisis involved, of what is at issue." The poet and critic Dale Smith, in his study of the Duncan and Levertov correspondence, articulates the challenge in terms of a rhetorical awareness as such: "The problem for any speaker or writer, given their particular social and cultural situations, is to speak through the chaotic accumula-

tion of positions.... It is a compositional struggle, to activate a presence of mind among others, reaching for the available means of persuasion, and perhaps, even then, still falling short of the peculiar sense of agency established by the moment." Certainly the Reagan administration and Jeffrey Dahmer spoke "through the chaotic accumulation of positions" to "activate a presence of mind among others." How? And how might a poet occupying an othered position today use such strategies to focus their texts, and us, on "what is at issue"?

Purdue University's Online Writing Lab defines *kairos* as "the elements of a speech that acknowledge and draw support from the particular time and place that a speech occurs." E. C. White says *kairos* is "a passing instant when an opening appears which must be driven through with force if success is to be achieved." The term, he notes, "has roots in both weaving (suggesting the creation of an opening) and archery (denoting the seizing of, and striking forcefully through, an opening)." The archer cannot aim directly but must instead calculate an arc that will bend, eventually, to her target. So the "chaotic accumulation of positions" through which a rhetor speaks may also offer the coordinates of her arc. The audience offers bodies, histories, assumptions, and prejudices. Site and circumstance similarly offer "material" for the speaker to "activate." *Kairos* is a visionary strategy in that it requires one

... how desire might buttress

to step, if only slightly, outside of ideology or of dominant modes of perception in order to make these into tools.[2] If archive fever always excludes as it includes, then artists and poets using *kairos* can not only choose the optimal time to deploy an argument, they can also spur audiences into making the excluded "documents" legible.

Los Angeles–based multimedia artist Daniel Joseph Martinez provides an example. David Levi Strauss categorizes Martinez's work by *inside manifestations* (complex, richly layered installations experienced in galleries and museums) and *outside manifestations* in which Martinez introduces language into public sites. Levi Strauss notes " ... the outside manifestations must be simple and direct enough to operate quickly and have an immediate effect in a very crowded media environment. The outside projects are intended to create public space at a time when public space is disappearing and the very idea of the 'public' is being dismantled politically in the United States." Levi Strauss borrows a formulation from Ralph Ellison when he notes that Martinez's work "bring[s] these conflicts into his art, where he asks fundamental questions that reveal 'the chaos which lives within the pattern of

our certainties.'" Though media savvy and direct, Martinez can also make such revelatory gestures, which disrupt our racial imaginary's archive, feel as subtle and intimate as they are startling. Take, for example, his contribution to the 1993 Whitney Biennial, *Museum Tags: Second Movement (Overture) or Overture con Claque—Overture with Hired Audience Members*. Martinez's assistants distributed aluminum lapel tags designed to look like the tokens of paid admission into the art institution. The "hired audience members" of the piece's title function as a wry commentary on the inevitably commercialized relationship between patrons and art institutions and to the way in which the piece conscripts otherwise unaware participants. Each tag had printed on it a different part of the phrase "I can't imagine ever wanting to be white." A spontaneous interruption of syntax occurred when one person wore a fragment: "White," "To Be," "Imagine," "I Can't," or "Ever Wanting." The isolated words and truncated phrases lent themselves to contemplative engagement; inspiring, perhaps, existential questions, and inviting individuals into an atomized experience away from the collective ritual of patronizing a grand art event. However, when a group formed by chance, the sentence reconstructed itself and called individuals into an interpretive community of sorts whose laughter, discomfort, or outrage extended the work's effects. Museumgoers might find themselves

---

[2] <u>Kairos</u> is a frightening power. Iago's declaration in Shakespeare's Othello "I am not what I am" echoes the "I am that I am" construction offered by God to Moses in Exodus 3:14 for a very good reason. Iago's ability to "activate a presence of mind" among others is a world-building power in that, like white supremacy in the U.S., it sets the terms and parameters for our perceptions and interactions.

racial construction.

considering how their own phenotypes and museum tag labels constitute a doubled and de-stabilizing moment of naming even as they are forced to ask themselves how desire might buttress racial construction.

In reassessing representations of black male bodies in the work of Robert Mapplethorpe, Kobena Mercer writes that "[i]n contrast to the claims of academic deconstruction, the moment of undecidability is rarely experienced as a purely textual event; rather it is the point where politics and the contestation of power are felt at their most intense." I bring Dahmer's *kairos* and mass incarceration to this letter to suggest some ways the intensity Mercer notes spills across any boundary that might cleave discourse (or art, or politics) from daily life. Richard Pryor's 1980 interview on the set of *Stir Crazy* turns a routine professional duty into a moral gauntlet that contests power at exactly the fever pitch to which Mercer refers. "I'm rich. I'm a rich, black, ignorant nigger," says Pryor. To the interviewer's entreaties of "C'mon Richard," Pryor responds, "I'm serious, shit. You didn't let my grandmamma talk. I'm talkin' this for Marie Carter." As the interviewer gets back on track by asking him-self, "Okay, what do I want to say here, I want to say ... " Pryor cuts him off with, "I don't care what you say cuz nobody cares what I think." When asked about influences, Pryor says, "I never had a comedian I looked up to, I look up

to the Bank of America... . I ain't no good, I ain't gonna try to be no good, this nigger should be in the penitentiary." When asked about Gene Wilder, Pryor says, "Gene Wilder ain't shit, he's a faggot." When asked to get serious, Pryor says, "He [the interviewer] want me to be intelligent, like Malcom X ... ahh, the Black Man, the reason the revolution has come down ... I don't know nothing, I'm lucky!" Apropos of nothing, Pryor interjects, "I just want to get out of Tucson alive," and "I ain't no good, I ain't tryin' to be no good, I just sucked three young white girls' pussy." He goes on to point to the dispensability of blacks in the movie industry, noting the recent firing of an extra on his set. As the interviewer tries to re-cover from this commentary Pryor asks, "Can I play with your dick?"

Gratuitous vulgarity is a stone; a poem, as Charles Olson showed us, can be a field; but Pry-or's dexterous rhetorical lunges and feints form an ugly constellation turning above us, a constel-lation complete with reference points by which we might navigate. Bringing years of stage ex-perience with him, Pryor spins from role to role, reminding us of his status as a commodity in the economy of Hollywood, lampooning accepted black public figures such as the militant intellec-tual, derisively outing his colleague, expressing a cold desire for his male interviewer's genitals, bragging about having sex with white women, and dedicating his statements in honor of his

...I can't make him my flag.

grandmother who, silenced by white supremacy, will have no other honor. These are only some of Pryor's articulations; he commands the stage of what would have been an interview for a full ten minutes before he is finally called back onto the film set. His sense of *kairos* uses, among other material, the occasion of being cast as an exceptional representative of a race expected to sell a product in order to undermine the very moment and to render himself unlikeable, uncivil, and unavailable to the interviewer's agenda and unavailable to the expectations of any audience Pryor could have anticipated at the time. For a sense of context, only two years before did Tucson, where Pryor was filming *Stir Crazy*, begin to integrate its public schools in earnest, and only after a prolonged battle in the federal courts. Though Pryor was ostensibly beyond such struggles and, in the particular exchange of this interview, occupied the position of power, he repeatedly calls attention to his criminal status and, as poet Dawn Lundy Martin said recently in a public lecture, to the trauma of knowing some bodies are more disposable than others. I would add, too, that knowing one's reprieve from that disposability is purely circumstantial and always tenuous augments such trauma. Criminal, Pryor reminds us, to be of a people who were property and to now be free. Hence, politically expedient and profitable mass incarceration. Hence, modern day variants on lynching. Hence, the racialized frenzy coloring encounters between black people and cops or vigilantes. And hence, Brittany Williams. Hence, Taneka Talley. Hence, Cheryl Green. Hence, Brandon McClelland. Hence, James Byrd. Hence, Trayvon Martin. Hence, Oscar Grant. Hence, Ramarley Graham. Hence, Timothy Stansbury, Jr. Hence, Amadou Diallo. Hence, Jordan Davis. Hence, Ousmane Zongo. Hence, Jonathan Ferrell. Hence, Renisha McBride.

I admire deeply Pryor's ability to resist the ways that civil interaction can actually be a means of coercion, a means to make us validate narratives that obscure the continuously unfurling scroll of disposed black bodies, the disavowed document of our racial imaginary's archive fever. Pryor, in this performance, is irredeemable in so far as my feminist and queer liberation values are concerned. But that's precisely the point: I can't take him up into my archive of heroes, I can't make him my flag. He self-immolates. In Mercer's terms, the "moment of undecidability" for Pryor in that situation, I think, is precisely the moment most of us would elide: it is the moment of being addressed. We respond because we need to be seen, and we are willing to accept the constitutive particularities of the address, the way the address positions us before we even speak. Pryor chose to contest that power. He tries to cast himself as object, I think, in order to claim a black subjectivity,

He self-immolates.

one perhaps more truly his than the double bind, offered by his celebrity, of being an exceptional representative. Pryor leaves me with questions integral to any poetics I might claim: What good are our gains in civil rights when they induct us into a middle class that obscures, as Michelle Alexander argues, the racial caste system on which it depends; and, what good are poetics, modes of testimony, documentation, representation, and legibility, if they serve to normalize this condition?

There seems to be much made of technology and its ability to usher us into new eras. Pryor's performance made his interview toxic to television and its role in reinforcing our racial imaginary. The digitized footage of that interview now has about a million and a half hits on YouTube. What Pryor did to absent himself from normative modes of representation now makes him a delicious curiosity to people who can laugh into the privacy of their digital screens. And these screens, moreover, are fast becoming sites where constructions of self are more wholly commoditized than ever before.

But that's only one way to measure an era. Another is by the uses of bodies, their unwitting availability to projections, and their inability to stop the bleeding. By that measure, time seems to nearly stand still. Pryor's example, though, can remind us to look about to see what materials are waiting for us to take up, circumstance to

circumstance, in order to be, if not dangerous for twenty years, then, to be dangerous for as long and as variously as it takes.

Works Cited

"3 Whites Indicted In Dragging Death of Black Man in Texas."
N.p., n.d. Web. 12 June 2014.
<http://www.cnn.com/US/9807/06/dragging.death.02/>.

Alexander, Michelle. "The Age of Obama as a Racial Nightmare." *Tomgram.*
N.p., n.d. Web. 12 June 2014.
<http://www.tomdispatch.com/archive/175215/>.

"Aristotle's Rhetorical Situation: Kairos."
Purdue OWL: The Rhetorical Situation.
N.p., n.d. Web. 12 June 2014.
<https://owl.english.purdue.edu/owl/resource/625/03/>.

"District History." *Tucson Unified School District.*
N.p., n.d. Web. 12 June 2014.
<http://www.tusd1.org/contents/distinfo/history/history9310.asp>.

Duncan, Robert, Denise Levertov, and Robert J. Bertholf. *The Letters of Robert Duncan and Denise Levertov.*
Stanford: Stanford University Press, 2004.
Print.

Harrington, Joseph. "Docupoetry and Archive
Desire." *Jacket2*.
N.p., n.d. Web. 12 June 2014.
<http://jacket2.org/article/docupoetry-and-
archive-desire>.

"Jeffrey Dahmer." *Jeffrey Dahmer*.
N.p., n.d. Web. 12 June 2014.
<http://karisable.com/skazdahmer.htm>.

"Jeffrey Dahmer's Victims." *Jeffrey Dahmer's
Victims*.
N.p., n.d. Web. 12 June 2014.
<http://www.angelfire.com/fl5/headsinmy
fridge/Victims.html>.

Lundy Martin, Dawn. Panel on "Poetry and
the Anthropocene," Naropa Summer
Writing Program,
Naropa University, Boulder, CO,
June 2, 2014.

"Lynching of African-American Male. 1960,
McDuffie County, Georgia.
Gelatin silver print. 7 x 10."
*Journal E: Without Sanctuary: Lynching
Photography in America*.
N.p., n.d. Web. 12 June 2014.
<http://withoutsanctuary.org/main.html>.

Mercer, Kobena. *Welcome To the Jungle:
New Positions in Black Cultural Studies*.
New York: Routledge, 1994. Print.

"More than One in 100 Adults Are Behind Bars"
The Pew Charitable Trusts.
N.p., n.d. Web. 12 June 2014.
<http://www.pewtrusts.org/news_room_
detail.aspx?id=35890>.

Pryor, Richard. "Buddyhead Presents:
Richard Pryor Loaded on Cocaine."
YouTube. YouTube, n.d.
Web. 12 June 2014.
<https://www.youtube.com/
watch?v=EvSgPowOO8c>.

Smith, Dale. *Poets Beyond the Barricade Rhetoric,
Citizenship, and Dissent After 1960*.
Tuscaloosa: University of Alabama Press,
2012. Print.

Strauss, David Levi. "Between Dog & Wolf:
To Have Been Dangerous for a Thousandth
of a Second." *The things you see when you don't
have a grenade!*
Santa Monica: Smart Art Press, 1996. Print.

White, Eric Charles. "Kairos."
N.p., n.d. Web. 12 June 2014.
<kairos.technorhetoric.net/layers/
metaphor.html>.

OPEN LETTER
A. VAN JORDAN

*If you don't intend to write about race but consider
yourself a reader of work dealing with race, what are
your expectations for a poem where race matters?*

The first time I read a poem aloud publicly, it was
in 1993 in an open mic, upstairs at It's Your Mug
coffeehouse, which is now closed down, no longer a fixture in Washington, DC's, Georgetown
neighborhood. Although the poem was pretty
sad, quality wise, it was an important moment for
me; it was a kind of first high that I would chase
for the rest of my life. At the time, my day job was
as an environmental journalist for a news agency.
I wrote about air pollution compliance, which
was a bit of a Sisyphean task, writing about com-
panies that didn't comply to the 1990 Clean Air
Act daily. The same regulation and the same in-
fraction, despite the subjects being different com-
panies, ensured the same story every week.

When I went to the microphone, it was at the
urging of a friend, Joel Dias-Porter (aka DJ Renegade). For most of that period in my life, I was
simply searching for some *thing* to fill a void, so
I started listening to poets and musicians in the
open mic scene, which invariably led to reading
more poetry. I was satisfied with that. But Joel
urged me to come back with some poems the
next time I came to It's Your Mug's open mic.
He's a pretty persuasive dude, so I did.

When I got to a line in the poem—and like I
said, the poem was pretty bad, so I no longer remember what that line was—I heard the crowd
gasp quietly, and a little farther down a few people laughed at another line. Through the rest of
the poem, the entire room was completely silent.
Everyone was listening to me, intently.

I want it to raise the rhetoric

The close listening caught me off guard in a way I had not expected. At that point, I was less concerned with whether people *enjoyed* the poem or thought it was good; I simply wanted them to *respect* the poem and, consequently, respect me. My biggest fear was of it becoming amateur night at the Apollo and having people boo me off stage. What happened instead was a new experience: It was the first time I felt a room of people listen to what I had to say without debate, without an edit, without someone fact-checking my work, and without someone suggesting that I consider another angle. As an African American male, I realized in my daily life, I had not experienced that kind of close listening before. And I realized I could offer ideas, emotional observations, and suggestions and have them taken seriously, whether anyone agreed with them or not. Over time, I came to realize that this is what—in my heart, so to speak—motivates me to write. This is also what I expect when I pick up a poem by someone else: I want to hear them, to paraphrase Mallarmé, *suggest* something about the human condition that causes me to consider that suggestion long after the poem has ended.

Often when I read the work of writers on the subject of race, I find that the work falls into two possibilities: (1) the poem completely underestimates the complexity—the nuance, even—of the subject, or (2) the poem says something about the subject of race from a point of view that uncovers a new perspective all together, which, like a good love poem, ain't easy to do. Unlike a good love poem, there isn't as long of a tradition of *great* race poetry. There are a lot of poems on the subject, though. Nonetheless, the challenge is that there are a lot of opinions on race and those opinions do have a long tradition. So, like any other poem, the question is what does one have to say in the poem that couldn't be better said in a debate or speech or essay or blog. The stakes are high with poems on race, so I want to see the same level of struggle to *suggest* something new, point-of-view wise.

Often my litmus test comes in the form of where the poem raises out of the lyric moment, the metaphoric, or the narrative to transcend the conceit of the poem; I want it to raise the rhetoric to an epiphanic conclusion. I'll ask, if the poem has set this scene or argument or conceit for itself, how does it work through the labyrinth to the "1" moment, the exit. It seems often that the greatness of the writer has nothing to do with achieving this moment. Indeed, I often find that the more renowned the writer, the greater his or her failure. I've had many debates about Faulkner, whose works seem to underestimate the complexity of race; Twain, whose works do, again and again, transcend and illuminate the complexity, masterfully; and Conrad's, whose *Heart of Darkness* tries but, I believe, fails on this subject. When I disagree, as in the case with Conrad and

to an epiphanic conclusion.

Faulkner, I'm often met with the argument that I'm not considering the character. If it's a poem, particularly by a poet of some renown, they argue that I'm not considering the *voice*. But I do. The voice needs to not simply mimic and show but, yes, tell. This is the rub: No one wants to *tell* when it comes to race in America. This is too easy to debate, to dismiss. Whatever the scenario is in a poem, whatever the conceit, it needs to find transcendence and use all of the elements within the poem to accomplish this—particularly with race. I say this because the opinions vary so strongly on the subject that without trying to say something acutely, the message simply falls flat. And the question comes back: Why did you try to say this in a poem if you weren't going to take it higher?

I think this is what Eliot was getting at in his "Hamlet and His Problems." Although he wasn't addressing race, the mission of the work is still relevant. The essay is often quoted by defining the "objective correlative," but the more important part of this, for my purposes here, comes directly after—italics at the end mine:

> objective correlative; in other words, a set of objects, a situation, a chain of events which shall be the formula of that *particular emotion*; such that when the external facts, *which must terminate in sensory experience, are given, the emotion is immediately evoked.*

In general, I'm actually not that interested in poems about race. Period. Race is the one subject I can say I get my fill of on any given day. If I do read one, however, I want it to raise the stakes in the poem and say something that will "terminate in sensory experience" and offer a conclusion in which "the emotion is immediately evoked." As a result, I do respect a poem on race that suggests more than I would have assumed in my daily life. I tell you, I don't really get off on these poems as subjects, so when they transcend and say much more about the human condition than one might expect—"Oh, not another white-guilt poem? Not another the white-man-done-done-me-wrong poem!"—I stand to attention. Yes, I want this in all of my poems, so why would I settle for anything less in a poem about race? If the voice cannot accomplish this, I stop listening.

OPEN LETTER
DAN BEACHY-QUICK

At this year's AWP, I sat on a panel of writers deeply influenced by Melville's *Moby-Dick*, but illness and weather cut our panel in half, and so with only two of us to present, we found ourselves with ample time to answer questions from the audience. Much of the questioning circled around the notion of *Moby-Dick* being the "great American novel." It is a mode of thinking that genuinely irks me, an assumption posing as a question, as if "greatness" were some empirical quality that can be measured by checking off every square on the check sheet known as "greatness." *Moby-Dick* is great insofar as it frustrates the validity of such assumptions by turning averse to the authority that underlies them. Its greatness lies in its very frustration of the term. Needless to say, needled as I felt, I was preparing my rant. But the question that came next wasn't the one I expected. A man in the crowd asked if *Moby-Dick*'s failure to deal with the racial issues of antebellum America disqualified it from being considered the "great American novel."

I should say the man who asked this question was white. I should say that the entire audience was white. I should also say that a certain tension ran through the room at the question; at least, a nervous tension ran through me.

And then, as it is with me and this book I love more than any other, I saw images from the novel, saw scenes from it, heard sentences, heard Ishmael saying, "Who ain't a slave? Tell me that." I answered by suggesting that Melville's *Moby-Dick* might be one of the earliest American novels to show what a genuinely multicultural society might look like. The harpooners aboard the *Pequod*—Queequeg, Dagoo, and Tashtego—

are Polynesian, African, and Native American. Their skill earns them more pay, and authority over, many of the white sailors with whom they've shipped. Merit, to a considerable degree, displaces race as a means of qualifying the worthiness of another human being. But there are more profound ways *Moby-Dick*, and Melville wearing Ishmael's mask, address race. In a chapter such as "The Quarter-deck," Ishmael ceases his first-person narration, and suddenly, the reader finds him or herself as if in a play, where every member of the crew on the deck speaks his own words in his own voice. It is as if the narrator has grown invisible; it is as if the narrator has disappeared. The beauty of it, and the ethical splendor of the chapter, is that Ishmael allows every character, regardless of position and regardless of race, to speak for himself, and to speak out of the deep individuality that indelibly marks the voice of the one speaking. Ishmael desires to recognize the reality of those lives that are not his own. The cost of doing so is to deeply mar the perfection of his own voice, to scar that suspension of disbelief a first-person point of view gathers around itself with a scoriating doubt. Ishmael's voice does the remarkable ethical work of diminishing itself in order to be responsible to another, and the only way to be responsible to another is to recognize in them a reality that supersedes one's own.

There's more, I said, there's more. There's Ishmael tied by a monkey-rope to Queequeg as his great friend balances on a whale floating in the ocean, and should Queequeg fall off the whale into the ocean, then so Ishmael will fall, and follow his friend to death. Melville shows us this monkey-rope as this primary symbol of our "mortal inter-indebtedness," that sense that in ways less tangible but all the more urgent for that fact, we find ourselves each tied inextricably to the other. There's Ishmael, many years after surviving the *Pequod*'s tragedy, tattooed over the entirety of his body, saying "I myself am a savage, owing no allegiance but to the King of Cannibals, and ready at any moment to rebel against him." So radically open is Ishmael's self when he says I, that the very word of self-identity shakes loose from its confines and widens, and opens, and propels itself not into itself, but toward the other. "I is other." Just as the poet said.

The man who asked the question looked to me somewhat abashed at having asked it. I left the room feeling I had defended this book I love from accusation it didn't deserve. But later that night, and still now these many weeks later, I feel perhaps I had myself missed the point I was trying to make, missed the import of the question. I kept thinking how different that question would have felt if asked not by a white man, but by a black man or a black woman, how I know the ease of my answer wouldn't have come so easily to me if the one asking the question had within themselves the pain of that very history they asked about. I thought, but Ishmael wasn't a slave; Melville wasn't a slave. I thought, he's speaking in a metaphor. I thought, my whole defense had appealed not to the excruciating history of slavery and racism and genocide that still poisons what it is to say, "I am an American," but to an idea, an ideal, a concept. I felt—I mean, I feel, that I had answered the question poorly for having answered it so well. I failed in that way I don't wholly know how to describe—in some secret way, some helpless way; I perpetuated some arrogance I'd meant to dismantle. Stupid hubris of the mind. Answer the human question. Answer what's human in the question. What is it to say, I tried?

SIGNING AND RESIGNING
JAMES ALLEN HALL

1. In the Chapel

Once, I was in love. This was in Houston, in the early part of the last decade. We rarely held hands—my boyfriend was not one to make public displays. But we'd been visiting the Rothko Chapel, where he sometimes indulged me. We were feeling romantic, safe. Forgive us. We forgot we were an interracial gay couple exiting a chapel into broad American daylight.

We didn't even notice the white woman. She was a whiff of overly perfumed air I can still smell. She was almost behind us when she said, matter of factly and to no one in particular, "Niggerlover." Then strolled into the chapel, past the obelisk outside dedicated to Dr. Martin Luther King, Jr.

Once inside, she sat on one of the benches and stared for a long time at the fourteen paintings Rothko installed in the place. She no doubt saw each of them as black, until her eyes adjusted to the dark. Then she must have seen the paintings shift and alter, color swimming up to the surface. The blacks reveal themselves as reds and browns, grays and blues. As she sat there, she must have given a passing thought to her deed for that day, a Tuesday.

But she did not think: I am this black.

2. In the Poem

I was writing a poem about the light in the Rothko Chapel. I wanted to capture how darkness—diminished light—could be made beautiful and sacred. I wanted to somehow translate the chapel into language. Not just language: art.

But I couldn't stop myself from including that woman's word at the end of the poem.

To be different is an

I couldn't make the poem without her. The poem was a failure, and my workshop leader let me know as much with his silence during a classroom discussion regarding it.

And, reading it now, years later, I realize that it overdescribes, overreaches, imposes its ideas unsubtly. It was a failure because I needed too much from the reader. I needed the reader to feel slapped as I had felt slapped.

I needed to be the woman at the end of the poem, with all of her power to redefine that moment for my boyfriend and me.

My poem did not say: I am this black.

It said, I am this white. How dare you try and take that from me.

The poem must face opportunities for transcendence for the speaker, or it must turn its back on them and lose face. This is the difference between epiphany and critique, gaining power and losing it.

3. Singing and Signing

Haven't you ever read a poem to which you had a visceral reaction, where you looked up from the page and saw through changed eyes? Dickinson's definition of poetry as something which takes the top of her head off comes now to mind.

A poet is a signer of the imagination. A poet bends and renders signs that stand for the real, takes sign (language) and recharges it into a signature of her or his imagination.

When the poet traffics in received signs, we say the language is boring, the poem lacks tension, the thinking is pat, the poet has not made it new. The poem fails to sing its signs.

Once, I tried to read a book called *The Education of Little Tree*, written as a memoir under a pen name by Asa Earl Carter, who also penned *The Rebel Outlaw: Josey Wales*. In the narrative, there's a scene where Little Tree, a young Native American boy, gets on a bus. For a reason I don't remember, the white citizens on the bus begin pointing out his differences, his ignorance about buses, and they laugh to each other. They are making fun of him. But Little Tree says he feels like he belongs there, and that these smiling people are welcoming him. He is glad to be among the welcoming white laughing people.

The Education of Little Tree remains the only book I have actually physically thrown across the room. Turned my back upon. (It was assigned reading for a series of lectures at Bennington College delivered by Ben Cheever; the lectures were titled "Bad Books.")

One reading of the scene might be that Little Tree is unfazed by racism and the ignorance of the white people surrounding him. That he sees himself as part of a community. That in depicting the boy as a naïve Native American knave, Carter praises his simpleness.

Bullshit.

education in and of itself.

To be different is an education in and of itself. W. E. B. DuBois, in "The Souls of Black Folk," describes that education as the development of double-consciousness: "It is a peculiar sensation, this double-consciousness, this sense of always looking at one's self through the eyes of others, of measuring one's soul by the tape of a world that looks on in amused contempt and pity." Carter never tried to see himself from the outside. If his language—his art—is porous, it is superficially so. It lets us in to a degrading and racist understanding of what it might mean to be different.

It was no surprise to me, then, to read Dan T. Carter's article "The Transformation of a Klansman" from the *New York Times*. Dan Carter acknowledges a probably familial link to Asa Carter before detailing what can only be described as a virulent and active racist agenda on the part of his distant relative:

Between 1946 and 1973, the Alabama native carved out a violent career in Southern politics as a Ku Klux Klan terrorist, right-wing radio announcer, home-grown American fascist and anti-Semite, rabble-rousing demagogue and secret author of the famous 1963 speech by Gov. George Wallace of Alabama: "Segregation now ... Segregation tomorrow ... Segregation forever."

He even organized a paramilitary unit of about 100 men that he called the Original Ku Klux Klan of the Confederacy. Among its acts, these white-sheeted sociopaths assaulted Nat (King) Cole during a concert in Birmingham in 1956. In 1957, the group, without Mr. Carter present, castrated a black man they chose at random in a Birmingham suburb as a warning to "uppity" Alabama blacks.

Carter's racist agenda is pretty focused: he wanted to warn "uppity" people of difference—not just to mark them, but to fix that mark. It is as if he believed that he could only be white if someone else was black; that whiteness had no meaning, no authority, no ability to achieve anything real, without blackness.

The poet speaks from a position of authority: At the beginning, a poem must establish its in/credible voice. By the end, it must abdicate its throne. All poems end in silence.

4. Tender Resignation

I remember a teacher in graduate school beginning his workshop by telling us, his students, "Language is power. Poetry is power. I can show you how to have the power."

What good is language—or power, for that matter—if it is used without care, without tenderness toward its subjects? Concentration of power is not, it seems to me, the end to which poetry aims. Consider Whitman's diffuse selves in section 24 of "Song of Myself"—the section that starts with his name, then the appositive phrase, "a kosmos." Consider Dickinson's even more diffuse selves—the speaker in 280, who feels a funeral in her brain, then is revealed to be dead inside of a box inside of her brain inside of her head. Dead and speaking, the most diffuse of selfs.

In her essay "Some Notes on Silence," Jorie Graham extols the poetic virtue of silence—not silence, but the struggle toward speech.

One can feel the weight of what the language is battling with every expectation of rhythm or tone or form that is not met. The poem doesn't hurry or slow because of whim, after all, but because of what the silence within or without demands, silence from who it is, in effect, won. Some poets win easily and always. One feels no *fight* for the poem in the poem. Some put up a powerful struggle. (Think of Berryman, all those breaks, twists in syntax, gaps, lunges.) Some often or always lose. I often feel in Dickinson, in Glück, that they have battled with a worthy opponent and been gagged by it.

She goes on to discuss several of Louise Glück's endings in order to surmise about her poems that

the silence supersedes, is, indeed, victorious. And it is the terrible muteness of the Fall that her endings act out, over and over, it seems to me, the betrayal of the spirit into the flesh, that great silence... . I think of Frost's comment: "There are no two things as important in life and art as

being threatened and being saved. What are the ideals of form for if we aren't going to be made to fear for them? All our ingenuity is lavished on getting into danger *legitimately* so that we may be *genuinely* saved."

A poem which does not at least try—or want to try—to abdicate its authority does not struggle toward speech. There is, in Graham's terms, no fight.

To speak from the powerless position toward power enacts that struggle to be saved, to be heard. It needs and yearns. It earns our hearts by losing.

RACING STEIN:
WHAT IS SEEN AND UNSEEN IN TAKING A HERO OUT
FOR A REREAD
JILL MAGI

Preface: Arriving at this Essay and Where Next?[1]

In the late '90s and early 2000s, when I was working full-time at the City College Center for Worker Education as an academic adviser and adjunct, I was also learning all I could, on my own, about what was being called "experimental poetry." I was learning this because I wanted to rewrite an auto-biographical novel that needed to "tell it slant"—it needed to be a long poem and not so front facing about a family story.

Recalling the Nuyorican scene of the early '90s, when I had been an audience member, and because I was living a racially integrated work life and social life, I noticed how this experimental poetry world was mostly white. Still, I was falling in love with writers like Scalapino, Hejinian, and Stein. Until I would later rediscover Sonia Sanchez and find Harryette Mullen, then Tracie Morris, Renee Gladman, Nathaniel Mackey, then reread Hurston and Hughes, and then the *Tripwire* issue on African American experimental writers, I was also asking: "Why don't black people innovate in literature?" Immediately, I sensed that there was something wrong with my question. I divided up the question into three: "Why is it that I am not seeing many black writers in innovative writing circles?" "What is the history of black literature?" "How is innovation a context-dependent notion?"

I built a personal curriculum around these questions and I still pull this curriculum into my teaching. It is informed by Henry Louis Gates Jr.'s *The Signifying Monkey*, rap music and hip-hop culture, and a love of jazz, particularly John Coltrane

---

[1] This review was originally published by Jacket in slightly different form in 2009.

I don't want to

and Alice Coltrane. I believe that jazz taught me how to listen to American literature and hear its hybridity: how innovation is made alongside and within tradition. And how innovative and experimental art can also be crystal clear about injustices and the desire for equality. I also learned to make space for two aspects of essentialism: the value of identity pride in fighting for justice, and yet how, like gender, race is a moving target and race-only allegiances and generalizations always beg for expansion and show their exceptions quickly.

The following review of Stein's works and scholarship on her is part of an ongoing "second semester" to my curriculum. I want to investigate the ways that white writers write race. Taking Toni Morrison's *Playing in the Dark* thesis to heart, as well as Tisa Bryant's *Unexplained Presence*, I want to chart omissions, brief mentions, truncated forays into race, or full-on engagements with race that might look like white writers writing about people of color, or writing black characters, as Stein attempted. With Robin D. G. Kelley's *Yo' Mama's Disfunktional!* in mind, I want to trace the historiography beneath their representations and discuss this in classrooms and in reviews. With Nell Irvin Painter's *The History of White People* in mind, I want to see if I can track how writers write white subjectivity, a moving target linked to power and privilege, often naturalized, so it may be harder, in literature and literary scholarship, to see and hear.

Riding the subway in New York City, overhearing conversations, I am aware of white speech. Women, in particular, have high levels of sibilance. And their sentences turn up at the end even when they are not asking a question. I am interested in tracking this whiteness that seems to value sounding unsure, even when one might actually be sure. Then I think of the privileged notion, in some literary circles, of "indeterminacy."

For my own writing and teaching, I have accepted the poem that needs to be direct—accepting the linguistic and scholarly complexity that looks like this: "Tell it like it is." I am listening more closely to the student whose poem makes a grand claim, who adopts a rhetorical posture of sureness, and how this might be a kind of signifying on "taking a stand." It is also possible that my studies of Stein and race may have led me back to fiction, storytelling, and an attempt to write with clarity about class and labor: to articulate my own class background and all that the workplace teaches me because I *have* to work: resulting in a manuscript entitled *LABOR* that questions the belief that you better have class privilege in order to survive as an "innovative" artist or poet.

dethrone a literary hero . . .

There are many ways to think about and read Gertrude Stein in *Selections*, part of the "Poets for the Millennium" series that is, according to the University of California Press website, "Global in scope, experimental in structure, and revolutionary in content ..." Each volume in the series is "... edited and introduced by a poet or scholar with a fresh and radical approach to the subject." Joan Retallack's thoughtful eighty-one-page introductory essay and her editing work stretched my reading of Stein into new territory. But in the series editors' self-proclaimed spirit of "revolutionary" and "radical," I want to ask some different questions of Stein. Especially in the territory of race and literary innovation—an area of significant contemporary relevance—I believe that there is a good deal more to consider.

The Problem of Privilege and the Construction of Whiteness

Gertrude Stein "was lucky to have income from a family trust that was adequate to live on," writes Retallack. I would like to point out that there may be an unlucky aspect to this privilege.

As Toni Morrison argues in *Playing in the Dark: Whiteness and the Literary Imagination*, whiteness, one kind of privilege, as it is usually imagined and constructed, distorts intellectual and creative work by creating incomplete and flaccid textual "others" and "selves." Stein may, therefore, have something to teach us about the intellectual and artistic *limitations of privilege.*

I agree that trying to decide how racist or not Stein might have been is a "futile" pursuit, but it's also futile to ignore the possibility that her "enduring capacity for contradiction,", a capacity often celebrated in those writers we deem "innovative," may have stemmed, in part, from the distortions of privilege. And though one might argue that Stein, as a lesbian, "could identify with the outcast condition of negroes," Stein might also teach us that it is possible to still fall down on race consciousness because of the functioning of other privileges.

A kind of disclaimer: when I described this review and my thesis to a friend, he gently reminded me, and I'm paraphrasing, "It's hard to do what you're doing—writing about privilege, the modernists, their issues with race. It is very difficult to be a writer and understand 'the other.'" I agree. I don't want to dethrone a literary hero—as if I could. Rather, I hope to add something to the conversation, to ask some questions, agreeing that "Stein's work leaves more questions than answers for her readers... ."

Extending the "How Racist Is It?" Question

In the "How Racist Is It?" section of the introductory essay, Richard Wright's fascination with Stein's use of black speech in "Melanctha" is relayed. Retallack points out that in Wright's published autobiography he omitted any reference to the "Negro speech" he admired in her works.

. . . representations of blacks

Wright "would choose not to use dialect in his own writing" and Retallack wonders: "Why did Wright have second thoughts about dialect as a literary artifice?" Instead of concluding, "One can't know," I believe one *can* and many scholars have. Whether or not and how to use dialect or vernacular is, in African American literary theory, a well-recounted debate among African American literati and intelligentsia of the New Negro Movement, and this debate was taking place also *in Stein's time.*

For readers and writers interested in questions of authenticity, representation, subjectivity, language and power and politics, the debate about vernacular and representation is—or perhaps should be—a central focus of study. I believe that this debate over vernacular and race representations is an important point of entry into a history-aware discussion of the literary postmodern.

Wright warned black writers that the use of black speech in literature could further ideas of a stereotypically uneducated, racially segregated, naïve black person. Those who thought as Wright did believed that it was strategic, and ever so political, to represent blacks in the "best" light possible, engaged in direct confrontation and struggle with white society and the white world, in order to argue that blacks were mistreated but fully human, able to be educated, hardworking, and deserving of equal treatment.

For black writers and those concerned with racial violence at the time, literature was to be part of a battle *to stop the horrifying epidemic of lynchings of black people at the beginning of the century* and to advocate for justice and equal treatment. Therefore, representations by blacks of blacks were debated, contested, and through carefully crafted calls for work and editorial decisions, sometimes tightly controlled.

Langston Hughes, Zora Neale Hurston, and others took up a different view regarding the use of black speech in literature. Celebrating Paul Laurence Dunbar's late-nineteenth-century works called the "minors"—poems in dialect that were very popular among white audiences, and this fact is part of what fueled Wright's argument against using black speech as he saw it as a potential kind of minstrelsy—Hughes and Hurston and others saw black speech as a point of power, poetry, and cultural importance. They did not equate the so-called "uneducated voice" or the distinctly black voice in vernacular with a less-than-equal person.

Henry Louis Gates Jr., in *The Signifying Monkey: A Theory of African-American Literary Criticism*, explains that regardless of the split between Wright's view and those who thought like Hurston, black writers of the time and in the US shared this: a deep interest in character *not* divorced from the larger social context, a commitment to connecting character to dignity, humanity, and political purpose.

by blacks were debated . . .

Hurston studied anthropology at Barnard with Franz Boas, essentially the founder of an American anthropology that was not based in eugenics or scientific racism, but rather the idea of culture in context, the practice of participant observation, and non-typology-based classifications and racial hierarchies. In the academy and in the social sciences, Boas's work began to undo the legacies of eugenics, of scientific racism that went hand in hand with the "Enlightenment." Boas and others were doing this work *in Stein's time.*

Empowered, in part, by her training with Boas, Hurston studied the speech patterns and the stories of black people in several locations, including the Caribbean, and including in her hometown, an all-black town in Florida. She was, incidentally, light skinned and the daughter of a minister. Her Janie Crawford character in *Their Eyes Were Watching God*, a representation of blackness that was unacceptable or unstrategic according to Wright, is a light-skinned poor southern black woman who speaks in vernacular, and who is both admired and at the same time despised for her light skin and her smooth hair—the result of a white schoolteacher raping Janie's mother.

This example of a kind of interior view of color and color lines—from within the community, well researched, lived, and therefore a vastly different view from that of Stein's—problematizes Retallack's claim that in "Melanctha" Stein is merely transcribing the color hierarchy that was "assumed by the whole of American society, black and white, with relatively few exceptions."

It might be more accurate to say that Stein *did not know* and wrote, perhaps even confidently and comfortably, what is usually the typical outsider's and uninformed view of blackness: the myth of the benefits-only aspect of being light skinned or of passing. Hurston knew well the intricacies of color within the black community and she knew that light-skinned blacks could be hated for their skin color.

Hurston's representational complexities don't stop at color. Though she doesn't write or read, Janie Crawford is in possession of a poetics in *Their Eyes Were Watching God*. Gates, in "Zora Neale Hurston and the Speakerly Text," points out that Janie pays attention to the philosophical riddles embedded in the mule stories she overhears. She is the character who listens to the stories that the Bahamian workers tell "down on the muck." Janie understands, as one could presume Hurston also understood, that black culture is not monolithic, in any way deficient, without a history, and devoid of literariness and intelligence. This understanding is achieved through study that debunks myths of otherness created by the dominant white society—an understanding born of interactions and observations, not only through being black, but through listening with ear and heart.

Where did Stein want to meet

Turning to Stein, how does a writer interested in character, in Americanness, in subverting grammar to free the language, remain silent on violence against an oppressed people to whom she simultaneously extends curiosity? Does interest in a people's speech patterns necessarily mean that there is love and understanding and a sense of equality in the listenings, in the mimesis?

The years leading up to and during Stein's book tour were terror filled and featured numerous incidents of false arrests, racist injustice toward black folks, especially the working class and poor. Do any of her writings on the sweeping and exciting 1934 book tour for *The Autobiography of Alice B. Toklas*—the event that starts off Retallack's introduction and provides the image for the book's cover—include how she experienced the extraordinarily tense racial segregation and violence of the US *at that time?*

In response to these questions, I believe it is important to point out that it is quite possible for white writers to consider themselves divorced from or unengaged with violent social realities, including racism—and they may believe that such realities for "others" do not affect them.

Stein has the potential to teach us that it may be a feature of whiteness, class privilege, and the Eurocentric modernist "make it new" idea to work with "words only" (a kind of intellectual segregation), separating words (and self) from social realities and separating even from the physical body. I want to argue that Stein should not be disliked for this possible approach—rather, she is an example of how this approach in literature is possible.

In a statement to conclude the discussion of Stein's use of black speech, Retallack claims that "there will always be a problem with mimicking the language of any people whose lives are affected by a culturally inscribed power deficit." I wish that this sentence read: "*as long as racism exists* there will always be *at best, a challenge for, and at worst,* a problem with *white writers* mimicking the *vernacular languages of non-whites.*" It is also worthwhile to note the pressure put on black writers during the Black Arts Movement to sound black. One writer's "problem," therefore, may be crucially different from another's.

I hope that my sentence rewrite acknowledges these things: That black writers have always been code switching in language choices—and here I'm thinking of slave narratives or Phillis Wheatley's poems—so do we call this mimicking and if not, how is it different?; and, that all people, regardless of who "owns" or claims which language as their home language, regardless of skin color, are affected negatively by a "culturally inscribed power deficit"—racism. Restated, and returning to Toni Morrison's thesis: racism affects us all, affects our living, intellectual, and aesthetic choices.

. . . a black person?

Melanctha: Segregation Celebrated and Simplified?

The Jeff Campbell character in "Melanctha" seems to be a Booker T. Washington "race man," a doctor who "loved his own colored people" and is always "thinking about what he could do for the colored people," a phrase and sentiment that is repeated numerous times in this selection. The world here described by Stein is a segregated world—Campbell and others go to "colored schools" and Melanctha has a "black neighbor" and there are no white characters except for the ghostly historical presence of the white family for which Jeff Campbell's people "worked" and thus got their name.

Campbell appears to be a segregationist who wishes for his people—and this is in the narrator's voice—"not to be always wanting new things and excitements, and to always know where you were, and what you wanted ..." Stein writes Jeff Campbell as then saying, "I don't believe much in this running around business and I don't want to see the colored people do it." Is this "running around" a portrait of a segrega-tionist's view of the NAACP's desires for integration? Is this piece a veiled or not so veiled portrayal of "know where you belong and everything will be okay" amid an environment of terrible racial violence?

Stein's Jeff Campbell character gets his winning ways and "free abandoned laughter that

gives the warm broad glow to negro sunshine" presumably from his father, "a good, kind, serious, religious man" who was "very steady, very intelligent, and very dignified, light brown, grey haired" and "was a butler" for a family from which the family gets their surname. Sounds to me like the stereotypical house slave or servant who, through a white narrator's simplifications, paralleled by the benevolence of a good white master or "employer," "knows his place" and does not desire anything outside this place, a segregated world, or a world where the only instance of desegregation is this kind of "employment" with its clearly delineated power hierarchies.

Where did Stein want to meet, on the page and in life, a black person? Where, in all her love for classification, did she want them to reside? Was Stein inscribing a simplified Booker T. Washington defense of segregation? I do not read her work as a critique of this—and I am thinking of the appearance of Hurston's Mrs. Turner in *Their Eyes*, a character who exists in order to further a critique of color and shade-based racism. How do Stein's inscriptions and representations here inform whiteness as a category? Does the racial hierarchy set up by Stein—dark-skinned "negro" as "brute" and light-skinned black as "very steady, very intelligent"—function to put whites at the top of such a hierarchy? How is this inscription naïve on questions of passing, legacies of rape, and problematic in its essentialism?

. . . formal innovation may

Do we ask these questions of Stein's work? Are we able to imagine how Stein "got" those views she inscribed? I believe that it is important that we *do* imagine how this is possible.

Interestingly, Hurston was a kind of segregationist—but her brand was one that sprung from a studied love of black speech, of black culture, perhaps of a simplified idea of "the folk," but at least an idea of them that sprung from understanding and recognizing the deep intelligence that a person may have despite their education level and literacy. Hurston's desires were not for black people to simply "know their place" but that they "take their place" and make for themselves a world free of racism's violence, albeit separate from whites.

Loving the People: Knowing Versus Classifying

I am looking closely at the verb "love" in Stein's sentence, "I love it that every one is a kind of men and women, that always I am looking and comparing and classifying of them, always I am seeing their repeating." Is there a philosophical match between eugenics and "her interest in scientific approach to character psychology," an interest that informed "her quest for a science of character into the discipline of a nondescriptive literary method"? If this innovative "method," "resembling what Stein was enjoying in the nascent modernism of the European avant-garde," was akin to eugenics, how could it be that an

iconoclastic, well-educated, intellectually curious mind such as Stein's would find so much agreeable material in this troubling framework?

This, to me, is a very important question to ask of Stein. It is a question of how it is that racism persists and is perpetuated, how it is tested and reinscribed in literature and therefore in reading. If Stein's typologies are in fact "less determinate than the atrociously airtight racial typologies of so-called social scientists in circulation at the time," which "social scientists" is this statement referring to? And if the works are "less airtight," do Stein's typologies push toward truth or myth about black people? How could white critics, then and now, know which direction they lean toward? What kind of integrated study is needed now?

Imagining Protection: How White is the Household?

In discussing some of the roots of Stein's innovations, Retallack argues that Stein was backing away from nineteenth-century novelistic romance, from novels with their tired plots that valorized the "viscous intimacy of families and other close relationships." I love this idea. (I have memories of throwing a couple Jane Austen novels that I was supposed to read and love across the room!) Further, Retallack describes traditional family as being essentially unhappy for Stein and so Stein's ability to create "her own

166

function as a mask . . .

secure household with Alice" is the refuge from which her innovative writing flows. Yet Stein's discontent with the world of those novels does not have to do with any impatience around the global economic systems—with racism at their cores—that makes possible those plots that rely on wealth and Victorian manners.

Perhaps it could also then be argued that Stein's class and race privilege, as well as suppressing her Jewishness for as long as possible, isolated her from the troubles going on outside the household. Perhaps it is possible that Stein's "self-identification with the normative transcategory of Americans, artists, and geniuses overrode a sense of Jewish identity."

In asking how Stein could have admired Weininger's *Sex and Character*, "[p]art racist and misogynist diatribe, part progressive approach to gender" (insofar as it entertained the notion of feminine and masculine not attributed to biological traits only), I believe it's important to point out that Stein could admire and entertain eugenics because her class privilege *provided her with the imagination* that she was protected from the day-to-day violence of these philosophies. Of course she was not—and that is how privilege distorts reality.

The description of Stein and Toklas in exile in the French countryside during WWII is frightening and devastating—I shudder to think how they made decisions to stay and how each day must have been filled with fear.

And while I shudder, along comes this anecdote, perhaps as proof that class, race, and history *do* in fact always exist and play out within the home: that Stein and Toklas "once briefly feared they might be denounced by a disgruntled servant." The white imagination may create the myth that a household is successfully isolated from the pressures of the inequalities that usually beget privilege.

Indeterminate Word Work: "An Elucidation" or Murky?

I want to entertain these questions, and I do so as a person who finds Stein's grammars incredibly exciting and generative:

Are Stein's word works, described as often "intractably indeterminate," a way to inscribe avoidance? Is it troubling or comforting or both to read Stein and conclude, among many things, that formal innovation may function as a mask or hiding place, a way of looking away, of not looking into the times? How revolutionary is an art practice that, in the name of innovation, possibly erases or at least swerves away from some of the most troubling historical events of her time, of our last century? Do some of our back hairs bristle when we are reminded to read, as Lorenzo Thomas has said regarding black literature and Toni Morrison suggests for all literature, with a sociological mind? Who can choose whether or not to read and write with a sociological awareness?

I am not advocating

Here I feel the need to be very clear: I would never want her works or the details of her life to be censored. I am not advocating for didactic literature. I am advocating for a kind of reading that sees race and privilege, even and especially when the one we are reading is white and even and especially when the one we are reading is considered experimental.

"What can now be seen in the living … ?"

In a last example of the important questions that the book raises, I'm grateful that Joan Retallack selects and includes a letter from Virgil Thomson to Stein in the "Documents" section, along with the *New York Times* review of the opera scored by Thomson.

In Thomson's argument for the use of an all-black cast, Thomson claims that it is "their rhythm, their style, and especially their diction" that has led him to this artistic choice, continuing by adding that "[a]ny further use of their racial qualities must be incidental and not of a nature to distract attention from the subject matter... . Hence, the idea of painting their faces white. Nobody wants to put on just a nigger show."

His explanation is a raced insistence that the artist, the performer is "naturally" raced white, so that to be black and to perform is to be "just a nigger." The *New York Times* review explains Thomson's all-black cast thusly: "Mr. Thomson chose a Negro cast, he said, because he felt they had ... a more direct and unself-conscious approach to religious fantasy."

These passages cause me to ask how many times, in our contemporary situation, are similar naturalizations made—that "experimental" is raced white, for example? That black writers, as Nathaniel Mackey has pointed out, are stereotyped into being read as "content" innovators mostly?

Racing "experimental" as white occludes certain textures of experimentation, and it occludes the fact that the first North American literary experiments sprang from colonialism, slavery, genocide, and the Middle Passage. Placing "the black Atlantic," as Paul Gilroy argues, at the center of any concept of "the modern" and therefore "postmodern" certainly cracks open practices of appropriation and alters definitions of literary innovation.

One can't begin to know how Thomson's sweeping and speculative claim is made possible without understanding the cultural power dynamic inherent in such generalizations about "the other." The Thomson document may teach us that art communities, even if experimental or counterculture, are not "above" racism or even interested in "countering" racism.

The introductory essay of this selected volume concludes by asking, "What can now be seen in the living with these words that we are doing?"

for didactic literature.

This book, for me, provides evidence that artists—especially those who operate within realms of privilege and segregation—no matter how revolutionary their forms, are entirely capable of inscribing and reinscribing distorted notions of race.

If this capability goes unmentioned and unread, then my fear is that we are thwarting the potential of a revolutionary now. Another question to ask might be: What might now be *unseen* in the living with these words that we are doing?

Bibliography

Gates, Henry Louis Jr. *The Signifying Monkey: A Theory of African-American Literary Criticism.* New York: Oxford University Press, 1988.

Gilroy, Paul. *The Black Atlantic: Modernity and Double Consciousness.* Cambridge, Mass.: Harvard University Press, 1993.

Mackey, Nathaniel. "Expanding the Repertoire." *Tripwire* 5 (2001): 7–10.

Morrison, Toni. *Playing in the Dark: Whiteness and the Literary Imagination.* New York: Vintage Books, 1993.

Stein, Gertrude. *Selections.* Joan Retallack, ed. Berkeley: University of California Press, 2008.

Thomas, Lorenzo. *Extraordinary Measures: Afrocentric Modernism and Twentieth-Century American Poetry.* Tuscaloosa: The University of Alabama Press, 2000.

Thanks to Paula Austin for historical discussions about segregation, and to Warren Orange for his lecture on Hurston and US history, which helped to plant some of the thought seeds for this essay.

EXEMPT, IMPLICATED[1]

RACHEL ZUCKER

All the people in my poems are white. Of course that's not true. But it sure looks like that. After all, I never say otherwise. Why? Fear of saying the wrong thing, of seeming racist. Being implicated. This semester I'm teaching a class called "Lines and Lineage: Contemporary American Poetry by Women" at NYU. I have a fantasy—shameful—that by teaching poetry by women, a whole class about women and women's poetry, having edited the anthology *Women Poets on Mentorship: Efforts and Affections* about women poets and their female mentors, that this makes me exempt. What I mean is that I have this idea that if I prove I am a feminist that means I am not a racist[2], that I am exempt from the charge of racism. Of course this is ridiculous.

The first week of the semester I ask the students who their favorite dead American women poets are and who the most important dead American women poets are. Then I e-mail them my list of links to "Foremother Poems." From their lists I see I've forgotten Phillis Wheatley ("important") and June Jordan ("favorite"). I add them to my list of links even though I pause for a moment, thinking, "I don't like Wheatley's poetry" and then wonder if this thought makes me racist.[3] I also add June Jordan's essay "The Dif-

---

[1] When I write essays I try to use the form as a field of inquiry, a way of figuring out what I think rather than as a tool for convincing a reader to feel or think a certain way. It's often a frightening process—forging ahead without a sense of direction, without knowing where I'm going or what I'll find. This essay was an extreme version of my usual essay-making process. When I saw the call for essays about race and poetry I thought, "How completely terrifying! I don't want to write about that! I have no idea what I would say about race!" As a proponent of "write what scares you most," these reactions made me have to try. After all what else is an essay—from the French essayer, to try—but an attempt?

I began with the word "implicated" and with the first thought that crossed my mind when I read the open call: "All the people in my poems are white." I had no idea where the writing would lead me. It was a painful essay to write and a scary essay to publish, but the more I wrote the more I was brought into contact with my own previously unarticulated ideas, my own history and context as a white and Jewish writer living in New York City. Months after the essay was published on the blog I was asked if I'd consider revising it for a print edition. I asked a friend to read the essay for me. One comment she made, "you're revealing yourself," seemed profound and shockingly obvious; it ran through my mind like a news update on a Times Square LCD for weeks. I wanted to revise the essay in response my friend's feedback but it also seemed disingenuous to do so in a way that too completely covered my faux pas and blunders, that made me seem more enlightened, less narcissistic, less racist or even a better writer than I was when I struggled through this essay the first time not knowing where I was headed. So, other than minor editing corrections, I've included my revisions as footnotes so that my missteps remain visible. To do so seems to be less of a whitewashing, which feels particularly important for a project like this.

[2] My friend says the essay fails to double back on its own statements. What do I mean by racist? What does that mean to me?

[3] My friend says by not defining "racism" my use of the word begins to feel flippant. I know that she is right. I see that in the essay I accuse myself of being racist without exploring what that would mean as a way of preempting the accusation from others. Merriam-Webster says racism is "A belief that race is the primary determinant of human traits and capabilities and that racial differences produce an inherent superiority of a particular race." No, I am not, according to that definition, racist. I do not believe race is the primary determinant of human traits and capabilities. I do not believe that racial differences produce an inherent superiority

ficult Miracle of Black Poetry in America," about Phillis Wheatley, which I hadn't read before and immediately love.

I'm embarrassed to have forgotten June Jordan. But loving her essay so much makes me feel just a little bit exempt again[4]. When preparing to teach it, however, I get tangled up in my own thinking[5]. The poetry of Wheatley's that we have was written under the tutelage (and strict influence) of Susanna, Phillis's mistress, and by the all-white (male) canon. Jordan writes,

> What did she read? What did she memorize? What did the Wheatleys give to this African child? Of course, it was white, all of it: white. It was English, most of it, from England. It was written, all of it, by white men taking their pleasure, their walks, their pipes, their pens and their paper, rather seriously, while somebody else cleaned the house, washed the clothes, cooked the food, watched the children: probably not slaves, but possibly a servant, or, commonly, a wife. It was written, this white man's literature of England, while somebody else did the other things that have to be done. And that was the literature absorbed by the slave, Phillis Wheatley. That was the writing, the thoughts, the nostalgia, the lust, the conceits, the ambitions, the mannerisms, the games, the illusions, the discoveries, the filth and the flowers that filled up the mind of the African child.

Is Jordan saying that Wheatley's published early poems—extraordinary as they are and written as they are by a black girl-woman—the first African American poet—that they aren't black poetry? This idea fascinates me because the course is about mentorship and influence,

---

of a particular race. In making this very basic statement, I am genuinely afraid to sound stupid. I hear a voice in my head saying "How could you ever feel otherwise?" as if even saying "I don't believe race is a primary determinant of human traits" makes me racist because such a belief should "go without saying." It seems distasteful to me, uncomfortable to me, to define racism, and part of me believes that only a member of a minority race has the right to define racism. So, here is another erasing as a way of trying to get myself off the hook.

[4] This line embarrassed me and I want to take it out. But I don't because here I think I'm hinting at my own definition of racism. I feel better when I love June Jordan because I want to prove (to myself? To the reader?) that I am not racist, which means I don't think poetry by white writers is better than poetry by writers of color. There is a ridiculous essentialism or tokenism to the idea that if I know and love x number (what number is enough?) of writers of color or their poems that I am, therefore, not racist.

[5] My friend asks if my whiteness makes it difficult for me to see something of value in Phillis Wheatley's work, to value her firstness even if I don't appreciate her work. Yes, I think so. If she were the first female Jewish poet I think I would have kept reading and reading until I understood her better or found something to love. Who is the first Jewish American poet or the first Jewish American woman poet? I don't know. Now that I think about it, I'm curious, but it doesn't feel like an important position to me somehow, certainly not as important as the first African American poet is or the first African American woman poet. Part of this has to do with literacy and with the difference between coming to this country as a slave or as an immigrant.

. . . I explain that Dr. Jew

about what happened to women's poetry when women poets began to be mentored, taught, influenced and inspired by other living female poets. I want to make a connection between race and gender. Between the white oppressors and the patriarchy.[6]

Jordan is saying, in part, that we don't know what kind of poetry Phillis Wheatley wrote after her owner (how horrible a word)[7] Susanna, died, after Phillis married, birthed, and buried three children and lived as a free black woman. This poetry is lost to us, says Jordan.

If she, this genius teenager, should, instead of writing verse to comfort a white man upon the death of his wife, or a white woman upon the death of her husband, or verse commemorating weirdly fabled white characters bereft of children diabolically dispersed; if she, instead composed a poetry to speak her pain, to say her grief, to find her parents, or to stir her people into insurrection, what would we now know about God's darling girl, that Phillis?

This moved me. I wanted to know about that Phillis, that poetry. I wondered if I would like that poetry more than the highly formal and to my ear allusive, religious, buttoned-up poetry that we have access to. I worried, though, that I was misunderstanding Jordan or using her for my own purposes and somehow doubly erasing Phillis Wheatley from my course as I'd almost erased Jordan. I didn't want to use Wheatley as a metaphor to talk about women writing in the language of the patriarchy. I didn't want race to be a metaphor for gender. This felt wrong.

This essay is starting to feel like a white apology.[8]

"There are almost no black people in my poems," I thought when I got the call for this essay. There are no Hispanics or "others." There are, of course, other people. My husband, my family, my children, all of whom are white. Also, my students, passersby, New Yorkers, other poets, some of whom are white and some of whom are not.

There are almost no references to race in my poems or to the issues surrounding race. I speak of Jews and Christians and once, in a long poem called "Welcome to the Blighted Ovum Support Group," I explain that Dr. Jew is a "nice Asian man." In the same poem I make

---

[6] Do I want to make the connection between racism and the patriarchy as a way of activating my own empathy and identification and therefore more closely and personally investigating Wheatley or because as a white woman I feel I have no right to talk about race in the classroom? It feels particularly remiss to avoid the topic of race when teaching a poetry course organized around the theme of identity identification (in this case gender).

[7] My friend wants me to expand or delete this parenthetical. By inserting "how horrible a word" into the text am I covering my butt, afraid to use the word owner without a little show of offense on my part?

[8] This is a line that shows up in several of the essays by white writers. When my friend calls attention to it I realize how the impulse to include it is similar to when one of my sons says "sorry" to me or to each other as a way of avoiding responsibility. Is it a real apology? If so, to whom am I apologizing?

is a "nice Asian man."

fun of a nurse's English. Do I feel emboldened to do so because of my anger for Dr. Jew, a nice Asian man, and permission to refer to Dr. Jew's race because he's nominally stolen my identity? He's "Dr. Jew" with great power over me (and indeed his actions left me with a serious medical problem) but I'm *the Jew*.

On my blog www.thehereinwhere.blogspot. com, where for thirty-five days I have posted one-sentence descriptions of the "real world," I have not, at the time of this writing, mentioned race in a single post. The blog is called "W(HERE): one way of paying attention." Does it mean that I don't attend to race? I don't see it? Of course not. I just don't write about it. On February 13 my entry reads, "Where, like a fisherman keeping steady pressure on his line, a woman pulls and pulls a young girl toward school or day care and the girl's Elmo (red wrist held tightly in her fist) dangles, jiggles and incessantly smiles, open mouthed, at the ground." There is a photo of the woman, child, and Elmo. It's cold and they're all bundled up and I've photographed them from behind. I know, because I remember, that they are African American, but only one finger of the woman's hand shows in the photograph. I've mentioned Elmo's skin color (!) but erased the race of the mother (I think, actually, she was the girl's grandmother) and child. Why? How does it feel

to realize this? Racist.[9]

***

[9] The reason it feels racist, suggests my friend, is not that I've erased their race, but that I have a judgment about the (grand)mother's treatment of the young girl. At first I resist this reading. I argue, no, I don't think she was a bad (grand)mother. Yes, says my friend, you do. She says I felt uncomfortable with the way she was dragging the little girl along. If I allow myself to be quiet and listen, to be brave enough to listen, I know she's right. And, the thing she has not said aloud is also true: I wonder if the way she dragged the little girl along was racially influenced. Do I believe that women of color drag their children or yell at them or hit them in ways that I almost never see white women (except for poor white women) do with their children? Not that I'm conflating race and class. The reason I noticed the woman and the girl was because what she was doing disturbed me. Is the reason I don't mention their race that I think the way the woman is treating the child may be related to her race, an idea I feel extremely uncomfortable with?

I want to stay open to the idea that what might feel racist to me about not having mentioned the (grand)mother's race is not simply that I am, in general, not mentioning it when someone I write about is of color, but that in this specific case not mentioning race was a way of avoiding explaining or exploring some of my feelings (and judgments) about the way in which childrearing is sometimes culturally, economically and racially influenced. There are several instances on my blog where I mention the interactions between grownups and children. The modus operandi of my W(HERE) blog is to observe without commenting, without editorializing, but when I write, "Where, at Hampton Chutney restaurant, a woman eyeing a mother with twin girls, admonishes her son who is sitting in the window seat bludgeoning stuffed animals, 'Remember Roofus, GIRLS don't like killing!'" It's pretty clear I think Roofus's mother is trying to publicly apologize for her son's behavior with a deprecating humor that is ultimately sexist and probably confusing to her son. When I write, "Where at Super Soccer Stars coach Justin does not give three year old Phoebe her stickers and Phoebe's nanny says 'I'm very disappointed in you' and Benjamin's mother says to Benjamin, 'We can't go to Phoebe's house now because she had bad behavior' and then, to Phoebe, 'You ruined

"I guess Philip Roth

I erase.

Racist.

In my NYU class the one Asian student in the class says, "I was put off when the authors [Arielle Greenberg and Becca Klaver] write about being white and middle class like Plath." I listen. I nod. I almost say nothing. Other students are nodding. I thought Greenberg and Klaver were saying they were white and middle class as a way of calling themselves out, recognizing their limitations, their perspective, acknowledging their bias, but now I see that the student just felt excluded. She thought, "This essay wasn't written for me." I want to hear her, to respond thoughtfully.

Greenberg and Klaver: "Our discussion of girlhood centers on a subject [Plath] who is white and middle-class, like Plath and like us. We acknowledge the limitations of and problems with this. Also, we are not hoping to offer any solutions to the many difficulties of girlhood described in this essay. Above all, we hope that this conversation might be a jumping-off point for others to think about the ways in which poetry is important in the formation of identity for young women."[10]

I am thinking about audience. I am thinking about being exempt and being excluded.

I'm thinking about how Arielle Greenberg and I, editors of *Women Poets on Mentorship: Efforts and Affections*, were taken to task by an anonymous reader for being two straight, white, upper-middle-class women who, s/he argued, because we were white, straight, and upper middle class, could not provide a diverse range of essays. There is truth in this. As we drew up our initial list of poets to invite, the list contained poets who were a lot "like us." By the time we'd submitted the book to the publisher, however, I felt that it did represent the diverse experiences

---

my whole day' and Phoebe just stands by the wall of smiling Super Soccer Stars looking at her feet," I am describing a scene in which I think several adults enacted a ritual of public humiliation on a very young girl that is shockingly inappropriate. Do I think that Roofus's mother and Benjamin's mother act this way because they are white? Maybe in part, I do. In particular, I was extremely upset by Benjamin's mother's level of cruelness toward this young child. I wanted so much to know what Phoebe had done to elicit so much scorn and spleen even when I felt sure that nothing she could have done would justify such treatment. I was also interested in the dynamic because I felt certain that Benjamin's mother would <u>never</u> have spoken to the girl that way if she'd been with her own mother rather than with her nanny. I wanted the nanny to protect Phoebe even if Phoebe had messed up. I wanted the nanny to punch Benjamin's mother in the face. The way that the abuse was being handed out and taken and accepted by everyone around seems white to me, seems like white, Upper West Side New York (and related to the interaction I mention later with the therapist in this essay). I mention these other posts not as a defense ("I think white people are mean too and sometimes treat children badly also so I'm not racist") but, rather, because yes, I agree, I do have ideas about people and race and there is a whole level of investigation I leave out by not writing about it.

[10] "Mad Girls' Love Songs: Two Women Poets—a Professor and Graduate Student—Discuss Sylvia Plath, Angst, and the Poetics of Female Adolescence," <u>College Literature</u>, Fall, 2009.

is my Sylvia Plath."

of a diverse group of women. Still, we were chastened.

I wonder, listening to my Asian student, if I find the Greenberg-Klaver essay meaningful, poignant, and interesting because, like the authors, I am white and middle class. I am about to say some of this when one of the two white male students in the class says that what he resents is Greenberg and Klaver's treatment of Woody Allen. He likens Allen's marriage to Soon-Yi Previn to Sylvia Plath's suicide. My mind is spinning. "I guess Philip Roth is my Sylvia Plath," he says. Now I can't imagine how to untangle this. The Asian student feeling excluded by the white authors. The male student feeling excluded by the female authors. The Jewish male student defending his hero for marrying a young Asian woman who may or may not have felt like his daughter and then likening the marriage (or perhaps the media's treatment of the marriage) to Plath's suicide (or the media's treatment of the suicide)? Where to begin? I am not, apparently, exempt. In fact, deeply implicated, I'm having trouble saying anything valuable at all about race in my class about women's poetry, and clearly there are things to say. I feel a flash of anger at the women of color we asked to write essays for our anthology who didn't come through. I'm ashamed. I want the women of color to have to deal with race. To make my arguments for me. I want to be exempt. I feel, wrongly, that I should

be exempt from this work because I am talking about feminism, because I am a Jew. Because I tried, more than I ever had before, to talk about money, in my latest book. These things exempt me from nothing.

I'm thinking about the sensitivity training workshop I went to at the University of Iowa where I realized, for the first time in my life, that I was white, that most people saw me simply as female and white or white and female. Embarrassing to admit that for the first twenty-six years of my life I'd thought of myself as female and Jewish. Does the student talking about Woody Allen and Philip Roth feel that being Jewish makes him exempt?

I have seven students in the graduate class. Two are male and five are female. Both the men are white (one is from Ireland, one is Jewish American). Of the women, one is Asian, one is Southeast Asian, and three are white. Last semester I had thirteen students: one black woman, three white men, one Asian woman, and seven white women.

How if I don't say anything it means straight. Means white. Exempt from mention.

When I read Major Jackson's essay "A Mystifying Silence: Big and Black" in *American Poetry Review* in 2007 I was surprised at how called out I felt. He wrote about "the dearth of poems written by white poets that address racial issues, that chronicle our struggle as a democracy to find

I was . . . one of the poets

tranquility and harmony as a nation containing many nations." I was one of them, one of the poets contributing to the dearth. I vowed to think about this, to hear Jackson when he says [about Tony Hoagland] "Yet, I would rather have his failures than nothing at all. At least his poems announce him as introspective in a self-critical way on this topic. Self-censorship should never be an option for poets." I vowed to stop censoring myself, to be willing to write about race even if it made me look bad, to be more willing to make mistakes, to blunder.

Four years later, there are still no black people in my poems.

There are, of course, I know they are there, but they're not called black or African American. I don't mention their race. I made everyone white. Racist.[11]

Both of my older sons, upon learning in school about Rosa Parks, asked some version of, "Did Dad ever have to sit in the back of the bus?" revealing their belief that because my husband is olive to my pale, he is African American. "We're white," I told them, astonished by their misunderstanding. They are taught, in school, to say that

people have "brown skin" not "black" and they seem to think that everyone is just a shade of something; there is no more "black" and "white." I'm glad that my New York City boys are so accustomed to diversity in their daily lives and so indoctrinated with a liberal, progressive philosophy that they are horrified to learn white people once enslaved black people. I'm glad when my boys are incredulous when they find out that some people ("people in other parts of the country") don't think gay people should be allowed to marry (they literally think I'm joking when I tell them this). But I'm uncomfortable about how this liberal humanistic indoctrination erases the history of groups, of genocide, how it makes these atrocities seem historical or elsewhere. I don't know how to proceed.[12]

[11] Now, with some distance, I wonder if the whole thrust of this essay is a way of hiding, of avoiding. I make myself a hero by admitting that I leave out race or erase race and for this I call myself (before anyone else can call me) racist. But really what if I've left out race because I'm afraid of what I might say about race, afraid of examining what I think and feel about race. Focusing on the leaving out is another way of avoiding, avoiding writing about what I do not say.

[12] I wrote this essay over the course of several weeks. It was a sensitive time for me as I was waiting to hear whether I'd gotten a job as a tenure-track professor at the University of Idaho. I was a finalist for the job and had had a three-day fly-out to Moscow (pronounced "mahs-go"), Idaho. My three days in Idaho were intensely stressful. Aside from the pressure of meeting so many new people and being "on" all the time, I taught a workshop, gave a job talk, was taken out to dinner, thrown a potluck by the chair of the department, was driven around campus, and interviewed by administrators. The whole time I was racked with doubts about what it would mean to move to a place like Idaho, to make my home there, to raise my three sons—Moses, Abram, and Judah—in a place like Idaho. Part of me thought growing up in a place like Moscow might help my children form a Jewish identity that would be more meaningful to them than the kind of liberal-secular Jewish identity we'd fallen into as a kind of default mode in New York. Another part of me thought that if we moved to Idaho my boys would have to change their names.

contributing to the dearth.

In my grad workshop last semester none of my students were Jewish. This surprised me. The first class of the semester fell on the second night of Rosh Hashanah, the Jewish New Year, but because it was a new job for me, I held class anyway. I thought surely several students would be absent but all showed up. They didn't even know it was Rosh Hashanah. None were exempt. Just me. By showing up I erased myself, in a way. But, because I am white, I can, in this country, pass for the majority. I am sometimes exempt but have never been really, truly excluded.[13]

"Motherhood is invisible work," I tell my students, none of who have children yet.

I am an example. Of:

I want my students to read Eileen Myles's essay on the VIDA website about women. Will it make my male students feel bad? One is exempt because not American. One because Jewish. Of course not, they are not. Neither exempt. Men. Is part of why I worry so much about my students' feelings because I am a woman? Maybe instead I should worry about how little I address matters of race in the classroom, in my poems, in my personal life—how easily I ignore or overlook race. I do worry about that. Feel ashamed. The shame isn't useful. Gets none of us anywhere.

When I was a grad student at the Iowa Writer's Workshop I worked as the assistant to the chief photographer at the office of University Relations. Part of my job was to go out and shoot "stock." These color photos would be used in the view book and other promotional admissions material. I was given specific, explicit instructions to "shoot students of color," and felt, I *imagined* feeling (never having hunted), like a hunter. I stalked the students of color. Looking for them, following them. Waiting for them to smile or talk to friends or walk by the capitol building and yes, I was not above (below?) asking them to walk by the capitol building again if I'd missed my shot, to "act natural" while I pointed my long lens at them. Day after day and throughout Iowa's two seasons I searched for those elusive Benetton moments when a "rain-

[13] I don't know why, when writing this essay, I chose not to talk about my job search. Perhaps, because they had neither offered me the job or rejected me. Or perhaps it all just felt like too much to include. Looking back on it, it's clear that the specter of a life in Idaho was on my mind as I wrote this piece. In Iowa I felt conspicuously Jewish, but in Idaho, I felt a level of Jewish anxiety I'd never felt before. The question of whether I would feel comfortable living in Moscow was on everyone's mind and almost everyone on the search committee addressed it in subtle or explicit ways. The English department organized a meeting for me with three local Jewish women (none of whom had much to do with the university and all of whom had been approached to recruit me solely because they were Jewish). What I heard, over and over, from everyone was that Moscow was unlike the rest of Idaho (read: racist, homophobic, anti-Semitic), that Moscow was a kind, quiet, inexpensive, beautiful place to live that allowed artists to flourish. I spent almost all of the time between meetings and classes crying in my motel or in the adjoining strip mall. I had decided that if offered the job, I would take it. I decided this, along with my husband, out of my own free will and with a combination of financial motivation and a sense of adventure, and yet, every time I imagined moving there, it felt like death.

I reconsider.

bow of students" in yellow and black Hawkeye regalia casually posed in front of the gold-domed capitol gleaming in the clear blue Iowa sky.

Who was I convincing? Was I part of a propaganda machine that tried to convince minority students to come to a white wilderness—tried to show them that others like them were here? Almost a lie. Or were we trying to prove to ourselves, by putting students of color in almost every photo, that we cared about race? Or were we trying to fool the white kids into believing that because Iowa City is the most cosmopolitan (code for "racially diverse") city in Iowa that it is remotely cosmopolitan?[14]

Diversity as a "value." A "priority."

I was looking at, looking for. But wrongly.

Token.

When I lived in Iowa City people often asked me if Josh (my then boyfriend now husband) and I were siblings. I would jokingly respond, "We're both Jewish." Did the knowledge that we looked different to the white Christians we met make me feel exempt from the discomfort and privilege of being white? What made me feel okay about my propaganda? How strange to have realized I was white at the same time and in the same place that I felt most conspicuously Jewish, most visibly part of a minority group.

[14] Was my Jewishness a kind of otherness that would make me more appealing to the Idaho search committee or did it make me less appealing—less likely (they might think) to fit in, feel comfortable, less likely to stay for the long haul?

Many of my students think feminism is over or no longer necessary. I hear the argument that if we'd all just stop making such a big deal about the differences between men and women then maybe these differences would cease to exist. This argument strikes me as facile, immature, and just plain wrong. I am compelled to challenge them, to talk this through, even when I'm confused about how to talk about gender without being "essentialist," without stereotyping or making sweeping generalizations. I do talk about it (because I'm a woman?) and when I'm wrong or mistaken, I apologize. I refine my thinking. I reconsider. I try again.

But (because I am white?) I feel unable to speak about race, afraid of making mistakes. How horrible to be called out as racist, to seem racist, to be racist.

As I write this I'm at Starbucks on 110 Street and Broadway where I used to frequently run into Rachel Wetzsteon before she killed herself. I'm thinking about how, in an effort to talk about gender I told my students about the very high rate of suicide among female poets. I think I was trying to frighten them, to get their attention. To make womanhood a life and death issue, which sometimes it is.

A black man just asked me to stand up so he could unplug his computer from under my table. I watch him. From his posture, clothing, gold bracelet, the way he buttons his tightly fit-

I try again.

ting trench coat, the way it takes him two full minutes to arrange the belt of his coat, the way he puts scented moisturizer on his hands and the back of his neck, I assume he's queer. I am so tremendously uncomfortable writing this. About describing his race, his sexual orientation. About naming his race for no apparent reason. About using queerness as shorthand to describe the way he moves his body. I'm in contact with him—breathing in the scent of his cream—putting him in my essay. Is this honest or just another kind of propaganda? Why am I writing about him? Because he's black. Because I said I never write about race. Does this make me exempt now?

What I learned at sensitivity training was that my students of color would see me as white, but I never had a student of color at the University of Iowa. They were all white. All Christian. All seemingly (but probably not) straight. They saw me as a woman (and mostly disliked me for that). I know they saw me as a Jew (and some felt anxious about this and said as much). Of course being white and teaching white students didn't make me exempt from needing sensitivity training. When I taught Toni Morrison's *Sula* the students only wanted to talk about the "message" of the book; they wanted to prove, in their discussion of the book, in their flimsy writing about it, that they were not racist. Would this vexed and unsettling experience have been less infuriating and painful if the class had not been entirely

white? If I did not feel the failure of being a white woman trying to teach white students about race in completely inadequate ways? What if there had been one black student in the class? Would I have hesitated to teach *Sula*? I remember vacillating between trying to get the students to focus on the book "as literature" and stop talking about everything in the book as a "message" about race and, then, turning 180 degrees and begging them to talk about race, to be honest about race, to think deeply and critically about themselves and the position of privilege and power they enjoyed as white people in America. It all seemed like a failure. Performative.

This week, at NYU, I'm teaching Lyn Hejinian's essay "The Rejection of Closure" and Katy Lederer is coming to visit. White, white. I avoid?[15]

---

[15] My friend asks me why teaching "Rejection of Closure" is an example of avoiding race. What I am not saying here is that I feel more comfortable talking about Hejinian and Lederer than about June Jordan's essay. I feel at home discussing Katy Lederer's essay in Women Poets on Mentorship: Efforts and Affection in which Lederer talks about the pain of differentiating herself from Hejinian even after claiming her as a mentor. I feel confident discussing the schism between LANGUAGE poetry and lyric poetry, about poets of the air and poets of the earth. Katy and I have an easy, friendly, somewhat argumentative rapport that I associate with the fact that we are both Jewish (she's half-Jewish) and both went to elite colleges and then to the Writer's Workshop (although we were not there at the same time). I feel that I can ask Katy serious questions about her poems without offending her and without embarrassing myself. I am at home in the intellectualized debate about thought and feeling, lyricism and experimentation, but it feels like a white kind of poetry

A weird, nervous laugh

Judah, my three-and-a-half-year-old son, has two close friends at day care: Melanie and Maria. Maria has two dads. "What do you think about having two dads?" I ask Judah after a play date with Maria. He thinks for a minute and then says, "If I had two dads ... I would ... I would ..." He trails off. "What?" I ask. "I would be African American," he says. A weird, nervous laugh escapes my lips. I take a deep breath. "Maria isn't African American," I tell Judah. "She's ..." I have no idea what to say. I don't know where Maria's biological family was once from—South America? Central America? She looks Mexican, maybe? I don't know any of the details of Maria's adoption—was it domestic or international? (I find out later that Maria is "from Queens" but do not yet know her dads well enough to make a joke about this or know if a joke about this will ever be funny to them.) "She's adopted." I tell Judah. He looks at me. Now I'm completely flummoxed. I've just implied that if one is adopted then one is not African American. Judah's other friend, Melanie, is African American and is also adopted. Melanie has one mom and no dad. Now that I think of it, I'm just assuming that Maria is adopted because she has

two dads and doesn't look like either of them (they're both white). I'm assuming all sorts of things and doing a terrible job explaining any of it to Judah. "Melanie is African American," I tell Judah. "Maria is not." Why am I saying this? Both Melanie and Maria are not white. Both are (I think) adopted by white parents. "If you had two dads you might have brown skin but you might have white skin," I tell Judah. Why is any of this relevant? But it is.

I'm sitting in a therapist's waiting room on the Upper West Side of Manhattan. A girl, maybe sixteen or seventeen years old, is sitting next to me reading from a textbook. She keeps dozing off, her head falling forward until the weight of her falling head jolts her awake. When she reads, she follows the line of text with her index finger. I can't see the name of the textbook but the chapter is called "Generations." Our knees are almost touching. Does she know I'm writing about her?

I am writing about her because she is black, and I'm writing about race. That's honest. Is it horrible?[16] What if she saw this? When her

---

that we'll discuss. What do I mean by that? I mean that I haven't done the thinking and reading necessary to figure out how race intersects with LANGUAGE poetry, with the projects and poetics of Hejinian and Lederer. I'm uncomfortable with how comfortable I feel when talking about this deracinated (by me) topic. My friend suggests "The Rejection of Closure" could have interesting implications in terms of race and poetry. I had not thought of that before writing this essay.

[16] "Why would it be horrible?" my friend wants to know. My friend says that when we write, we don't say anything about our subjects but only about ourselves. She says this in the most offhanded way as if everyone knows and accepts this as true. But to me, this is a stunningly new idea. So shocking that I have trouble listening to the other things my friend is saying. Writing is not an attempt to understand other people but an attempt to understand myself! My friend feels certain that my readers know this, understand this, and expect this. Am I the last to know?

escapes my lips.

phone rings she turns the book over in her lap to answer it. She's reading *Reading Culture* by Diana George. "I'm tired," she says into her phone and begins to speak quickly in another language. I can't tell what it is. I know it's not Creole, Spanish, French—the only phrase I can understand is, "Chase card."

I'm ashamed. I notice. I write.[17]

I'm ashamed. But not because my white, well-off son just spoke to me rudely and dumped his things on the floor of the waiting room and not because I've just objectified him in my writing. (Do I think he's "mine" to objectify? Because he's my child, of me?)

There is no connection between Maria's race and her being adopted. Although there might be. There is no connection to this girl's following the text with her finger as she reads and her race or (more likely) nationality but there might be. I don't know. I should probably shut up. Not put my foot in my mouth or the pen to the page. Implicate myself. To feel exempt from being implicated.

Part of what I'm always doing when writing is figuring things out, figuring people out, figuring the world out, noticing. I'm always writing into

what I don't know, about what I don't know. I've never liked that writing adage, "write what you know." I'm often advising my students to write in order to understand.

I've taken pride in my career as a writer in "telling the truth," in avoiding sentimentality when sentimentality is a kind of propaganda or mythmaking.

I've said, in my writing, harshly honest things about my children and husband and family. I've mocked the Jews. I've prided myself on not caring, in my writing, about being liked. But what else can explain my total avoidance of writing about race if not the fear of being hated or disliked?

I feel that if I notice, in writing, that the sixteen-year-old girl across from me follows the text with her finger, that this is a way of knowing her, discovering her, describing her. But I fear that if I write, "the sixteen-year-old black girl across from me follows the words of *Reading Culture* with her finger as she reads" that I've said something demeaning about all black people even though some black people (particularly people for whom English is not their first language) read haltingly and some do not as do some white people. If she were white, I might mention it. But to say something, anything negative about a person of color, feels to me racist. But if I don't mention that she is black I've erased her race, I've made all the people on my (writing) world seem white.

---

[17] Writing is about paying attention. But perhaps what I'm paying attention to, as my friend says, is myself, not others. Does this make things more or less embarrassing? There is less danger, I suppose, of objectifying others because I'm not really (ever) talking about others, but more danger in revealing my own racist thoughts and feelings if I'm really always writing about myself.

. . . abusive,

Also racist.[18]

There is a poem in my book *Museum of Accidents* about a horrible event I witnessed. A young boy was lying in the middle of Ninth Avenue and a group of teenage boys—middle school kids, I think—were stomping on his head until a group of girls chased these boys off. They were boys and they were not white. I mention only that they were boys.

I want to talk to the girl in the therapists' waiting room. I want to ask her where she's from,

what language she was speaking, what she thinks of that heavy textbook. I want to know more about her because I'm curious and because I want to present her "multidimensionally." What does that even mean? Why do I want to do that? So that I don't appear racist? But how can I strike up casual conversation that doesn't lead to "what are you doing here?" in this therapists' waiting room? She is black and I'm white. I'm almost forty; she's barely seventeen. We are almost touching, alone together in a foyer the size of a closet—so intimate. When she talks on the phone I pretend not to hear her. When she catches me glancing at her, I pretend to rub my eye. I imagine my handwriting to be too illegible to give me away and anyway she's not really looking at me. Is it because she doesn't care or is too tired to bother or too polite?

A woman, obviously Jewish, in her fifties, comes out of one of the offices down the hall. "Did you go back to school?" the white woman asks the girl in a very loud voice. "Do you go on Tuesdays?" "I don't go on Tuesdays," the girl mumbles, looking down. I can hear the soft accent in the girl's voice but still can't place it. A boy—maybe ten years old—comes down the hall behind the white therapist. He is very beautiful and unmistakably related to the girl. He has close-cut hair and very dark skin. There is a blueness or grayness in the brown of his skin. In seeing his beauty I notice how beautiful the girl

---

[18] So, what makes her interesting to me? What makes me notice her? My friend wants me to be honest about what white privilege means to me, about what "racist" means to me. I notice that I notice people acting badly: a woman yanking a little girl's hand; a man walking down Broadway in Manhattan wearing in expensive looking clothes and saying into his cell phone, "Honey, I'm stuck in Fort Lee, the traffic is terrible"; a woman waiting for her daughter to come out of therapy berating her husband over the phone for his failure to lie convincingly to her friend. I assume and am suggesting that the woman is not treating the little girl nicely, that the man is having an affair, that the woman is a shrill harpy and probably responsible for her daughter's need for treatment. I was about to say that I notice things that startle me, that intrigue me, that perplex me, that my noticing is a way of finding things out (okay, finding things out about myself and not about others) and that what I'm noticing is "difference." But as soon as I turned this thought over I realized that what I <u>mostly</u> write about—my obsessive field of inquiry—is my inner life. The culturally uncomfortable thoughts and feelings I have about my children, husband, parents, friends—my boredom, lust, dissatisfaction, desire, anger, jealousy, and now, I suppose, I must add racism, or perhaps more accurately, racial identity or perhaps more accurately whiteness. Right? I'm writing about myself then I'm writing about whiteness and when I write about people of color I'm also writing about whiteness.

intrusive, wrong.

is and wonder why I didn't see it before, why she became beautiful to me in her resemblance to the younger boy. The boy puts his backpack on and waits for his sister to gather her things. The therapist walks away without saying good-bye to either of them, which shocks me, angers me. The boy goes out the door, and his sister turns to me and smiles as if we shared something, which, I suppose we have. "Good-bye," I say, smiling, happy to have something to say.

A writer, it seems to me, has two options: to objectify her subjects or to assume the subject position of the "other." I'm uncomfortable about how uncomfortable I am when poets write from a subject position that is not their own. For example, I recently read a manuscript of poems by a young father about his wife's first pregnancy. There were many wonderful poems about his impending fatherhood. There were also a series of poems, sprinkled throughout the book, in which he writes from his wife's perspective and these, well, they bothered me. I am uncomfortable about my discomfort because, in theory, I want to believe that assuming another's identity can be an act of radical empathy, not to mention an interesting writing move. But in practice, I'm not so sure. In practice, the embodiment of another (in poetry but not in fiction, at least to my ears) feels abusive, intrusive, wrong. But the alternative—to objectify, to be always pointing out the other as *other*—feels wrong too.

This morning when dropping Judah off at day care I watched Adia[19] rub her hands all over her son Desta's face and neck. She looked up at me, smiled and said, "Sorry, it's a black mom thing." "What do you mean?" I asked. "We're just so dry," she said. Her "we" hung in my mind. "Why?" I asked, stupidly, but determined not to just smile politely and let it drop. "I don't really know the biological reason," she said, "but we're meant to live in a moist climate." Her "we" did not include me. She went on, "Some black kids get a sort of gray skin; Desta gets white patches." I thought of the boy I'd seen at the therapist's office, how his skin had looked gray to me, how I'd been embarrassed to record that detail but forced myself to include it. I was not embarrassed to hear Adia talk about this, only interested, but any thoughts of my own—connections between Desta and the black boy in the therapist's office (connections based on race) were uncomfortable. "I probably should be using shea butter or cocoa butter instead of Vaseline," she continued. Now I

[19] Before publishing this essay online, I asked if I might use the names of the people I name. Adia (who is not really Adia) said no. When I asked her what name she wanted me to use, she told me to choose. I was then in the strange position of searching for African-sounding names for her and her son (their real names are African), of trying to find fake names that would communicate the kind of black family they are as if their real names could do that. It was one of many strange moments during the writing and editing of this piece that made me think about my subject position when writing about people, real people, whether I mention or avoid mentioning race.

understand her fleeting apology; she thought I'd have a judgment about petroleum jelly, but all I was noticing and thinking about was the gentle roughness or was it rough gentleness with which she rubbed her son's face and neck and the completely relaxed way in which Desta submitted to her. It was the kind of moment my writer's eye notices and records and often works through later on the page. It wasn't only a maternal moment, a human moment, it was, as Adia said (but as I don't think I could without quotes) "a black mom thing."

This essay is one of the most uncomfortable things I've ever written. It isn't really an essay except in the sense of the word *essayer*, to try. I'm getting nowhere, I feel. Only making a spectacle of myself. Implicating myself, at least, for a start.

AND HERE HE COMES SMILING INTENDING NO HARM
A POETICS OF INVISIBLE
FRANCISCO ARAGÓN

California, 1989

Hoisted the girded slab of concrete. Above 40th in north Oakland. Waiting to board a train that will dip into the bay. Commuted to college that year. The year before: Barcelona. The years before that: Le Chateau Residence Club south of the Berkeley campus.

The sun low, the air brisk, the station's sparse—the middle-aged couple nearby fingering a map. She's in a vest, he a parka. Our eyes lock briefly but I'm too shy though at the ready with directions if they ask: I'm proud of my native city, having lived so far away.

They say nothing.

What am I wearing? Jeans probably. A hood, a shoulder bag of colored woven cloth. Then *he* emerges from the top of the ascending stairs, college-aged like me. They spot his lighter hair, and something is aglow as they walk toward him, us.

"Excuse me, could you tell us how to get to Union Square," their eyes on him the entire time. He answers, they pivot, migrate back to the edge of the platform, which begins to tremble as the metallic-gray convoy shudders into MacArthur.

———

The scene depicted above—
I've mostly kept to myself
Twenty-two years.

———

"If you have never written consciously about race why have you never felt compelled to do so?"
—Claudia Rankine

"Racism is enacted to

Recently, in an e-mail (altered to protect the guilty and the innocent), this:

"Years ago, I met [ ] at her poetry class up at [ ] University. The occasion was a guest lecture by [ ], and I was an unofficial part of the Cave Canem delegation that [ ] had invited. We got into a brief conversation about poetry, and she asked me, "Are you a Cave Canem fellow?" I told her I was not, but that I *was* part of a collective of Latino/a writers in the Bronx called Acentos. I had more to say, but she quite literally cut me off midsentence, utterly uninterested, turned her head to the right, and started chatting up Cave Canem poet [ ] instead. I've never felt more erased in my entire life. [...]

I tell you, I will never forget that experience for as long as I draw breath."

Erased. Erasure. It's a term I hear, am more aware of, these days. What I experienced, felt, at the MacArthur BART station in northern California twenty-two years ago was precisely that. Standing on that platform, the possible reasons engraved themselves, remain deeply etched:

Did they think I didn't speak English because of my complexion?

Did they think I wasn't American?

But it's never seemed like "material" to me, that episode, or another like it.

"I will never forget that experience for as long as I draw breath."
  —Rich Villar

Until now.

Indiana, 2003

Bordering South Bend on the Saint Joe we drive through Mishawaka onto Grape Road ...

Glass doors slide open at our footed approach. A sale on wide screens.

And here he comes smiling intending no harm.

Looks in my direction before something—what?—pulls his eyes away, his words floating not toward me but the man standing next to me, though I had been the first and only person to speak.

When he finishes his sales pitch, I speak again, posing a follow-up. He's clean shaven, blond, thirty. The Best Buy logo on his chest looks stretched so that his polo seems tight fitting.

But he doesn't shift his gaze back to the person

absent the parallel actor."

who spoke and asked him the question, instead keeps it on my companion, who hasn't uttered a word. "How about that model over there," I say, pointing—looking directly at him now.

The expression on his face: a mixture of bewilderment and confusion. He doesn't seem aware of what he's been doing. Again he addresses his remarks to my partner—a Caucasian man. So I interrupt, thank him for his time, and we both walk away.

———

"Racism is enacted to absent the parallel actor."
    —J. Michael Martinez

———

Who knows what the store employee was thinking, but it was that subway platform in Oakland all over again: erased, invisible—in the country I was born and raised in.

———

What might this look like in another sphere?

In July of that year (2003) I joined the staff of the Institute for Latino Studies at the University of Notre Dame, easing myself into the role of literary arts administrator—conceiving of, implementing initiatives that, as they increased in number, became Letras Latinas: a gesture that sought and seeks to enhance the visibility of Latino letters.

But to address this question of visibility, I had to see what was out there.

In October of the same year, *Poetry* magazine published the work of two of my favorites: August Kleinzahler and Jim Powell. The magazine had fallen off my radar, but with a new editor at the helm and a recently acquired bundle of money, it was now back on.

The books reviewed in the back pages of that issue, or rather, the poets whose books landed a review, were: Harvey Shapiro, Christopher Logue, and Sam Hamill.

It was then I decided, as part of my efforts to see how Latino poetry would be covered, to make a mental note of the books *Poetry* reviewed. I began to track them, month in and month out, year in and year out. A monthly, *Poetry* devoted space, however brief, to as many as ten titles in an issue.

2003 came and went.
2004 came and went.
2005 came and went.
2006 came and went.
2007 came and went.
2008 came and went.
2009 came and went.
2010 came and went.

Number of books by Latino/a poets reviewed in the magazine in those years: **0**.

. . . to render invisible an

At one point I penned a Letter to the Editor that appeared in the *Boston Globe* one Sunday, in response to a piece they ran about the new and improved *Poetry*. I pointed out that although *Poetry*'s new editor had stated in print that they were committed to reviewing a "range of books," the magazine continued to render invisible an entire community.

Could this be happening elsewhere, in this sphere of American letters?

A native of California, I peered west.

"New California Poetry"

"The New California Poetry series presents works by emerging and established poets that reflect UC Press's commitment to innovative and aesthetically wide ranging literary traditions."
   —University of California Press
      website (2011)

"According to the 2010 US Census, California's population was 40.1% Non-Hispanic White, 5.8% Black or African American, 12.8% Asian, .4% American Indian and 2.6% from two or more races. 37.6% of the total population are Hispanics or Latinos of any race.

"Demographers have speculated that California will have a Hispanic majority by 2020."
   —Demographics of California, Wikipedia

California, 2000–2008
For
Carol Snow
New California Poetry, 1
2000

Enola Gay
Mark Levine
New California Poetry, 2
2000

Selected Poems
Fanny Howe
New California Poetry, 3
2000

Sleeping with the Dictionary
Harryette Mullen
New California Poetry, 4
2002

Commons
Myung Mi Kim
New California Poetry, 5
2002

entire community.

The Guns and Flags Project: Poems
Geoffrey G. O'Brien
New California Poetry, 6
2002

Gone: Poems
Fanny Howe
New California Poetry, 7
2003

Why/Why Not
Martha Ronk
New California Poetry, 8
2003

A Carnage in the Lovetrees: Poems
Richard Greenfield
New California Poetry, 9
2003

The Seventy Prepositions: Poems
Carol Snow
New California Poetry, 10
2004

Not Even Then: Poems
Brian Blanchfield: Poems
New California Poetry, 11
2004

Facts for Visitors: Poems
Srikanth Reddy
New California Poetry, 12
2004

Weather Eye Open: Poems
Sarah Gridley
New California Poetry, 13
2005

Subject
Laura Mullen
New California Poetry, 14
2005

This Connection of Everyone with Lungs: Poems
Juliana Spahr
New California Poetry, 15
2005

The Totality for Kids
Joshua Clover
New California Poetry, 16
2006

The Wilds
Mark Levine
New California Poetry, 17
2006

I know I am not alone

I Love Artists: New and Selected Poems
Mei-mei Berssenbrugge
New California Poetry, 18
2006

Harm
Steve Willard
New California Poetry, 19
2007

Green and Gray
Geoffrey G. O'Brien
New California Poetry, 20
2007

The Age of Huts (compleat)
Ron Silliman
New California Poetry, 21
2007

It's go in horizontal: Selected Poems, 1974 – 2006
Leslie Scalapino
New California Poetry, 22
2008

rimertown: an atlas, poems
Laura Walker
New California Poetry, 23
2008

Ours
Cole Swensen
New California Poetry, 24
2008

Number of books by Latino/a poets published
in "New California Poetry" between 2000 and 2008: **0**

━━━━━

And then:

Virgil and the Mountain Cat: Poems
David Lau
New California Poetry, 25
2009

"How did this world find me? I grew up in a Chicano-Chinese and Anglo household in Long Beach, California, always driving, sometimes surfing, and passionately playing orchestral music in the age of Snoop and Dre."—David Lau, "Discretized Vortices of the Superfluity," Poetry Society of America (New American Poets)

━━━━━

Over at *Jacket2*, the poet-critic Craig Santos Perez, in his recent playful piece, "Why Are White Editors So Mean," quotes the previously cited Rich Villar, who has identified what largely afflicted me during those years, and still does, though to a lesser degree:

in this TOC Anxiety.

"Table of Contents Anxiety arises when the first reaction to holding a new journal or anthology in your hands, before you even read one line of literature, is to flip open the Table of Contents and quickly scan it for black folks, or Latinos, or Native Americans, or anything, ANYTHING, besides the usual Smorgasboard of the Unsurprising when it comes to editors and their lists. I know I am not alone in this TOC Anxiety."

Two TOCs

American Women Poets in the 21st Century:
Where Lyric Meets Language
(Wesleyan University Press, 2002)

Rae Armantrout
Mei-mei Berssenbrugge
Lucie Brock-Broido
Jorie Graham
Barbara Guest
Lyn Hejinian
Brenda Hillman
Susan Howe
Ann Lauterbach
Harryette Mullen

American Poets in the 21st Century: The New Poetics
(Wesleyan University Press, 2007)

Joshua Clover
Stacy Doris
Peter Gizzi
Kenneth Goldsmith
Myung Mi Kim
Mark Levine
Tracie Morris
Mark Nowak
D. A. Powell
Juliana Spahr
Karen Volkman
Susan Wheeler
Kevin Young

Number of Latino/a poets included in these anthologies: **0**

"If you have never written consciously about race why have you never felt compelled to do so?"
—Claudia Rankine

This never felt like "material" ... until now.
—Francisco Aragón

TOC Anxiety *is* an affliction, an over-preoccupation that saps energy, mental and otherwise, from more interesting and satisfying work. There were

. . . debate focused on black

stretches of time when I grew weary of it. And yet the nature of my day job wouldn't allow me to ignore these numbers. I felt, rightly or wrongly, like I had to work to lessen TOC Anxiety for others in my literary community, as well.

One of the things I tried to do was make the case, as tactfully as possible, for an ethos of inclusiveness (I'd grown weary of "diversity") to people in decision-making positions. Most were genuinely surprised when I'd point out some of these numbers. My efforts sometimes bore fruit when a one-to-one relationship could be forged, one based on good faith and mutual respect.

When I was based in South Bend, Indiana, my work took me to Chicago, mostly because of Palabra Pura, the reading series I cocurated there in collaboration with the Guild Complex. This brought me into contact with the Poetry Foundation—particularly, in the beginning, with those who worked for the website and did their events programming.

The Poetry Foundation became a partner, once a year, for one of our Palabra Pura readings—including events that featured Victor Hernández Cruz, Lorna Dee Cervantes, Juan Felipe Herrera, and Valerie Martínez, among others.

But there was one wing of the Poetry Foundation that remained, in my view, aloof.

Until one day when I heard from a newly hired senior editor at magazine. What I learned was both instructive and a revelation. This editor

shared that he'd in fact tried to assign for review, on more than one occasion, *The Wind Shifts: New Latino Poetry*—the anthology I'd edited for University of Arizona Press, which appeared in 2007. But nobody in *Poetry's* stable of writers would touch it. They didn't feel (I'm paraphrasing here) "qualified." They didn't want to say the wrong thing. They couldn't read Spanish. Etc. Etc. The editor, to his credit, and with whom I have since forged a cordial professional relationship, expressed sincere frustration—this resistance is what he mostly encountered when he tried to assign a book by a Latino/a poet.

It tempered, considerably, my public position from then on. I came to view the senior editor in question as an ally. I believed him when he said he was trying find writers who would take on the assignment of reviewing books by Latino/a poets.

And yet hearing about book reviewers declining to take on a book of poetry by a Latino or Latina writer felt, once again, like I was standing on that subway platform, and these reluctant critics were stand-ins for that middle-aged couple averting their gaze, not wanting to look me in the eye for any length of time.

———

Did they think we didn't write in English because of our heritage?

Did they think we weren't American?

and white—omitting brown.

In 2006, the poet Cornelius Eady became a colleague and friend at Notre Dame. In our extended conversations those years, he hypothesized that I was experiencing and feeling what he and other African American poets felt and experienced ten or fifteen years prior—before Cave Canem helped alter the poetry landscape some. In other words, there was a time he perceived that African American poets were being largely omitted and kept invisible, erased from the pages of mainstream journals and anthologies. There seemed to be a lag time for us Latino/as, and the necessary advocacy would have to continue, not only for Latino/a writers, but writers of color in general.

It all reminded me of what Richard Rodriguez had been saying since the nineties. America, mainstream American media, when it came to discussing issues of race in American life, was keeping the conversation and debate focused on black and white—omitting brown.

An additional strategy on my part, then, was to forge relationships with other poetry communities of color. The joint programming that Letras Latinas has carried out with Cave Canem experienced its best moment, I think, in the summer of 2010. In June of that year Chicana poet Brenda Cárdenas and I spent a week among Cave Canem fellows at their annual retreat. Cárdenas, in her capacity as "guest poet," was able to share her work with a new and receptive audience. It was also an immense pleasure getting to meet Carl Phillips and Claudia Rankine, as well other CC faculty, and the fellows, of course. My conversations with Rankine in particular proved fruitful as it was during that week that we conceived of a possible future volume in the *American Poets in the 21ˢᵗ Century* series with Wesleyan University Press—one that would include, though not exclusively, a number of Latino and Latina poets, thus presenting an enriched mosaic of American verse and criticism.

In the April 2011 issue of *Poetry* magazine, *Bird Eating Bird* by Kristin Naca was reviewed. In one passage, the reviewer writes:

> "When her uneasily bilingual poetry incorporates Spanish, she at once draws English speakers closer to her own experience—a Filipina American, Naca grew up with Spanish and English in her ears—and alienates those of us who don't know the other language well. Like the Nuyorican Poets, Naca occupies one of America's many linguistic borderlands, and seems at home neither in Spanish nor in English: when using one, she must negotiate with the other. In *Bird Eating Bird*, that discord echoes through the reader's experience too."

"we are / the insides /

This is a start.

This is not a complaint.

This is the beginning, finally, of a conversation.

There is more work to do.

California, 2009–2011

Sight Map: Poems
Brian Teare
New California Poetry, 26
2009

Transcendental Studies: A Trilogy
Keith Waldrop
New California Poetry, 27
2009

R's Boat
Lisa Robertson
New California Poetry, 28
2010

Green is the Orator
Sarah Gridley
New California Poetry, 29
2010

Writing the Silences
Richard O. Moore
New California Poetry, 30
2010

Voyager
Srikanth Reddy
New California Poetry, 31
2011

Dark Archive
Laura Mullen
New California Poetry, 32
2011

Metropole
Geoffrey G. O'Brien
New California Poetry, 33
2011

Latino/a poets published in "New California Poetry" in 2009, 2010, and 2011: **0**

And here he comes smiling intending no harm

Last year the Yale Series of Younger Poets competition designated its first poet of color—distinguished poet and former Cave Canem faculty member Carl Phillips—to serve as judge. For the first time since the prize was established in 1919, the winner is a Latino/a poet: Eduardo C. Corral.

Corral's manuscript, it should be noted, relies considerably on Chicano Spanish to achieve its full aesthetic arc.

# of your body . . . "

I'd like to think that Phillips experienced neither "alienation" nor "discord" when taking in Corral's literary art.

=========

And yet I continue to believe that the poetry community in the United States—the sliver it represents in our national discourse—is a microcosm of said discourse. And therefore, there *are* those in our literary community for whom inclusiveness is simply *not* a priority, at least not high enough beyond lip service. And there are those for whom it is—which becomes evident by concrete gestures and acts. My job satisfaction derives from working with the latter.

When I encounter and experience the former, I find myself mouthing to myself the end of Chicano poet Francisco X. Alarcón's prophetic poem, "Letter to America," published in 1990 in his book *Body in Flames*:

America
understand
once and for all:

we are
the insides
of your body

our faces
reflect
your future.

(translated from the Spanish by
Francisco Aragón, with the author)

Charles McGill, **<u>Once Upon a Time in a Land Far Far Away</u>**, 2011

Sculptor and illustrator Charles McGill has an obsession with golf—its symbolism, its land use, its fashion, its membership, and its bags. He locates these used bags, deconstructs, reassembles, and decorates them until they reveal a story from American history; one of toil and leisure, inequity and exclusion. MKC

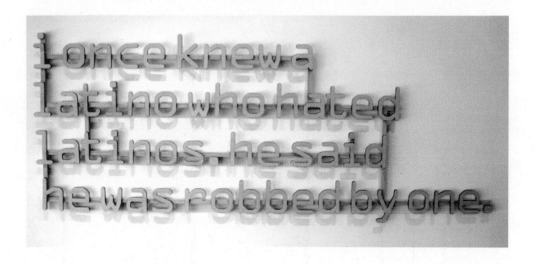

Nery Gabriel Lemus, **I Once Knew a Latino**, 2010

Hiding beneath this anecdote is the reductio ad absurdum of facile racial disparagement. Lemus mirrors this too common fallacious syllogism with a damning reflection of self-loathing. MKC

Amitis Motevalli, **Looking for the Birds**, 2005

Iranian born artist Amitis Motivalli has a gift for the acidic editorial, as seen in this work from her series, Re-Aiming the Cannon. Presumptive Jihadis, one wittily depicted wearing the jersey of Pittsburgh Steelers' Pro Bowl quarterback Ben Roethlisberger, shoulder rocket launchers supplied by the American military. MKC

Edgar Endress
Street Photography, 2010

After thirty years, Mr. Apollinar Escobar is the last photographer using this ancient German camera that produces "one-minute" photos on the streets of La Paz, Bolivia. A miniature darkroom, the camera produces a paper negative and positive print inside the camera. Though the image is black and white, Don Apollinar often, at the request of customers, retouches the negative with red ink. This results in the subjects looking "whiter." Thus, the colonized internalize their inferiority by imitating the colonizer. MKC

CRITIQUE

By which I mean simply that I can't find a clear thread. If no one is willing to speak unless they are offended, then offend them. **I think that's important to remember: how personal this all is.** Now I get to be naïve and contradictory. **I knew on which side of the border I belonged, but I crossed it anyway, entering a place where I was not welcome.** Your effort alone is not enough.

OPEN LETTER
KASEY JOHNSON

Dear Claudia,

I am submitting some thoughts on race given the discussion that has opened up recently on your website. Race as we know it is a social construct. We see one another as racialized subjects only because we live in a society that has constructed us that way. So, race is something we have inside of us, an ontological concept that has become naturalized. What are we to do with this naturalized concept? Hold on to it forever? Reproduce the xenophobia of our forebears? I hope not. Neither do I see race as a critical category falling away anytime soon. Just as feminists call for a strategic use of "woman" for organizing against oppression on the basis of sex and gender, so too racialized subjects can and often must appeal to essentialized notions of race in order to fight oppression with any sort of recognition or visibility by the powers that be (in a dominant culture that has constructed them as such and continues to oppress them as such).

There is a culture of shame about race in our society. We are ashamed to admit our own confrontations with whiteness, blackness, yellowness, or redness, not realizing that though we are constituted through and through as racialized subjects in the political and social discourse of our society, it in no way dictates the limits and leaps our minds may make. Now I get to be naïve and contradictory. I am saying that we are constituted through and through by race, and also that race does not define us. And I am sticking with those contradictory remarks. Race is an ineluctable part of the social dialogue of our times; it is part of our historical past and there's a lot out there to suggest it is not going to go away anytime soon. However, the racial landscape is changing, and changing quickly. A generation ago the visibility of particular writers of color was not what it is today. What inspires me most about our current moment are the young and old who examine literary and cultural productions for the lacunae that exist; those who are intent on dismantling and struggling against hegemonic cultural centers that are not representative of both material that is out there and of their own experience. These times are changing.

This is not to suggest a narrative of progress. I am not suggesting there will ever be an idyllic future free of struggle. Even if we move past our own atrocious and sordid American racial history (but how will we and should we? What should remain a part of the social memory? How do we both respect and honor our past and also heal from it?), there will be some other incident in which there is an "us" defined against a "them." I am not hopeful, it's true, about people in general. I think that horrendous acts are justified and committed daily based on unsound, hypocritical human judgments. And it's simply unfair. And it keeps happening. But the world continues to turn and as long as it does, there are those who are brave enough to question the status quo and challenge even their own thinking and assumptions.

So yes, race feels very present, a historical narrative that has followed us from our colonial past into the present (still colonizing) moment. We cannot ignore race because to ignore race is to ignore the very subjects that the dominant culture has racialized and oppressed. However, to recognize ourselves as racialized subjects is not to stop there or to flaunt stereotypical, racist thought or attitudes. To acknowledge our racialized selves is in some way to transcend those forces that confined us there in the first place, that made us ever think that what mattered about us was the color of our skin or other phenotypic racial signifiers. At the same time, we should be able to discuss the color of our skin and the resonances, historical, social, political, that that coloration has for us; without dialogue we are lost. As we are, ultimately, a planet of separate peoples, separated geographically, culturally, and separated by the very membranes that keep our bodies together, then it follows that dialogue and the translation of our shared feelings and thoughts are necessary.

Here I go sounding naïve again. However, perhaps a little naiveté is necessary, perhaps an unschooled, unsophisticated approach to ourselves and others is part of what we need to feel for each other, to make the leaps necessary to imagine positionalities other than those defined by our racial relationships to one another.

In peace,

Kasey

FEELING COLORED
DIANE EXAVIER

What I often find most problematic when it comes to writing race is how I'm supposed to feel about writing race. I am a black woman. I know that. And if you're reading this, you know it as well. It's not something I think about always; but it's clearly not something that I forget. With that said, I feel like race isn't something I always want (or need) to talk about; but it is something that other people won't let me forget. And that's where I get frustrated—when the choice is taken from me, when somebody decides that I need to address race because they're looking at me and seeing someone who is colored and, therefore, must have something to say about it.

But I am not tragically colored. There is no great sorrow dammed-up in my soul, nor lurking behind my eyes.

I first came across Zora Neale Hurston's essay "How It Feels to Be Colored Me" when I was seventeen years old—by way of artist Glenn Ligon's appropriated text in one of his well-known door paintings hanging in the Whitney Museum of American Art. On one of these paintings, in black oil stick against a white background, read the words:

"I do not always feel colored."

I remember thinking, looking at the painting at the time, that I do not always feel colored. I am from Brooklyn, where I grew up in a predominantly Caribbean community. My family is from Haiti. I am first-generation American. Even with such a seemingly obvious example of Other, I never felt like I was. Never felt different. Never felt like something else.

I first felt colored when I went to college in Western Massachusetts. The leading factor in my

Recognition is

sudden awareness of skin tone was an external and aggressive demand to identify as, stand for, and say something—none of which I had ever been forced to do before. It made me react with refusal to actively join the conversation.

Several years later, I find myself continually asking: Because I am black, because I am Caribbean, because everyone knows this, am I somehow more accountable, more responsible for handling, explaining and sharing this history?

You want to talk about race? Fine. Let's talk about race. But these conversations often happen in academic, intellectual, and—in those ways—private spheres, where race becomes an idea completely disconnected from itself in action. And what is the point of that? You're going to talk to me about the issue of race in America as an "issue" of "race" in "America." I do not need to be turned into an idea to understand who I am.

My history is dripping all over me, always. It is in my hands, in my face, in the bags under my eyes, in my gaze, in the tips of my fingers, in my feet. I don't need to tell you about it in order for you to know. But there are also times when I do feel inspired to drop knowledge and talk about why and who and what it all means. For me. I think that's important to remember: how personal this all is. Race and culture are both very, very personal.

All of this is incredibly difficult to make sense of because the United States of America is so young a country, living its history while that history is being made. The time lines are all messed up and blurry and crossing each other constantly. In his essay "Stranger in the Village," James Baldwin writes:

"People are trapped in history and history
  is trapped in them."

This is the story of America: the trap—the enslavement of an entire people, the robbery of land, the violence, the oppression, the silence. Also part of America's story is the freedom from the trap, the moment of getting loose: the wars fought, the rises from struggle, the movements, the many, many songs. The trap and the freedom from it will forever be intertwined. We are all of these things. Always. We are all colored by a history that we have no choice but to participate in as we live it and make it over and over again.

I truly believe that it is the recognition of the Other that ultimately leads to unification. Recognition is awareness, not definition. Unification is balance, not sameness. The Other is anything that is not you, not living in your body. I do think (and hope) there are ways to talk and write about race so that we are actually sharing, learning and experiencing. This is what I offer:

Give yourself and others the right of choice.
Remember that this, all of this, is America.
Respect history; but be willing to change it.

DIANE EXAVIER

awareness, not definition.

Let your point of departure be somewhere
inside of you.
Listen always, preferably before, and
especially as, you speak (or write).

OPEN LETTER

BETH LOFFREDA

Many years ago, in the late 1980s, I attended a university in the south, very white, highly segregated. I had a friend, a young white man, more aware and more well-educated than me in things that mattered, who took a class in African American history taught by a well-known black civil rights leader. My friend acknowledged—with astonished, lacerating shame—that there was a moment in class when the pressure of his own racial identity became so unbearable to him that he found himself imagining shouting *nigger* at the professor. This was a whiteness inside him he had not before come in contact with—had been cushioned from. Cushioned, in that paradoxical fashion of whiteness, by the very fact that he was white and thus did not need to know it.

My friend also told me that one day during class, the professor looked out the window—it was a first-floor classroom and the large windows were only a few feet above the ground—and saw an African American woman he knew, another professor, of literature. He leaped out the window to greet her, left the class behind. Riding the wave of the white students—racial hostility and shame, right out the window.

At least, that's how my friend described that moment. But what did he, or I, know really, beyond our own projections? That classroom was for my friend a theater of endless self-contradictory projection—anger at the teacher and then an envious, mournful resentment that he had left—the peculiar, roiling emotional machinations of whiteness, of the particular kind of whiteness I wish to think about here: well-meaning whiteness, whiteness that means no harm, that thinks it has *it* mostly figured out. I've reconstructed that classroom as my own theater too here, for my own purposes, a curiosity about what happens when the projections turn back inward. Which is another way of saying that when the cushioning's removed, you realize it's a mess in there, in the white mind. Which is a start.

I didn't know how to think about these things in college; at that time, I only knew that I wanted to. I went to graduate school. In graduate school, in the 1990s, it turned out that "race" was something you needed to know about. I do not mean to imply that this was an unsalutary development. It was a hugely powerful development in my own education. I feel that most of my education has come from books and the small but remarkable group of teachers who have been their interlocutors. In graduate school, the books stripped off that cushioning and in its place gave me a chastening, freeing distance. The usefulness of temporarily exiting my own confused and cushioned mind. I could offer a long list here of the books that did this; a list that I try still to convert on a regular basis into syllabi for the classes I teach. Maybe most powerful for me was the experience of reading the writers of the Harlem Renaissance, for they taught me in a sustained way that white liberals like myself were a problem. The ones who think they mean no harm. And are a problem still, for many reasons, including their feeling that their good intentions inoculate themselves against racial self-awareness.

It was good then, that in the '90s "race" was something you needed to know about. But it has had its other effects. In the academic world today it is possible to encounter smart white people who feel the presence of people of color is optional, since they already know "race." Whiteness is resilient that way.

Another effect of this period was that white people began to praise each other for talking about race. It was brave to write about it. But saying it is brave to write about one's whiteness is not unlike saying it is brave to live inside a house. White people are often so defensive on the subject of race because to be white is to feel a certain perhaps unsought, perhaps uncultivated, but still palpable if you look for it, sense of unmistakenness. There has been a test you didn't even have to take and you got the answers right (points subtracted for certain errors—your mistaken desire, perhaps—but still. You did well). White people don't like to be mistaken. They would prefer not to take any more tests. They passed! And when they write about race, they would like you to give them an A for effort. Because they were brave.

One way, if you are white, to take note of your whiteness is to pay attention if you feel a little p.o.'ed, a little *restricted*, when asked to think if your race matters to what you write or read or think; or when asked to consider that your writing about race has a content that you have not

There is something

sufficiently considered. That your effort alone is not enough. It is not that I know for certain that race always matters. I'm honestly not sure how to calibrate this. But it may matter more often than a white writer thinks, and it may matter in ways she doesn't realize.

I suppose what I am trying to say is that it is important, valuable, for white people to write about race. But not because it is brave. Let us reserve that term for more truly dangerous endeavors. Saying it is brave makes it special, optional, and somehow unchallengable. When it could instead be unremarkable, a matter of course. Not easy, mind you. Hard. But not brave.

For many well-intentioned white people, writing or talking about race is hard, but not in the way I want to mean this word. It is hard for us because there is the feeling, back there in your mind, that there might be a skeleton in the closet you don't know about, or one you don't remember. That you said or wrote or did something that someone will use against you. I feel that fear raised up in the back of my mind as I write this. What can I be accused of? It's there. Many white people react to that question with defensiveness or fear, which are both forms of avoiding the truth. Because there is a skeleton in the closet. There is something to be accused of. Because you are white. And you grew up in a racist country. And there was a moment, or many moments, maybe even whole decades of earlier

life, when you didn't sufficiently transcend those conditions. You have been wrong.

So what? This is the wrapper that must come off, unremarkably, as a matter of course. What I mean by hard is something different. What is difficult is the education you must commit to as a white person, the long and necessary education. A long and necessary education whose primary condition is that it never ends. You are never finished.

In a book I wrote about the murder of a young gay man in the town where I live, I tried to counter the blanketing whiteness of the town by counterposing some voices of color against the comfortably unaware voices of some of my white interview subjects. A white colleague told me that was a predictable move. It was a move, of course, a use. I didn't worry too much about this, in the sense that I mainly tried to do it well and stay alert for mistakes. This is obvious: it seemed worse to leave some subjects out because to "use" them would be "a move." This orchestration might not have been "natural" to me as a writer; but unnaturalness, unnatural engagement, was the best I could do at the time. I believed, still do, that whiteness was part of what made so many of the white people in my town react in certain ways to the murder, a reaction that became the dominantly reported reaction, because they were white. I also believed it might be useful to at least somewhat dislodge

to be accused of.

this dominant reporting. Did I use people of
color to do this? Yes I did. I interviewed people
of color because I reckoned they knew things
I didn't know, things that weren't optional to
know. I wanted the point of view to not settle
in a single body. I wanted people to hear themselves, to hear people other than themselves—
I wanted the book to do that for everyone. It was
all moves. It was writing.

You try hard not to make mistakes, you accept that you will make them. You try, if you are
white, to not use "race" as yet another open field
for your endless and praise-hungry self-assertion.
You don't run people out of the room when you
don't get an A. In one way the question is what
writing is for. I don't have an original answer to
this. I write and read so that I can finally think;
and I write and read to hope that it might be possible for me to construct a vantage point on what
I don't yet know how to know. These two things
do not feel like separate endeavors. Is it impos-
sibly idealist for me to believe that when I read,
say, Richard Bruce Nugent, I both am and am
not myself, as he is both himself and not? Not a
transcendence, but a chance to halfway get out
of one's own mess of a mind in order to get back
in. You don't write to get clean. Writing's not hy-
giene. But I write in the hope that writing clears
some room for something else.

OPEN LETTER
SORAYA MEMBRENO

To Whom It May Concern:

The issue of race in writing is a tricky one, depending on who is writing, who is reading, the tone in which it is said ... and the discussion of race in writing seems a never-ending one. Personally, I think ideas of race don't exist separate from their history. If it were not for the historical fact of slavery, I'd be skeptical that we would even notice race as an important part of someone's being. Then again, I may just be naïve.

The closest to writing about race I've ever come to is an origins poem; and really I wrote about culture. I have not felt compelled to write about race because I do not think it should matter, or at the very least, I do not think it should be the primary factor attributed to my writing. I would hate it if people read my work *looking* for the bits of the Hispanic girl to show through the writing. I am Hispanic, yes, but that's not your business. It does not need to show through in my poems if I do not explicitly want it to. And so far, I haven't. I don't see my race as something that should permeate everything I write. And I don't want the expectation that goes along with advertising the fact that I am a "this" writer, or a "that" writer. I am just a writer, and what I look like shouldn't matter. I do, however, have to recognize that there is definitely a certain expectation that goes along with writing, particularly poetry. We recently had a class discussion in which it was brought up that the book we were reading didn't have the author's picture anywhere on the book. I thought it was interesting, but honestly didn't make anything of it. I was incredibly surprised to hear the discussion progress; it went beyond just a simple curiosity, people *really* wanted to know if the author was black or white, as if suspending judgment until they found out. Some even vocalized that, once they found out the race of the author, it changed their view of the book. But if the book is already written, and you'd already read it and formed opinions on it, what difference does it make that the author is black or white? Race undoubtedly casts everything we read in a certain color, and the degree to which this is true is astounding. But I don't know if this says more about the poet, or us. Our society is obsessive about race, overly cautious to be polite about it, and completely underhanded in the way it attempts to not really deal with it. Race is never confronted, it is something to be tiptoed around, but smiling at it won't make it go away. Everyone is too scared of saying the wrong thing, so no one says anything. There is no such thing as a truly frank, honest conversation about race. This is where poetry *should* come in.

I'm torn when asked the question of whether I have any responsibility as a poet to my audience. Which consequently begs the question: do I have a responsibility, as a Hispanic poet, to a Hispanic audience? In all honesty, I haven't arrived at any conclusions about that yet. I want to say no, to yell *no*! But ... I'm also aware that it's not that simple. I suppose, to some degree, my experience is unique, as is everyone's, and so there is some merit in exposing your experience to things an audience may never have been exposed to. But this seems to be at the cost of pigeonholing yourself indefinitely. I want to speak out on behalf of the imbecilic way my parents' country is run, my home now, and the desperate resignation of its people, but if it comes at the cost of being a mini Sandra Cisneros for the rest of my life ... I'm not sure it's worth it.

Race does not define me, it is my culture, but it is not *me*. Therefore, I can only assume that race does not define you either. I think it can, if a person chooses to let it be a defining factor in their lives, but I do not believe that it necessarily ingrains anything in you. My "race" becomes an issue only when other people seek to place me in some category, and depending on the occasion, they arrive at different results. Therefore, for me, race is something that gets attributed to me from external forces, and so I do not think it any inherent part of me. There is nothing about an individual that can, or should, ever be decided by someone else before the individual himself.

It should be the role of poetry today to address that which is usually kept silent. And if it means stirring shit up, so be it. If no one is willing to speak unless they are offended, then offend them. These issues can't be pieced together if people are hiding crucial pieces in their pockets, so let's have poetry that can put everything on the table.

Thank you for the opportunity to put our opinions out there.

TRESPASSES
LACY M. JOHNSON

i.

At the northeast corner of our farm, roughly a stone's throw away from the narrow gravel road that led past our house, stood an old, sap-crusted evergreen tree. Nailed to its trunk a white sign with red letters read Private Property / No Trespassing. This sign marked the border between our forest and the forest belonging to our neighbor, who didn't live on the property, and whom I had never met. The trees on our side of the line looked like the trees on his side of the line. Our underbrush like his underbrush. Because the border lacked a fence, birds and deer and rabbits crossed and recrossed it at will. I knew on which side of the border I belonged, but I crossed it anyway, entering a place where I was not welcome. (It thrilled me.) Anyone driving by on the gravel road would never know I didn't belong there.

ii.

In a recent comment thread on Facebook regarding an article I had posted about an author writing in a dialect associated with a racial group (not his own), a former classmate told me he finds all writing in dialect offensive, even if—to my surprise—the writer is writing in his/her own dialect. He explained:

> Part of the problem may be that we tend to associate dialect with class, and we presume that writers are educated, and of a means above that class. That is, the writer has become a member of a group more privileged (WE ALL HAVE SO MUCH MONEY, RIGHT) and is therefore no longer a member of the socioeconomic

group she or he claims to represent. Any representation of a group's speech patterns, to me, seems less than genuine.

I responded:

Hmm. An interesting point. Though I think some of what offends me about dialect work is trying to mimic non-standard pronunciation on the page. Altering spelling to mimic speech and whatnot. (That bugs me to no end, and is why I still can't stand reading Mark Twain.) I find representations of non-standard grammar less offensive, though. Or if not non-standard grammar, at least regionalized syntax. I occasionally do that in my own work, and in doing so, sort of re-tune to a certain language already/still in my head. Getting educated didn't silence it, but rather taught me how/why that music was "wrong," which I now kind of resent.

iii.

During dinner, my husband asks what I've been working on. I try explaining how the term *white trash* is a racial slur. He puts down his scotch and raises his eyebrows.

For many whites, I say, whiteness is the invisible, unraced center of an otherwise racialized world. These same whites use the term *white trash* to differentiate between themselves and

poor, low-status whites, and in doing so, inscribe differences that are not just social, but material, physical—visible on their skin, in their manners, morals, and behaviors—making *white trash* a marked, racial, and degraded form of whiteness.

He points his finger in my direction and interrupts: you should say that this is only the case in America. In South Africa, say, or China, the relations and the reality would be totally different.

I say, Thank you. I will consider mentioning that. I sip my wine and pause before speaking. The server comes to retrieve our empty plates, leaves a dessert menu by our elbows.

As I was saying: because they're marked as not quite white, *white trash* do not experience the same effects of white privilege as middle- and upper-class whites.

Not quite white?

Right, not quite white. Their skin is white, but the way other whites treat them is not.

iv.

Around the same time I took my first poetry workshop in college, I started changing my speech. I said "am not" instead of "ain't." "Should have" instead of "shoulda." I dropped "ma'am" altogether, and instead relied on "Doctor," "Professor," or "Ms." By the time I was accepted to graduate school and started teaching my first writing class, I'd gotten pretty fluent, though occasion-

The passer cannot

ally overcorrected when nervous or intoxicated. Because it wasn't a word I was used to saying, *not* was particularly troublesome and almost always came off sounding a little British. A lot of people must have noticed, but only one person ever gave me grief: a student of mine from an affluent suburb, who spent the whole semester coming to class late, interrupting me during discussion, turning in assignments a week after they were due, or not turning them in at all. During the midterm conference, I pointed out that his grade was suffering. He pointed out that his father was rich and his taxes paid my salary. On his end-of-semester evaluation, he wrote that I was an idiot and needed to drop my "affected accent." "Ms. Johnson," he went on to say, "has no business at this university or any other."

He was right, of course. Social norms and conventional wisdom dictate that white trash (or their variants: hillbillies, rednecks, and crackers) are incongruous with the college classroom, even more so with the lectern at the front of it. This symbolic divergence stems partially from the downward, degrading force on these cultural figurations of whiteness—stereotyped as thick-headed, ill spoken, backward, lazy, immoral, violent, and illiterate—and also from the upward, elevating force on the figurations of the academy itself—consider the ostensibly class- and race-neutral terms *academics, intellectuals,* and *artists*—in effect, building an invisible fence around any academic, intellectual, or creative enterprise, such work being the private property of a relative few.

In the years since that initial course—the one with the pain-in-the-ass student who tried to out me—I've become a fluent speaker of standard American English, though I tend to lapse into dialect when I go home for a visit. I've also changed my clothes and my teeth and my hair—a slow and gradual process. I cover my tattoos any time I need to be taken seriously. I own a house in an affluent suburb and teach writing at the university.

No one knows I don't belong here.

v.

And then there are the invisible lines of maps, which have no corresponding mark upon the ground, in the soil, through the trees or the grass or the air, though it is possible to cross them. To cross the line, to toe it, to pass over an unspoken but understood border. And then there are the visible borders of cities, which are not so much clear and definite lines of demarcation as intervals of either condensation or dissipation, depending on whether you are arriving or leaving.

And then there are the invisible differences among people, which have no corresponding mark upon the skin, in the hair, under the fingernails or eyelids or lips. But there are words they speak to one another, and then there are words

unpass or pass back.

they speak to you, the outsider, and the difference lies not so much in the words themselves, which mean very little when it comes right down to it, but in the history of people speaking to one another in that place, which you could not possibly know unless you happen to also be from there, in which case it doesn't need explaining.

vi.

The tricky thing about passing is that it only works when the passer is invisible. For that reason, passing only works in one direction. The passer cannot unpass or pass back, since in the act of passing the passer becomes visible to those who recognize the truth. Maintaining invisibility can therefore become all-consuming—whole lives spent keeping up the ruse. For that reason, the benefits of passing must outweigh the effort and anxiety expended in pulling it off, or no one would do it. Certainly, the benefits vary for different individuals, but might include the thrill of getting one over on the dominant culture, access to power and privilege, invisibility itself, or the sheer joy of sticking it to the man.

Let's be clear, though: the benefits of passing never include real, structural change. Under no circumstances can passing be considered an act of subversion; in fact, passing actually reinforces systems of oppression that operate by bestowing unearned advantages on some and denying them to others. It is only through a kind of semi-otic sleight of hand that the passer takes on the symbolic form of a privileged other: though the passer's actual, physical, material form remains the same, its signification changes. Passing does not, therefore, challenge or condemn those symbolic forms, or the advantages they bestow, or the structure of the system, or any individual who reaps its rewards. Instead, passing exploits an arbitrary relationship between a certain physical form and its symbolic signification.

Once we acknowledge the terms of this phenomenon, we find its manifestations abound. Consider the following: if we agree that a discrete social identity ("whiteness," for example) functions as a symbolic territory (it is finite, has boundaries), then we might also agree that any given literary genre (poetry, for example) occupies a similar sort of territory (it is also finite, has boundaries), in that language performs a sleight of hand in order to pass as "poem." One problem, then, with genre is that the mode and manner of our articulations are limited by the parameters of what will pass in that territory. Which raises some questions: What passes as poetry? What passes as nonfiction? Where is the border between verse and prose, fact and fiction? Who has drawn it? Who polices it? And according to what aesthetic?

vii.

One day in late spring I was sitting poolside with some of my friends from school. Some were drinking beers or chilled white wine. Several floated on inflatable rafts. I sat in a lounge chair—a wide scarf covering my pregnant belly, just beginning to swell—reading a trashy celebrity magazine and drinking Diet 7-Up from a plastic bottle. It was turning out to be a fantastic day. Near the grill, two of my fellow students began arguing—I couldn't help but overhear—about the sublime and the beautiful. One quoted Matthew Arnold. The other, Komunyakaa. I thought to myself, *for Christ's sake. It's fucking Saturday.*

Days later I was sitting on my bed, fans blowing on me from every direction. I had been reading who knows what—maybe student papers, maybe poems from workshop, maybe postcolonial theory or an Irish novel or any number of other things. The point is, one moment I was reading, and the next I was looking out the window, and then the words were already bubbling out of me and I didn't stop typing until they ran dry. I cried the whole time like some kind of blubbering idiot. And then there were my words. My real words—naked, visible, with all my linguistic imperfections laid bare.

Me. Mine. My own.

And for once I didn't try to revise the piece into something recognizable to my academic peers. Because although I've learned to correct the ways in which my native idiom is often ungrammatical, I've also learned that there's something about my experience growing up in a poor farming town in the Great Plains that gets lost in the translation to standardized academic verse. I've read that piece in public several times, and because I can't read it without falling back into my native pronunciation, with each reading I out myself: A hillbilly. A redneck. A white-trash class-passer.

No one tells me I don't belong here.

OPEN LETTER
EVIE SHOCKLEY

Dear Claudia,

This is my fourth or fifth attempt to write a response that addresses the questions you raised and satisfies me to some degree. I find that I want to say far too much for the space and time available to me here and now. There are the ideas about the relationship(s) between race and poetry, politics and aesthetics (ideas I've been grappling with for a long while) that I want to do justice to, and now, having read the many diverse approaches offered in the open letters already posted on your site, there are the "amens" and rebuttals and questions that have bubbled up in response to them. I can't distill it all. The issues, the history, and the possibilities are too complex. By which I mean simply that I can't find a clear thread that will take me directly (or indirectly) through the points I'd like to make, briefly enough that anyone would stop to read it all.

In fact, much of what I'd like to say here appears in the two books I've been working on for the last few years: one a collection of poetry, recently published, and the other a scholarly take on poetry and poetics, forthcoming later this year. But I can't import them into this document or sum them up easily (see above), so in lieu of that, I offer the following two points, just because they feel particularly urgent tonight.

First, to those who see the election of President Obama as a sign of the inevitability of further progress on matters of race in America, going forward, I recommend Paula Giddings's biography of Ida B. Wells (*Ida: A Sword Among Lions: Ida B. Wells and the Campaign Against Lynching*). Not simply a personal biography, it is really a history of the post-Reconstruction era as it unfolded around the life of a nationally and internationally respected journalist, political activist, and clubwoman. Reading about how the passage of the Thirteenth, Fourteenth, and Fifteenth Amendments, and the political, economic, and educational gains made by African Americans during Reconstruction infused black and white people with both hope and a sense of certainty about racial progress—only for them to see lynchings increase to the point of 231 in a single year (in 1892) and the swift rise of Jim Crow in the South and de facto segregation in the North—will put the changes we've seen recently into perspective.

And, second, when I'm thinking about race and poetry, I'm not only thinking about the dynamics between whites and African Americans—or between whites and any other group of folks. I am concerned with the ways that African Americans and Latinos, Asian Americans, and Native Americans, for example, are engaging with one another. What are the analogies, the parallels? What are the telling differences? I've not been thinking about these questions all my life—being a product of a very black-and-white Not-So-New South—so I'm still working on the learning curve that will enable me to write about these concerns with the kind of knowledge and nuance I always aim for. But they are on my mind and already inform some of my poems. Similarly, I think a lot—and write an increasing amount—about the interconnections and inter-

actions (and divergences) among black people in the US and those in other parts of the diaspora and in Africa itself. This is just to say that, from my vantage point, inquiries into the meaning and operation of race do not necessarily focus on *interracial* issues—and, even when interracial concerns are at stake, they don't necessarily center on white people (or guilt). Another way of putting this might be to say that *race* is not the same as *racism*. I often find great pleasure in writing about race, just as I often take deep pleasure in my race, despite the painful contexts and histories that are also at stake.

With gratitude—
Peace,
Evie Shockley

Liz Cohen, **1987 Trabantamino 607 Deluxe**, 2007

Liz Cohen's project of converting an East German Trabant into a Chevrolet El Camino is an allegory of transformation. Combining Pan-American and Jewish diaspora cultural influences, Cohen toggles the evil twins of assimilation and mongrelization to produce a delightfully choking confection. MKC

William Pope.L, **White People Are A Desalination Plant in Puerto Rico**, 2001

This nonsensical declaration by William Pope L. is a piece of dada poetry, or absurdist theatre. It treats race, rightly, us a capricious designation—made more laughable by the faux scientific touch of graph paper. The humor, though, is a bitter notion; it declares, we agree, and then promptly forget the lesson. MKC

Amitis Motevalli, **The Last Centerfold**, 2010

Using the objectification of women and the demonization of Muslims as her recipe, Motevalli mixed this potent image of sexuality and dread, prurience and hostility. MKC

Ian Weaver, **<u>Black Power Helmet</u>**, 2008

Chicago artist Ian Weaver accesses power and confesses vulnerability in this work from 2008. In channeling the fantasy of a chivalrous past and yoking it to the struggle for equality, the artist is a self-made conqueror, chivalrous in lineage, instead of a three-fifths man, unmoored from his history and circumspect of his future. MKG

Liz Cohen, **Lowrider Builder and Child**, 2012

Desert prophet, Madonna and child, and bandana-wearing odalisque, Liz Cohen's self-portrait conveys her dominion over humans and their toils. The exploded lowrider, of her own invention, shields her from the setting sun as she suckles the child, also of her own invention. In this self-coronation she proclaims, "Look upon my works, ye mighty, and despair". MKC

Todd Gray, <u>**Shaman 33**</u>, 2005

Physician, heal thyself. Todd Gray is trying. After buying land in Ghana (on the advice of Michael Jackson, for whom Gray was once personal photographer) he set out to reconcile his western immersion with a notion of lost spiritualism. His results were dispiriting. The realization that he was irredeemably from Los Angeles, born and bred, can be seen in his Shaman series, where he pleads for mediation from African spirits who no longer recognize him. He is, at last, left to his own conjuring; his art school education and album cover skills render Africa intelligible to anyone familiar with Hollywood. MKO*

POETICS

The dream requires something of me. **It feels like choosing a violent failure or a violent failure—to say something or to not say something.** But I do find myself wondering where, in this community, is the room for stammering and stuttering? **It's always about the privileges that fear grants a man.** I doubt that any white person can look at a person of color without registering it, nor do I believe that repression desirable. **I write at race, or around it, instead of about it.** There's such power in looking—in being the one who looks and not the one who runs, slithers, limps, or glides under the gaze. **When "political" realities are ignored, reality is distorted.** What is the sound of me shaking my head? **I work to recognize the systems of racism we all function in, and I work to understand my own complicity, as well as my own survival, within these systems.** I suppose I want to be protected by the spaciousness that seems afforded to white writers, or especially those writers who don't get asked after a reading why they don't write again and again about their ethnic identity and experiences. **I try to make words shift/bend, but I still want to answer to their meanings.** Already the discursive machines are at work, making it difficult, for those of us watching, for the horror to set in, the body to feel it, the imagination to conjure. **It seems annoying and weighed down because history is heavy, but to write and to think that nothing has ever happened before I sat down to write is reckless.** Sometimes it's about what I wish I had said, sometimes what I wish I had not, other times something I wish someone else had said in (my) stead.

LOVE THE MASTERS

JERICHO BROWN

Every poem is a love poem. Every poem is a political poem. So say the masters. Every love poem is political. Every political poem must fall in love.

━━━

The political poem has an aim, whether the poet is aware of it or not. When I say I love you, I mean for you to understand that I exist in relation to you. And to your view of me.

━━━

Every poem challenges or supports the status quo. So say the masters. Poets whose work supports the status quo often fail to acknowledge that their poems are just as political as poets whose work questions it.

━━━

The love poet is not afraid of isms or phobias. She believes her love, the love she pours into her poems, overpowers. This belief makes her a vulnerable person on this planet where weapons are known to be sharp or explosive.

━━━

The political poet loves me. He says so in his poems. I meet him with my extended hand; he opens his arms. Literally.

━━━

Dear Reader,

Are you a poet who has produced what you meant to question current circumstances only to see half or more of your readers say it supports current circumstances?

You can't love me if

If so, I'm sure your political person, your love self, was willing to say, "Oh." Or weren't you willing?

Yours,
Jericho

―――――――

Every poem loves.

―――――――

Dear Cleanth,

I'm sorry, but seeing the poem as artifact without seeing the history and culture embedded in the poet suggests we read without any history at all. This may be a convenient way of reading for those who have a history they can't face.

Good manners move beyond the professional into the reading of the work when writing the poem about race. Even Audre Lorde and Lucille Clifton wouldn't be poets we know and love if they treated black women badly.

Missing you,
Jericho

―――――――

In the political poem, each character is a figure meant to represent some aspect of the whole. I write "Derrick" in a love poem thinking men other than I are in love.

―――――――

No matter how imaginative our poems may be, we write our lives. In the case of poems about race in America, each line is a testament to our lives as well as an art object.

―――――――

Dear Laura,

If a community of black women keep questioning a poem you wrote ten years ago, you too would start wondering about it. It's okay to question anyone who wouldn't.

Yours,
Jericho

―――――――

You can't love me if you don't love politically.

―――――――

When two good readers read an obviously political poem and say, "Its aim is to challenge the status quo," and two other good readers read the same poem and say, "Its aim is to support the status quo," then the poem has not reached its aim, has failed at love, is, yes, a bad poem.

you don't love politically.

My dearest Major,

I know exactly what you mean. Bravery may be beautiful, but it does not equal art. Since when does trying to jump make anyone a ball player? A poor discussion of any subject must be rejected. Given our nation's history, a poor discussion of race is the opposite of poetry.

Thanks again.

Your friend,

Jericho

Hope is always accompanied by the imagination, the will to see what our physical environment seems to deem impossible. Only the creative mind can make use of hope. Only a creative people can wield it.

Poems built around the idea of art as expression an idea that makes me want to pull my hair out! What one chooses to wear in the morning is expression. Art is not.

Some "drafts" suggest that because a feeling is prevalent that prevalence is enough for the poem, but drafts born from this sense are not poems; they are reports.

Poems change landscapes rather than photograph them. They have language and line break enough for us to see beyond any poet's ignorance as a person.

Dear Mr. Merwin,

I hope you're absolutely right about history taking care of it. Though I have to add that, because of being a black poet for whom time is collapsed and anything can be made metaphor, I'm always wondering what to let go and where to be an activist. History would not have taken care of me had activism not marched.

Today, we think of that activism as history, but once upon a time, many people, both black and white, thought, "Things will eventually work out, so why push?" Activists, on the other hand, think things like, "Why wait to be regarded as a human being?"

Best,

Jericho

Do you love me? So say the masters.

What is the sound of me shaking my head?

Racists can find themselves identifying with poorly written poems and excused because of them.

We look to literature to see what we hide from within ourselves.

An event happening ten minutes or ten years ago matters if anyone can indeed feel the effects of it now.

I will never understand the spirit of my ancestors, but I know it. I know it lives in me. I write because my writing mind is the only chance I have of becoming the manifestation of their hope. I write because my writing mind is the only chance I have of becoming what the living dead are for me. I exist because I was impossible for someone else to be before me.

Love,
Jericho

AN ABRIDGED VERSION
REGINALD DWAYNE BETTS

Neither Malcolm X, Martin Luther King Jr., Harriet Tubman, Ida B. Wells, Sojourner Truth, nor Rosa Parks have found their way into my poems. Therefore, if we judge by February's standards, I do not write race. George Washington, the Ku Klux Klan, Mississippi, Alabama, and Georgia have not found their way into my poems. Wallace, the secessionists, whites-only water fountains and water hoses have not found their way into my poems. Therefore, if we judge by America's standards in the '60s, I do not write race. Neither Elijah Muhammad (or Elijah Poole if you're hip), Marcus Garvey, Ella Baker, Stokely Carmichael (Kwame Ture if you're hip), George Jackson, nor Angela Davis have found their way into my poems. Therefore, if we judge by Black Nationalists' standards, I do not write about race. Neither Bessie Smith, Billie Holiday, Big Mama Thornton, Marian Anderson, Etta Baker, nor Etta James have found their way into any of the poems I've written. References to Jim Crow are also missing. As are for Coloreds only signs, any talk of John Henry, mention of Miles Davis, John Coltrane, Monk, and Ralph Ellison's *Invisible Man*. There is no underground railroad in my poems. No endorsements by the NAACP. No mammies. No Uncle Bens or Toms. There are no chain gangs, no Africas, no minstrel shows. None of my poems first appeared in the *Crisis*. None of my poems have been read at Klan rallies, have been recited while people boycotted in Montgomery. There are no shouts that scream *race*.

But is the question of writing race simply about reveling in and revealing racial trauma and triumph? We call *Native Son* a protest novel, and we say it discusses race—but is it more than a

I love rumors

narrative about a young black male coming of age in a racially divided city? Isn't it about Bigger Thomas making decisions so intractably tied to race that it's foolish to look at it otherwise? We ask if black writers write race, as if white writers don't write race. We write race whether we recognize it or not, because we write of America, and America's story is still one of race.

Yet, for me, the truth of it is that writers imagine a world, imagine worlds, and in breathing life into them set the stage for readers to discuss what they want to discuss. We have turned myopic in our views about race, and discuss it as if it is a costume that can be taken off or on at whim. Postracial seems nothing more than a cloak of invisibility that allows some of us to walk around America without the more obvious stressors that come with being black. And as writers, wearing this mask leads us to see the world in just one learned and morally bankrupt way. If you navigate the corporate world, the academic world, the medical world—any world outside of poverty, you can pretend to have no knowledge of the world of WIC, underachieving schools, and violence that is as natural as daylight. But even if you do this your work comments on race by posturing publicly a pretentious obliviousness, be you white or black.

If I write race, I write it slant. I write it scat. I write it slipshod. I write it in the same manner I live it. Letting my work embody contradiction and delight. I love rumors about black men. I love

the attention on the street in daylight. I smile at little children who want to touch my hair. Enjoy the seat beside me on the Amtrak that usually stays empty. Yet, when I put this in a poem, it's always about the privileges that fear grants a man. And for it to be art, it has to say that and more.

White and black writers sometimes imply that the Black Arts Movement, the Protest Novel, and the Harlem Renaissance have the market on race writing cornered. That to write about race now is to limit your vision. That worries me, makes me feel I am trading in my veil for a blindfold.

The markers of identity in my poems are chosen because of sound. The name Amir appeals to me, and I've always loved the *a* that ends the names of so many black women. The streets that haunt my poems are from memory, the version of legacy that you get when you don't have a history of college and middle-class home ownership in your family. There are people broken and breaking in my poems, people healing despite the cauldron of chaos they live in.

My poems are about race in the way their lives are about race. Race is liminal in America. It is both border and veil. Both what you cannot escape and what distorts your vision. Because race is intricate to the American narrative, and not just the African American narrative, but the American narrative, any questions of writers writing race is moot. The better question is what do we choose to know, both in life and in print.

REGINALD DWAYNE BETTS

about black men.

I don't tattoo race onto my poems, don't drop the name of Jesus and Steve Biko to signal I'm hip. Poems that talk about the racial legacy I've inherited as an American will become polemic, will begin to sound less like a man who knows the names of too many prisons, knows too many people in prisons, in poverty, in jobs that seem a product of complexion and their zip code rather than any real or imagined talent, and more like diatribe, like shout & fury, if I rely more on sledgehammer than the beautiful shades of gray that makes a man hunger for more life. For more of all of it, the beauty and the stares that make you want to hide in your skin.

I know that when writers refuse to engage in ideas, everything verges on a minstrel act: a performing of a past performance. So all of my poems, in their offering up the beautiful ugly of the life I know and imagine, are almost always only reaching for the ideas that might shift my own understanding of America. And that's okay, because writing, itself, is the most awkward race of all—where we shape all we know into words we hope will reveal what has long been hidden in the open, and do it knowing we're always chasing our own version of an ever-moving finish line.

OPEN LETTER
IRA SADOFF

I was born in Bensonhurst and spent much of my early childhood in the North Bronx: both neighborhoods were mostly populated by minorities: African Americans, Puerto Ricans, Italians, and lots of other Jews. The other minority kids were sometimes friends, sometimes strangers, sometimes enemies who would beat you up or fill your little satchel with snow. But we also played ball in the schoolyard together, spent time in the same classrooms (until the school system segregated us into advanced and remedial classes), and we did detention together. In common we were taught by the culture (most immediately by our families) to be suspicious of one another: for Italians, the Jews killed Christ; for African Americans, Jews were thought to be money hungry, evidenced by exploitative local merchants. We Jews were trained to be suspicious of "schwarzes" who were ignorant and lazy and—the worst sin of all—dirty. These messages were often primal and got under our skins. I spent my late adolescence in an informally segregated suburb (fearful of the decline of property values, our neighbors took up a collection to buy my mother's house when they heard she might sell to a black couple). My wealthier neighbors had black maids and, for many of my friends, their maid was the only black person they knew. I knew I wanted to take flight from the homogeneity, parochialism and class aspirations that blossomed in my neighborhood (and in most suburbs), so on weekends my best friend and I would go to jazz clubs like the Five Spot and The Half Note, where the artists were African American and the music was collaborative and "swung." That experience was an important part of my education, going back to the city, a site with enormous nourishment, some danger, astonishing vibrancy and curiosity and plenty of difference.

For most of my adult life I've taught at expensive private colleges with far too few minority students. It's impossible to elide the difference between a class with minority students and those without, especially when we're discussing minority literature. I experience this homogeneity as an absence; in the absence of the real I believe we're all forced to invent another, a one-dimensional other that elicits fantasy and often terror or idealization. No great discovery, but Fanon explains the phenomenon with great lucidity: I'm nowhere near exempt from this blindfolding. So how could I not write about race? How could anyone in this country who felt any stake in forces larger than the personal or familial, fail to respond to any one of the above circumstances? How could anyone live in America with his or her eyes open and not be deeply affected by race? Even setting aside broader understandings about race (segregation in housing and schools, the media rendering minorities invisible), children in my neighborhoods had a lot to untangle to really honor the complexity of another human life (seeking out all the correspondences and differences in our histories) while not succumbing to our fears and projections. I try to bring those aspirations to my poems, but of course no one forges poems around being a model citizen. We

work in a medium whose pleasures include the infinite suggestions of language, the sound play of multiple musics, metaphors we can never decipher, thankfully, with an act of consciousness. Nevertheless, writing's relational: we write lines to be read by others. For those of us who write to be more attentive, to probe our relationship to the world, we should be held responsible for the poems we want others to read. I'd like to set aside those reductive claims bemoaning censorship or that meaningless phrase *political correctness* in poems about race: a poem can be smug, pre-determined and morally superior, and should be judged as such. No one need be deprived of being ignorant either: we don't send assholes to prison. But it's self-indulgent to elevate "working on the dark side" (cf. Toni Morrison), exploring our own fantasies without the depth of vision that requires asking the hard questions in a poem (suggesting the resonance of larger forces that contribute to it). Nor does a reader have to declare "How brave you are for exposing your bigotry." Baudelaire's poems explore the degrading elements of desire; but there's always an echo of the counter, a puritanical Enlightenment culture that drives the questions of his poems and prose poems. For those who raise the specter of political correctness (many of these same folks think politics has no place in poetry—huh?— in order to justify their own limited aesthetics), their poetic worlds seem to me, frankly, too small

But I hope my words don't

to create a poetry of depth and vision. I think, don't they ever go to the store, or who taught them to write, what does a tax cut mean for the education of their own children? Should we not write about these matters? That's self-imposed censorship. So for me it boils down to *where do I live* in a poem. If I'm writing a poem that turns out to be about race—just as I try to feel deeply about those issues in any poem—I think about positionality. Late in the revision process, I wonder if the poem asks difficult enough questions? I think about cultural forces on my language—where did that feeling or phrase or idea come from: am I appropriating someone else's pain? Am I self-indulgent (sentimentality or melodrama asks a reader to feel more than the drama offers). And of course I watch for tone: if I'm satirizing I think hard about who's the object of the satire and what arenas might I overlap with those people I've reduced? If I'm satirizing racism, is the satire sufficiently fresh and nuanced to characterize another?

The most important question to ask of any poem: is the vision clichéd? Am I globalizing, stereotyping, over-generalizing about a group of people, white or black? Am I writing about people I know and understand? If not, do I honor their strangeness? Do I make myself culpable without making the poem about my large feelings (here I think of a filmmaker I ordinarily love, Claire Denis, who in *White Material*

makes a movie about racism and imperialism in Africa, but from the point of view of the white star—Black Africans have almost no speaking parts). I'm not afraid of appearing ugly in a poem, unsettling my audience, or examining unintegrated parts of myself; but I never want to romanticize that morally fallible part of myself to be "provocative": there's narcissistic display in the stance of "look at me, how ugly I can be."

Are there other questions I can inhabit more than a prescribed image of another? Is there a moral lecture under the surface of the poem that's parental, that was a willful condescending finger at the audience? In other words, to the degree that an artist can discern his or her own work, is the poem superficial or is it surprising and does it inhabit sufficient difficulty and complication? I admit to considering once the poem's done, whether the poem's familial or racial, what's at stake here? If holding someone else responsible for ugliness needs to be part of a poem (I'm not very worried about the feelings of a war criminal), does investigating my rage result in an authentically moving and necessary experience? Simply put, is the poem written of necessity? The test of a poem about race strikes me as the test of any great poem: does it reveal simultaneous breadth of vision and attention to the charge of language?

I compose without a subject and without censorship. A phrase, a word, an image interests

come at the cost of others.

me and then I pursue its associations: that's how I perceive the improvisational aspect of writing poetry. When the work goes well I relax my will: inevitably my concerns and obsessions will surface. But before I let the poem go out to the world I want to make sure as I can of its value—is it worth listening to, does the poem intensify experience so it's moving? For complex reasons—many of the difficulties suggested above—it seems like I've had more opportunities to fail in a poem about race than in more personal lyric poems. Perhaps I have less access to what motors those feelings. Retrospectively the poems failed either because of a limited vision when I was writing the poem "from the outside." Early on when I wanted to write about how jazz changed my life, the poems valorized Black folks. Their inner lives were full of suffering and feeling and mine was not. I made them instrumental. In short I exoticized those African American artists (Richard Wright's story "Slave on the Block" movingly tells the impact on the minority when treated in that manner). I was a child: they were heroes, but in the poems it was their job to serve, take me out of my vacuity. Or I unconsciously simply wanted to be a "good person" so the poems posited me as an ally, elevating the lyric self as a special case, an exception, exempt from those racist qualities I perceive in American culture and myself. One danger of globalizing, of assuming, for example, that every white person's

a racist: the effect of such a poem is a kind of dishonest fatalism, another kind of cliché: it tells the reader you don't know your subject(s) well enough to make distinctions. I don't think my failures are original or even of very much interest. I failed the way many others have failed before me. I'm not sure I've succeeded in writing a really good poem about race yet. I don't mind failing or falling short. I see holes in the vision and I learn from them. I don't want to ever censor myself as an artist. But I hope my words don't come at the cost of others. I don't mean to suggest that poems should avoid the risk of saying the hardest thing; I don't write to have good manners or to be civilized. I just do not want to put out into the world poems where language is in the service of unexamined conventions, or generic thinking. A therapist's first rule is "do no harm," and I'd like to think my poems minimally begin with that premise. And I'd want to be responsive and not defensive in cases where I misjudged the effect of the work.

Efface difference. I doubt that any white person can look at a person of color without registering it, nor do I believe that repression desirable. But instead of turning those projections, your own racial history, on others, ask the poem questions about where those feelings come from.

SCHIZOPHRENE: TEXTURE NOTES

BHANU KAPIL

To write race is to write its schizophrene. Tongue clicks and eye rolls as: stronger triggers for: psychosis than a race "event." A race riot. And so on. The chair smashing over the head. My father was walking home once, from a subway. That day, in class, on the day corporal punishment became illegal in the UK—a boy in his class, an eleven-year-old skinhead, smashed a chair over him, my father, shouting: "You can't touch me, Mr. Kapil!" That night, on the way home, my father was mugged. His briefcase was slashed with a knife. When we opened the door, he was shaking. He had lost a shoe. But what happened that night led to a several months long attempt, on the part of my mother and father, to save "green shield stamps." When they had accumulated enough, they went to a storefront shop and submitted their booklet. Then scanned the catalogue to find it: a leather briefcase with a gold lock. A woman in a pale blue nylon midi dress went through a door into "the back" and got it. A replacement. It was lined with faded rose silk. A silky material.

Was it that my father was a man? Was it that there was alcohol, on Friday evenings, passed between men like him? Was it that it was obvious? Was it that he shook, like an animal, discharging the attack from his nerves? Why do some forms of violence strengthen the psyche rather than—disrupting it? Radical modernity requires something of me—requires me to experiment with an aesthetics of violence. To write the larger scene. The race riot. Every day, I try to write the race scene for Ban, but at night, I simply dream of exiting a subway stop at the interface a car would make with the M25. The commuters are processing around—what else?—a roundabout, their hands on imaginary steering wheels, their wing-backed loafers shuffling on the tarmac, the asphalt, the black road: like wheels. They are playing. Evening editions of regional newspapers tucked sharply under their arms. The dream requires something of me. It requires me to acknowledge that my textual creature (Ban) is over-written by a psychic history that is lucid, astringent, witty. No longer purely mine.

I sometimes think I am doing a very weak thing as a writer. But in the classes at Naropa, we have another conversation about abandonment. About identifying the weakest place in a text and incubating it in another place. A different page. We read Lily Hoang's *The Evolutionary Revolution* toward this: the evolutionary, or generational, loops a narrative might make. The students write an essay: "What is a page for?" The short essays are very good. They take up the question of what is lost, what is weak, and what repeats. How a piece of dirt, as Melissa said when she visited our class, is the thing you "turn over." To see something stuck beneath. Glitter. Gum. And how you can take that glitter, that dung, and create a text from that.

Thus: Ban is the weakest thing. And yet to historicize her, to bring her forward—to give her an existence—will be to ask her to perform a diasporic act. To bring her molecules, her dirt, into the present time. How can I write a body without writing it out of the time in which it be-

longs? Note to self: research "aperture." Research: The Hindu occult. Who can I talk to about Asian vampires? About the capacity to bi-locate? I thought it was Ban I needed to catch. Her circulating matter. Her black spots. And keep. Or trap. In a glass net. But now I think it is me. I think I have to go: there. All year, I have been trying to write something that would attract her. Bring her here. I was wrong.

A ghost makes a click. A whirr. (Ban.)

I thought about the race clicks to make her. Their chronic, rather than acute, production. Translate to poetry. Translate to the long line. Phonemes, for example. And semicolons. As glottal sites. A sub-register: of dismemberment. The way a part of the soul gets caught on a hook, like meat. A comma is a kind of hook.

This is a brief note without literary examples. I wanted to respond to Claudia Rankine's open letter. Her question about linguistics and race. I wanted to write about the parts of the sentence that are shiny, blanked out, but also mirrors. Mirrors a person could walk through.

<http://jackkerouacispunjabi.blogspot.com
/2011/02/schizophrene-texture-notes.html>

E-RACING LINGO . . .
TRACIE MORRIS

In response to Claudia's call, I couldn't help but be alerted to the medium.

This is an electric conversation through wires and wireless, the 1s and 0s of snatches of conversation.

There's an erasure implied in these snatchings and I think that scraps of discourse are often the source, inspirations of racial utterances.

―――――――

I end up talking about race in my poems because I only write when I feel like it. Racial conversations, like love, *make* me/put pen to paper.

Sometimes it's about what I wish I had said, sometimes what I wish I had not, other times something I wish someone else had said in (my) stead.

The "memory hole" of topicalizing, momentary, atomized discourse, the trivialization of all data through its immediate access compels me to remember what I actually experience/have/experienced in my radicalized past: What New York was like during the Giuliani years, the distinct presentations of race in the 1970s, '80s, '90s, what my people went through, what young people go through now that they can't quite put their fingers on. The language for it has atrophied /made quaint and everything looks okay online —where everybody looks to see what's happening.

I *feel* like I have to sometimes remind folk/myself what has happened—it's so easy to forget—to vivify the tongue of what we wish was said.

A SLANTY KIND OF RACIAL(IZED) POETICS
TAMIKO BEYER

It has always been difficult for me to talk and write about race. My level of discomfort or fear depends on the context and the audience; this kind of very public declaration is particularly hard. Yet I am participating in this project because I know that allowing my unease to silence me is one of the ways that racism persists and thrives. We function in a society built on institutional racism where white privilege is hidden and masked, particularly by language.[1] We employ all sorts of euphemisms to avoid facing race head on, or even sideways: "ethnicity," "diversity," "postracial."

As a poet interested in both the materiality and the communicative performances of language, I want to examine how our language is complicit in sustaining racism, as well as how it might work toward dismantling it. Also, I'm cognizant of how often—and for very understandable reasons—discussions of race in this country narrow down to, literally, black and white. I want to add my voice to this discussion as someone outside of that binary.

My experience of my own race is complicated and fraught. I am mixed race—Japanese and white. I have light skin, brown eyes, brown hair, and facial features that seem to be read as white much of the time. I grew up in Japan—a very

---

[1] I come to poetry from a social justice work background, so I am employing the language of antiracism work throughout this essay. I understand racism in the US as a system of white supremacy—by which I don't mean we are ruled by the KKK, but that institutionalized racism is pervasive, ever present, and not undone simply by individual white people who claim to be "color blind" or not "personally" racist, nor by the mere existence of laws that ostensibly guarantee equal rights.

I've been working on

racially homogeneous society. There, I was un-doubtedly a racial outsider. When I was almost a teenager we moved to the US, to the suburbs of Seattle. In this mostly white context, people didn't know quite what to make of me. Full of pre-teen angst and negotiating severe culture shock, I tried my best to fit in, which meant, among oth-er things, figuring out how to "act white."

In short, I am not white, but I often pass as white. As a result, I have experienced both light skin privilege and racism. I am a border dweller, a border crosser. After many years of attempting to make sense of my racial identity and experi-ences, I have come to identify myself as a woman of color who takes seriously my light skin privi-lege. I work to recognize the systems of racism we all function in, and I work to understand my own complicity, as well as my own survival, within these systems. When and where I can, I at-tempt to name and dismantle systems of rac-ism and oppression.

I believe poetry exists to name—or at least invoke/evoke—and give access to what is other-wise unnamable/hidden/silenced/disappeared. And so, then, poetry must be a place/space to at-tempt to approach race and racism. At the risk of sounding reductive or simplistic, I think there are (at least) two ways that poetry can do this.[2]

---

[2] I want to acknowledge, too, the artificiality of talking about a racial/ized poetics as if separate from other elements of poetics and oppressions. That is to say, my understanding of both poetics and politics is also informed by my experience as an able-bodied, queer, middle-class woman.

Many poets of color have written about the importance of poems that describe experiences of race and racism. In this societal system of white privilege, where white people's experi-ences are universalized and the lives of people of color are "othered," these poems are vital for our survival. (I'm thinking here of Audre Lorde's line, "we were never meant to survive," and Lucille Clifton's, "come celebrate / with me that everyday / something has tried to kill me / and has failed," in particular.) It was important to me when I first started writing poetry to create poems that explicitly dealt with my mixed-race experiences. I was able to give voice to and un-derstand better my experiences for which I oth-erwise had limited language.

Today, I'm interested in the problem of de-construction. And I have some questions. If race is a social construct with real, tangible effects and consequences (and it is), and if I am attempting? How do I use (poetic?) language to write—into (alongside? across?) a social construct that relies heavily on masking language and a "not seeing"? That is to say, if we (in US society) rely on the cues of language to *not* face racism head on, is it even possible to employ a deconstructed poetics to write race?

Taking to heart Emily Dickinson's famous exhortation, I've been working on how to write it "slant" where the slant is not about avoidance

TAMIKO BEYER

how to write it "slant" . . .

but about an angled approach that—because of its instability—gets us as close as possible to the heart of both the construction of and real-life devastation of race. Like this essay's title, for example, and its sidelong acknowledgment of a racial slur.

I learn and take cues from other poets who I think are also working through these, or similar, questions. These poets are creating a poetics of race that, in addition to naming racism and naming the experience of being a person of color, also are grappling with how our very material of our craft is complicit in the racism we experience. I'm thinking of some of my own favorite poets—Myung Mi Kim, John Yau, Harryette Mullen, Claudia Rankine, the poets in the Black Took Collective (Duriel E. Harris, Dawn Lundy Martin, and Ronaldo V. Wilson). When I initially started this essay, I was deep into a reading of Cynthia Arriue-King's wonderful book, *People are Tiny in Paintings of China*, which seems to be enacting both a poetics of naming and a poetics of deconstruction, sometimes within the same poem. It is the development of this kind of poetics that both enacts and deconstructs race that I think I am working toward.

The strength of the first kind of poetics that I describe is that it names and gives voice to experiences and realities that are silenced in a white supremacist society. The second poetics is valuable to me because it gets to the language root of racism and attempts to disrupt it. Both are vital, both are necessary, both need to exist together to do the poetic work to create change in our racist society.

ON POLITICS AND ART, THE WRITER IN SOCIETY
JANE LAZARRE

"The conundrum of color is the inheritance of every American, be he/she legally or actually Black or White. It is a fearful inheritance, for which untold multitudes, long ago, sold their birthright. Multitudes are doing so, until today."
—James Baldwin, from the preface to NOTES OF A NATIVE SON

Because I believe with Baldwin that race and American race history is fundamental to American identity, I write and have written, in a variety of genres, centrally as well as peripherally, about race. But writing about race as a white writer is complex and problematic.

One's work may be dismissed or misinterpreted in a variety of ways. Furthermore, the publishing industry, from the large, corporate houses to the small, literary presses to the university presses, are as segregated, by and large, as other American institutions. The occasional Black editor, or small Black-owned publishing company, or imprints in major houses such as Amistad/Harper, focus, reasonably enough, on African American writers. The majority of editors in the United States are white and, like other white Americans, tend to stereotype people of color and art by and about people of color. When they are not denying the importance of race altogether, by assertions of color blindness, insistence that racism is a thing of the American past, or through the homogenized category of "diversity," they often find individual works to be lacking in "universal implication," in "emotional impact," or in "broad marketability." Thus, in the publishing, as in the academic industries, African American writers and literature are hyphenated as though this tradition were not quintessentially and emblematically American. Easily, an antiracist white writer, trying to explore this realm out of personal experience, imagination and artistic conviction, as I do, may fall through many cracks.

As epigraphs to my novel *Inheritance* (published in 2011 by Hamilton/Stone Editions) I used passages from three white American writers

(Herman Melville, William Faulkner, and Russell Banks), all of whom have thought and written with consciousness and beauty about the great historical American inheritance of racial bigotry: of whiteness as an idea, a political ideology and a system of oppression that reaches as *deep-in* as our most personal myths, our very bodies—their shapes, their colors, their sex—and as *far-out* as our social and economic institutions. I identify my work as inspired by these writers, a part of the tradition they exemplify.

I decided to structure the novel into three different times in American history—from slavery to the present, although not in linear order—so I could trace the very changing yet also in some ways tragically consistent ways the idea of whiteness as a sign of human superiority has persisted over time, right into our present moment. I believe that racism against Black Americans, its social and political history and its spiritual legacy, is not only a great evil that writers cannot ignore if we are claiming to be creators of *American* literature, but also an evil that can stand for bigotry and tyrannies of many kinds, and that is why the African American experience speaks to readers across boundaries of culture, race and class. The novel follows the generations of one Black family as they interact with a variety of non-Black Americans (of British, Jewish, and Italian heritage) in order to explore the genealogies of skin color prejudice as well as of antiracist consciousness among whites over time. The idea that peoples' racist actions and beliefs are to be explained away because they are "only people of their times" is one I wish to refute. History and contemporary life both tell us that there have always been white people in all walks of life who wrestled with American racism and its consequences—a minority, certainly, often imperfectly and even unsuccessfully, but more than enough to demonstrate that awareness, through writing and organized action, was widely available and possible for all.

Three central characters in the novel are white women. Louisa Summers is the daughter of a slave owner on the western shore of Maryland, living several decades before the Civil War. She is naïve and self-centered, but a passionate girl whose early belief in the evil nature of slavery and eventual love for one of her father's slaves, to whom she bears a child, turns her into a committed abolitionist. Hannah Sokolov, the daughter of Russian Jewish immigrants, married to a successful dentist in Norwalk, Connecticut, in the early 1900s, responds with her deepest sexual and emotional being to a black man and a black woman (his wife), but betrays what she feels out of anger and shame, reverting to the ease of socially pervasive forms of racism. Ami Reed is a writer of fiction and a white woman of immigrant Italian heritage in late-twentieth-century New York. She is the mother of a

. . . politics and art as

grown black son and a grandmother to his teenage daughter. She moves from a belief in "color blindness" to a change in racial and personal consciousness in part as a result of her love for her family, in part due to her relationship with two black women. One is a fellow writer, known for a searing memoir of her father's history, whose story is slowly uncovered in the novel. The other is Ami's new daughter-in-law. The overall narrator and in may ways the main character whose story is in some ways the center of the book, is the granddaughter, child of a Black father and a Jewish mother, who is searching for her identity as a Black woman in part through retelling and researching the stories of the three central white women. I am describing the novel in the most general, thematic terms, of course. The *story* of these people as they interact and discover mutual legacies over time is what the novel is most intimately "about." The original title of the novel was *Three White Women*. The idea of "inheritance" came to me recently, was reinforced when I came across Baldwin's words quoted above, and may or may not be more apt.

The idea that all art possesses explicit or implicit political agendas, versus the idea that "great" art is above and apart from political point of view, is a problem that has been argued by critics, academics, publishers, and writers for centuries. An essay by Albert Camus, "Create Dangerously," traces the argument brilliantly for the interested

reader. Clearly, I find myself, as an artist, in the tradition that sees politics and art as inextricably interwoven, a tradition that is represented by many living critics and writers, notably Toni Morrison, Chinua Achebe, and others, and goes back to Shakespeare, Greek dramatists, most non-Western traditions, as well as by African American literature. The contemporary distortion of this problem is to condemn fiction that takes a clear political stand as "didactic," rather than understanding the divisions of aesthetic perspectives in the US and elsewhere, then judging a work on its own terms. To take the pertinent example: fiction by white writers that takes a strong stand against racism is often dismissed as "too political," or even "didactic," while white fiction by white writers that ignores race and the presence of people of color entirely is seen as "not political," instantly granting it a higher place within the hierarchies of artistic excellence. But clearly, fiction is compelling and beautiful depending on the truth and complexity of its reflections and insights, the poetry of its language, its clarity of intention and authenticity of voice. For me, these are central components of what we mean by "literary imagination." When "political" realities are ignored, reality is distorted. When point of view is murky or self-deceiving, the reader, also, is in danger of being deceived. When the machinations behind plot, scene, or character are obvious, a work can be uncomfortably didactic, but this is

inextricably interwoven . . .

common in much contemporary fiction, including works which have no claim to political point
of view.

I write out of a belief in the power of story to
reveal our lives and our world, to ourselves, to
others; to use language as much as possible to expose layers of experience beneath what Virginia
Woolf (in her essay "A Sketch of the Past") called
"the cotton wool of daily life," and to try to expose
injustice, in particular in this and in some other
work, the injustice of racism. It is my aim, effort,
and hope that the last desire and motivation will
not obfuscate or undermine the first two.

"NEGROES MAKE ME HUNGRY" —SOME NOTES ON RACE

R. ERICA DOYLE

Once someone black told me that she couldn't tell that I was black from what I wrote. It was a pretty highly sexualized unrequited lesbian love story slash meditation on time and place. In it, one of the characters says, "'Negroes make me hungry.'" I really thought that anyone reading would know that only a black person would have the audacity to make that statement with impunity.

I understood what she meant, though. When I first read Audre Lorde's *Zami*, I didn't think she was that black, either. I didn't see my own experience as a young Caribbean American lesbian in the 1990s reflected in her experience as a young Caribbean American lesbian in the 1950s. In my teens, reading Toni Morrison was like reading Flaubert, it was so foreign.

Further back, when I was eleven, I remember reading a collection, *Negro Short Stories,* in my parents' library and being disappointed in the black writers because they didn't "sound black." Most of the work was written in Academic English— like this is—and the dialogue was in a phonetically spelled black dialect I could barely read. I was annoyed at the stiffness of the language and at the cartoonishly raced speakers.

I was operating out of parochial constructions of race based on my own experiences in a Trinidadian immigrant household, in a mostly Caribbean immigrant neighborhood, in Queens, New York, in the 1970s. There was very little outside of our community that reflected our multiracial, multireligious reality. So, just as I spoke one way around family and another around friends and in school, I developed a double consciousness around race— one as an insider and one as an outsider. And, in the great brownwashing of becoming American,

I subscribed to the idea of a monolithic blackness, desperately sought my own reflection, and balked at textual encounters that challenged my "ethnic notions."

It was not until I had a more sophisticated understanding of systems of power and privilege, imperialism and colonialism, that I was able to understand the complicated tapestry of identity that I'd been trying to negotiate in both my parents' library and in my basement apartment. Once I had that understanding, I was able to access texts without feeling betrayed by them. Once I found writers who interrogated oppressive signifiers outside of the realm of the narrative, I began to expand my own poetic repertoire. And I began to discard texts that I found offensive and small-minded, that did not do the work, somehow, of justice. It's not just that I find them insulting, but antithetical to my existence on the planet.

My initial frustrations with monolithic views of race in the United States actually fueled a lot of my writing projects—poems about my family and their history, short stories and novels about race, culture, class, and gender through my own lenses. The way I write about race tends to be through the examination of a "racial moment," like my poem "Cardinal Points," where two queer black American women in Africa confront the myth of "the motherland." Or the racialized process of jury selection in "Juror Number Twelve."

Or predatory photography by tourists in "Don't Explain." I write at race, or around it, instead of *about* it. Race is a made-up thing that makes us sick and crazy. My work tends to interrogate those "racial moments" of dis-ease, insanity, and inadvertent joy.

I think about identity particles all the time; they hover like bees or clouds depending on my mood, I contemplate consciousness beyond the body itself, my poems circling piranhas tearing out a chunk here and there. It's okay if you can't tell what I am. I know.

I know. I am trying to stay awake. I am trying to do all of this with love.

OPEN LETTER
SANDRA LIM

I see myself and my work as always in process, and I want the freedom to employ whatever it is I am inspired by or troubled by to enlarge my sense of what poetry is, what it does, and what it can engage. I get inspiration from so many different places. When someone comes up to me after a reading and asks why I don't write more about my Korean American identity (and this has happened more than a few times), I am perhaps at first naively baffled, then I realize all over again the gravity and flexibility that the effort of living and writing fully takes. When I don't write about a unified, singular, and yet broadly representative Asian American self, some people like to say I write "experimental" or "postmodern" poems.

Like any writer from a bicultural background, I share a doubled consciousness, but I don't always consciously "mark" my racial and ethnic identity in my work. It's not that my ethnic identity is not in play in the writing somehow (I don't see how it can be separated out of my consciousness, whatever I'm writing about), but I'm not interested in constantly naming it in the work. Maybe it's an inadvertent, reverse racial drag of a sort. And like drag, it exposes a tricky yearning to claim some kind of authenticity (in this case the authenticity of dispassion, of neutrality) even as it imagines itself to be foregrounding the fictionality of racial representation (or non-representation).

I suppose I want to be protected by the spaciousness that seems afforded to white writers, or specifically those writers who don't get asked after a reading why they don't write again and again about their ethnic identity and experiences (those experiences just being human experiences, of course). I want my writing to have in it something beyond forms of only personal racial identification.

It occurs to me that some readers who have asked me about my choices of subject matter have asked me this because they think of my Asianness as something I'm in danger of losing. But that presupposes a remarkable shared experience, shared beingness, too—"My people," wrote Kafka, "provided that I have one." Exactly.

So: hypervisibility or invisibility. There are so many ways to be unseen and misseen.

Well, there is not much poetry from which I feel excluded. I don't imagine myself above personal identifications (I'm hardly colorblind), but I might have to insist upon a lack of allegiance, upon my prerogative to have a multiple sensibility. My ideal is for the poetic imagination as violent and marvelous free space, a space to think and feel without stinting, to court ideological inconsistency, to express feelings of (at times dire) cultural contingency.

I don't believe for one minute that we have passed over into a postracial world. But I want the kind of amplitude that allows me to write of the contradictory currents of my Korean American heritage as well as to write as a speaker who doesn't "come from" an Asian America that speaks with only one voice, one style, one history, one sociopolitical reality.

I hope that the poems I write can withstand and oblige the contradictions of my selves and my imagination.

OPEN LETTER
HOSSANNAH ASUNCION

I haven't yet found the metaphor as a way into writing about race. Perhaps it is because of proximity—of my skin to witness.

I know enough of the imprecision of talking about race. It feels like choosing a violent failure or a violent failure—to say something or to not say something.

And to write about race, directly? How to do so? How to make such precise cuts without debilitating self-injury? How to know where to cut?

And where would I start? Would I start with an experience in graduate school in which one comment from a white peer was, "If I (a white woman) feel compelled to write from the perspective of a Black woman, why shouldn't I? Why should I limit my imagination?"

If I had said, "You should not write about being an 'other,'" would I have been a poet oppressing another poet? Would I be assisting in the failure of poetry?

In moments like those, it's difficult to translate my skin into a well-formed polemic.

I am being asked to make a choice: poet or Filipina? It is a constant inquisition.

———

So, then, it's me alone with a page.

I write about my mother's hands. I write about her skin.

Is that writing about race?

I have written poems about a Seattle man who killed a Filipino woman he found in a catalog.

Or is that writing about race?

In a line I write *pamilya* instead of *family*. I don't include footnotes. I don't translate. I don't feel the urge to defend the choice.

Or is that?

If so, is it enough?

RACE AND ERASURE

CAITIE MOORE

As a white poet in a racialized society, I think I have to distinguish writing about race from writing as a race. The former can be a tool of exposure and the latter ranges from a tool of a suspect neutral politics to one which completely erases socially constructed positions. Presenting unexamined racial politics is analogous to poetics of erasure, in that it is not always clear what the stakes, meaning, or valences of the source text are—it's not always clear what's being contrived or reworked by the poet. I sometimes utilize poetic erasure to enter, understand, or pay homage to prose I'm reading, and I often feel the threat of silencing the original.

I was raised, poetically, on transcendentalist, imagistic works that privileged the oblique over the overt. Emily Dickinson and H. D., Gerard Manley Hopkins and Robert Duncan, etc. I tried, in my master's thesis, to write about the US/Mexico border and Islamophobia in circuitous, oracular ways, all the while feeling like I was denying the content of reality. I worried no meaningful phrases were coming across, and worse, that my languorous prosody was an implicit endorsement of the situations that repelled me. I still read within this poetic tradition, but it answers to my everyday needs less and less. First, because my needs are not always psycho-spiritual. Second, because I find it is often stuck between the anxieties of appearing either quotidian or moralistic.

The letters of Robert Duncan to Denise Levertov are instructive in studying these parallel fears. In 1969 Levertov was involved with more and more movement work: organizing demos, lettuce boycotts, prison letter-writing campaigns, and fusing her poems with these daily experiences. Duncan received her letters and enclosed poems with less and less pleasure. On November 10th of that year, he quips in verse: "from the isolation cham-

Compulsive language is

bers and torture rooms / of Federal prisons / from the immediate contempt for the people daily / I take my esthetic distance." By October of 1971, he has amplified his artistic insults. On the 4th he questions her theme "Revolution or Death," writing that "the book clearly isn't 'revolutionary' in the sense of the poem." It isn't because, he contends, she/the poem is not truly angry. On the 16th he writes "Of course *you* are not Kali: one of the troubles you have as a poet is that even the flickering moments in which the grand vision of apocalypse might arise and some outpouring of the *content* of world-anger come, you cannot give it free imaginative expression, cannot identify with the anger, but must moralize and humanize." He tells her to stop/he exhorts her to go further. This argument traps me in an aesthetic conversation that pretends not to have material consequences.

Duncan is asking Levertov to move toward a compulsive space/compulsive language. Can compulsive language pay homage to harm without enacting it? Compulsive language is often harmful, if only because language is trafficked through spaces of systemic violence. So what we seek to channel through writing, we would apologize for in life. In the space of invention/reception (both of which are conceived in the spirit of query), do I become careless? Does the conduit make me hateful? Harmful? In the end (at the time that the poem becomes product) has

my harm been excised? Should I excise (read: cover for) my harm?

Grappling with utilitarianism during graduate school I asked a friend—a cis-male poet of color—what he was trying to solve in his poems. He was incredulous, as he often is, and answered, "There are no solutions." Last year in my kitchen we played out the Levertov/ Duncan debate over the purported "futility" of police brutality protests. And what did I say? Did I say a sixteen-year-old Black boy has been shot by a cop? Did I say we can't talk about this like this? Probably. But not in a poem. In a poem I said "behind them the racist curtain with the racist air behind it filling the racist room," which was not in reference to him, but to daily life in New York City. The line stands as an erasure of all specificity.

I try to make words shift/bend, to not be fixed, but I still want to answer to their meanings. For better or worse, meaning is part of the medium I've chosen, and even when I succeed in making the words bend, and even when I succeed at channeling energy, if something I say compulsively comes out as racist, I want to answer for it. Because even if it's the system of language that's fostered the possibility of that compulsion, words aren't racist in themselves, but in their formation, and poetry is form built by hand, in this case my hand. And if my explanations remain inadequate, I hope to be taken to task. Critique, terrifying

often harmful . . .

as it is, is not as terrifying as harm that stands uncontested.

Art is set apart from utilitarianism by its welcoming of unoccupied spaces, ambivalences, fragmentation, erasure, and the destructive/ illuminant mental zone that assures these aberrations. I want to stay true to the dual meaning that can free us by creating openings and escapes. However, I want to be clear that those openings should be big enough for bodies to fit through. I mean language to be a tool I use to navigate a space packed with bodies. Dead or alive, ignored or attended to, bodies with functions, predictable physical functions, bodies which sometimes contrive to create unforeseeable horrors played out on other bodies. I acknowledge that we're granted access to uncharted "inscapes," to use Hopkins's term. But if, as Duncan offers, "often I am permitted to return to a meadow" and if it "is not mine, but a made place" that meadow is so made not only by spirits, but by history, and I am not the only living figure and not all of the other bodies are basking in permissiveness. What this place lacks in censorship, it makes up for in responsibility.

OPEN LETTER
KRISTIN PALM

i.

I write about cities, so I necessarily write about race. Or, more specifically, I wrote a book about a city (Detroit) and race necessarily entered this story. Addressing race in the historical section of the book was not difficult. It would have been impossible to trace the city's origins, development, or decline without it. I'm inclined to say that including race in my personal story was scary (I am white). But truthfully, I'm not sure it was. It entered the story quite naturally, as I spent the years following my departure from Detroit thinking about the interactions that occurred there and how they shaped me. And I think the fact that I was reflecting back is part of what made me comfortable including race in this story. I had had years to ponder the events I wrote about, let them float in and out of my consciousness. I was able to strip them down to their essence and write about them in a way that, I hope, reflected that.

> In line at the grocery store a young boy turns
> to me he's black he asks is this where the white
> people live yes I say I mean this is where I live

This is the particular passage in my book to which I keep returning. This exchange is about race, of course, but it's also about two human beings interacting in the complicated, often inarticulate ways human beings do. The journalist in me would have felt compelled to take this instance and derive one conclusive, universal point from it. And I have written about race, specifically as it pertains to Detroit, in this manner as well. But in this case, the poet in me had permission to hold this event up to the light, examine it from many angles and, perhaps most importantly, write about it in a way that speaks to the emotional impact it had on me. I am comfortable (or comfortable enough, or I was comfortable enough in this instance) writing about race when what feels foregrounded is what? I am having trouble defining this. But it has to do with our basic humanity, the ways we interact in our most unguarded moments, what happens when we let go, however unintentionally, and stumble and stutter and admit that sometimes we're going to say or do things, or risk saying or doing things, that make us feel uncomfortable or shamed or remorseful or otherwise *not in control*. It occurs to me that what I am talking about here, or at least one of the things I am talking about, is humility. That is a vantage point from which I feel comfortable writing personal stories in general, and this includes stories that deal with race: I had this experience. It troubled me, it transformed me. I am willing to share this with you.

ii.

Of course, by virtue of publishing a book, I have entrenched myself a little deeper in the (experimental) poetry community, thus opening myself up to greater opportunities for criticism from my peers. This is perhaps my biggest fear around writing about race. One of the things I find simultaneously amazing and distressing about this community is the degree to which we hold one another accountable. Because I think it is critical that we ask questions like, whose history is being told here? And who has the right to tell it? And, especially if we are speaking from the viewpoint of the dominant culture, what kinds of assumptions are we making? Where are the gaps in our believing, our knowing, our telling? If we're going to tread in this difficult territory, we need to be able to answer these questions. But I do find myself wondering where, in this community, is the room for stammering and stuttering? For humility? I'm not saying that room doesn't exist, just that I'm not sure. Just that there is work out there that I have read that I felt was compelling and moving and made me think, but that I have heard others describe as "problematic." And personally, I find that word problematic. That is to say, it doesn't tell me much, least of all what the effect of the writing was on the person who read it. No matter how vulnerable the writer may be making herself in order to address the issue of race (or just the issue of being human, which naturally includes the issue of race), the critic is revealing no vulnerability of her own. It's an unfair position and the fear of having it directed at me absolutely enters my consciousness when writing about, or thinking about writing about, race. I will continue to do so if it is germane to my project. It would be too irresponsible not to. But I worry this fear affects how deep I dig and what I ultimately end up saying.

OPEN LETTER
DANIELLE PAFUNDA

Dear Claudia, Dear All,

Identity markers—race, gender, sex, sexuality, age, disability, nationality, ethnicity, religion, class, and so on—are basic units of power. The moment our bodies are born into culture, we start accumulating (or hemorrhaging) power. We enter a system of kinship and repulsion that predates us, and will in some mode or other outlive us. At the same time, this system is desperately dependent on us to reproduce it, which we do almost effortlessly. In fact, the greater effort comes in trying to stall or alter that reproduction.

If we follow the money/power, we can usually trace it back to the accidents of birth. We might then spend a lot of time telling others about the disparity, but I'm not, as a poet, interested in *proving* the disparity. It's self-evident. There if you notice such things and as dull to quantify as it is deplorable. I prefer to *describe* the disparity. *Embody* the disparity and mess around in its most abject dynamics. Is it remedial? Cruel? Vulgar? Juvenile? Maybe.

I begin all writing with gender because:

1) I do gender compulsively, and

2) in every culture, at every historical moment, gender is a *most basic* unit of power.

But I also begin all writing from my cozy swathing of Whitedom. When beleaguered by the myriad ways in which this world hates a girl, I can slink into whiteness (hetero-breeder stylings, middle classness, or the like) and rest easier. I walk into a store and purchase or not purchase whatever I can afford without incident. I take my children to the park and look like a mama on a magazine cover, like feminine *normal*. Especially if I keep my mouth shut.

Gender issues and race issues aren't *equivalent*, but they're *analogous* in ways I find fascinating and valuable:

—The traumas of racism and sexism can be mapped one on top of the other. Some crucial features will line up, others will diverge remarkably.

—Where race ostensibly suggests a common geographical point of origin, gender suggests a point of origin in biological sex. In both cases, the lived reality is far messier than that.

—Though across these lines we're all the same species—blood, brains, DNA, disease, function—we've been historically segregated. Rather than slightly variant bodies within the same species, white male bodies are marked as human, while bodies of color, female bodies, and intersexed bodies get marked *deviant, animals* of another bent.

It's grimly funny that the voices least sanctioned to speak come from the bodies most on display. There's such power in looking—in being the one who looks and not the one who runs, slithers, limps, or glides under the gaze. The power of looking is magnified by speaking about what one has seen, and in such speech acts, we lodge ourselves somewhere in the matrix of domination. Look: the body *is the thing*.

And oh, do we have feelings about the body. We cannot see a body without cataloging, critiquing, and reacting (attacking). Sometimes one might feel driven to explore the meanest and sleaziest reactions she experiences. This exploration might even be a public service of sorts, but the right to speech is not the right to approbation, thank goodness. If I sketch a series of sleazy feelings I had about another body, if I fail to frame or critique these feelings well, I will be called out.

Which is why, sure, I'm afraid to write about race, and why despite my fear when I do write about race, I'm not being *brave*. Or any courage on my part is beside the point. When I write about race, I acknowledge my existence as a human-with-a-body. I don't strain foppishly to transcend that body, I don't pretend power buys me out of the biological death march. If you're not writing sometimes-somehow about lived experience in the human body, I don't like you or trust you and I won't be having dinner with you. That may be no great loss to you, but for me it's quite a gain, a newfound ability to dislodge and relocate *the center(s)* of our culture(s).

On the first day of kindergarten, I was assigned a line partner whose hand I would hold as we walked to and from recess. My partner was the only black child in the class, and I thought *they know there's something wrong with me*. Clearly, my teachers knew that like the black girl I didn't belong. I burned with discomfort. One of my line partner's braids soon became tangled in the strap of my jumper. We were tangled, we were same, and I was exposed a fraud of a little white girl.

Well. I was chronically ill, which was sometimes visible. I was a Jewish-Catholic mix. I was doing *girl* wrong most of the time. I was often told "don't stand like a fag." I was told I'd need electrolysis. Those were little things. In more ways than not, no matter how different I felt, I was *unmarked* or able to shake my *markers* (if not my money maker) and pass.

To be fair, I'm now comfortable telling you because I was such a small child, you probably won't hold me responsible. Let's hold my parents responsible! My super-white town, my teachers, my *Free To Be You and Me* that just didn't do the trick. I've carried my line-partner story around like a puzzle and a shameful brand for three decades. The kinship, the repulsion, the projection of my internal difference onto her external difference, and, worst, the complete inability to process her personhood.

Personhood. We shouldn't have to earn it, but we do, and that makes it a suspect privilege. The speakers of my poems and stories mutate. Often, they're corpses, or pigs, or pearls, or vampires. They're always feminine, though non-normatively so. They're often female. They're mostly white. They're never able bodied in our conventional sense. They're pathological hetero-breeders more often than they're recognizably queer. They're me and they're not me. There's a lot of drag in my work, but I've thought so long on authority and speech and power, I'm cautious of what I wear. I don't make edifying work. My speakers revel in abjection, and I'd be afraid to place a woman of color in that dynamic. A *white* girl has just enough privilege to dissemble before your eyes, repulse you, and not risk losing her personhood (or not care if she does). Or so I feel, thank you Sylvia Plath. Can I say as much for a girl of color?

Sometimes while teaching, or at a dinner party, I fear I will reveal myself a monster of privilege. I am this thing that built its fortune on the backs of other humans. But I am also that back on which has been built. How to own up to it all?

It may have been boring to read so much about *me*, but that's one of the troubles of knowing you are a body with limits—you begin to realize you can't speak for everyone else. You can't speak in a chorus. Still, for old time's sake, let's ask *what is to be done*? What should *we* do? How do we mitigate our privileges and permeate the body's boundaries? Here's one way: if someone from the marked or marginalized category tells us we've fucked up, it's a good idea for us, no matter how wrongly accused we feel, to shut up, sit down, consider what we've done from new and many perspectives. It's also a good idea for us to tell our egos and shame spirals to can it. To consider that the current hegemonic center may be a dying star, that new centers may be blooming all around us. To keep stepping into the dialogue, humble, ready, eager for a new, non-toxic dynamic.

Yours,
Danielle

WRITING ABOUT RACE
BETTINA JUDD

Writing is attached to the body. This statement is quite a literal for me; it is my Black woman, queer-identified, round-bodied hand that puts pen to paper, to keyboard, and creates whatever I create. I recognize that my writing is read and recognized through this body whether I like it or not. I am not invested in erasing this paradigm, as many writers of various identities argue for, combat, etc. I like seeing my round brown hand typing, scribbling away because this moment is not an accident. It was fought for. To erase that as a part of what my writing is, whether it be a grocery list or poem, is to pretend as if this was given to me and to refuse to acknowledge that history for the sake of *some* folk getting to feel comfortable about reading it (potentially).

To say that my writing is attached to my body also recognizes the particular mode of thought that does not separate mind from body and spirit to which I closely attend. I don't find any creative freedom in detaching these things. To detach these things because they may constrict my writing also presumes that the rest of my identity is constricted, in itself unfree—even in my imagination. That's a depressing thought.

I'd like to think that my being Black, woman, queer, round bodied, and all of the "et ceteras" that highlight my privileges as well as my underprivileged race: US based/"American," English speaking, first world, able bodied, educated, cis gendered, middle class etc. have the potential to free my view *as long as I am aware of these things as opposed to trying to forget them.* As long as I recognize privilege as privilege and oppression as oppression I can write carefully and fully rather than reckless and mindlessly. So that's the politics of this. But I suppose in writing about how

I write *about* race rather than how race is implicit in my work (my thinking is that race is implicit in everyone's work especially when the race is white), I should go into the *why* of it.

As far as I can think in this moment, there are three central reasons why I write about race: I write about race in order to make sense of my place in this thing called race. I write about race because I can't only write about gender, sexuality, etc., without writing about race (I know some people think that they've achieved this—but trust, they really haven't). These things are all connected, all of these things are "colored" by the other things. Finally, as a larger project I write about race because it seems like some of the most responsible writing work I can do as a US citizen in order to begin to engage in larger discussions in the world. So I guess it would be fitting now to note my genres of writing in order to contextualize why I think of my writing as a project, as well as a life-practice: academic prose, poetry, mixed-genre, and love letters.

Perhaps it is because I'm US born. Perhaps it is because my mother is very politically minded and therefore fed me books on race. Perhaps it is because the books that didn't praise my Blackness as a child had white faces in them and yet presumably were *not* about race. Perhaps. See, it is as early as that. I'm a product of the US. I am a product of the Americas whose central project has been this race thing and I have not escaped it. *Neither have any of us.*

I write about race for the same reason people write about God, or nature, or their mother's wedding dress. It is in and around me like air and it is in my presence of mind and memory. Even now as I type this in some hipster coffee shop in Baltimore—I cannot ignore the fact that I am the only black person here. I am the only Black person in a coffee shop in Baltimore. Baltimore. I'm in Federal Hill. Saying that neighborhood's name makes my previous statement make sense. The name "Federal Hill" in Baltimore brings with it the flavor of race relations in US urban geographies. *That side of town, not this.* Race is in and around that sentence. While I sit here, I can't help but notice the metal design in the chairs across from me, the backs of them shaped into the Akan symbol "sankofa," which means to look back. People say the symbol is so common in metalwork in the US because Akan metalworkers were enslaved here and forged the symbol in wrought iron gates and fences. The design is so pervasive it means nothing. But it also means everything. The chair that is across from me, the café in which I sit, the old market across from it, history, and memory, all of these things are raced. It seems annoying and weighed down because history is heavy, but to write and to think that nothing has ever happened before I sat down to write is reckless. What exactly would I be writing about? In whose chair? And whose hand is moving across this page?

WHO'S WATCHING ANYMORE, ANYWAY?

DAWN LUNDY MARTIN

When Ronaldo V. Wilson, Duriel E. Harris, and I started the Black Took Collective over ten years ago, we did so to launch a critical investigation into questions of representation and race via poetic practice, performance, and play. I won't speak for my compatriots but, at the time, I was bored and slightly offended by what I perceived as an onslaught of reifying means attending to the representation of the black body in contemporary poetry. I want to call this the *phenomenon of true identity* or some kind of *collard-greens-in-the-blood phenomenon*—you know what I mean: *authenticity*. "Blackness" in poetry, particularly American blackness, it seems, as much as it is a framework for a cultural similarity in this phenomenon, is too a performance of language and the body—speech and gestures. Tongue of blackness, a way of speech or bodily gesture behind speech, a set of references and understandings, a realm of taste and tastes, a category of discrimination and struggle, a believed or imagined home place, a container.

I worry about the effects of these reiterative poetics because increasingly I'm of the mind that they are more than just annoying, but damaging. When the signs of blackness are inscribed via a limited lexicon and set of cultural biases, it might be that that determination, that lasso around the raced identity within the constraint of what has already been perceived, is dangerous. I, of course, understand the desire to be a part of a cultural group, to have a fear of dogs, let's say, or a weekly craving for Sunday black-eyed peas with ham hocks, or a predilection for "getting happy" in church, etc. There's something sweet about the neighborhood barbershop and something wonderful about community as it might be con-

You're all in this

structed or imagined there. I suppose I'm grinding my ax because of what happens when the field of view becomes so narrow one wonders from where the language and images themselves come. Is this, in fact, discourse doing its diabolical work? Or, discipline? Are we recipients or inventors? This is why I have a fondness for critical theory and philosophy—no matter their forms (could in fact be poetry itself). In those fields of study one is often encouraged to question or doubt what we see with the naked eye. A photograph we know is not simply a transparent representation.

Right this moment, I'm traveling via Greyhound Bus from Manhattan to Pittsburgh where I work as a university professor. It has been at least twelve years since I've been on a Greyhound Bus (so long ago I can't remember the details of the last trip) and I'm struck by how successful my deliberate class climb from the working class neighborhood in Hartford to a dual-city citizen has, thus far, been. It strikes me, too, that class is not merely about money but about an internalized sense of priorities and a casual performance of the body. *Don't ever rush. Better to be a tad underdressed than overdressed as you'll appear too eager. Use phrases such as "a tad."* I'm the sensitive genteel type now, so I'm boggled and made uncomfortable by my ragtag group of traveling companions. The young woman behind me as we pulled out of Philadelphia spent about

ten minutes on the crowded bus popping wrapping bubbles; the woman next to me is wearing so much cologne, I'm having a sneezing attack; and, despite the driver's very clear admonition that cell phone ringers are to be turned off or put on vibrate, ringers keep alighting in a cacophony of indecipherable song. This context has little if anything to do with race. Except. Except I am a black American woman traveling on a bus—clearly the least attractive and comfortable means of travel that one might choose—and on this transport mechanism, one cannot easily set one's self apart. My fellow travelers are from a mix of racial and ethnic backgrounds—most unidentifiable to me—though, mostly people of color. But here we are the same, or similar. The bus driver is mean to all of us without cause as if to say, *You're all in this shitbox together.* And we are. Race, I believe, and its complicated structures—its projections and internalizations—is all about one's sense of self via encounters with another. This other need not be another of difference, but can as well be an other of similarity as in, *I (mis) recognize you.* That encounter in the act of reading is not exempt from this premise. The racial image acts on us, creates us as we see ourselves reflected there in language and made manifest in flesh, fitting sometimes strangely against our senses of self.

To say in the work, *This is who I am* or, *This is who* we *are (or not)* with conviction and sta-

268

shitbox together.

bility, I believe, forecloses the very possibility of liberation that the work often seeks. To some, this contention might appear counterintuitive, but to paraphrase Erica Hunt, conventional language produces conventional meaning. And, by extension, I would add, conventional bodies and conventional selves. Also, we are long past the efficacy of screaming the parameters of one's existence from the mountain tops. I recently read the phrase *erasure of identity* as it regards a poetics whose attention is not focused directly on the *phenomenon of true identity*. Or, at least, this is how I understood the use of the phrase "erasure of identity," in the context within which it occurred. As it relates to the United States, at least, and much of the Western world, this phrase seems antiquated, to me, and limp. The power of the colonial enterprise and its regimes of negating power were direct and could be fought (perhaps over a great time span) with equal straight-eyed precisions. But what we need now is innovation, to cross out the script and rewrite what it means to be a raced being in the United States, of what it means to pay attention to the problems of race using art. We need to do this because these are desperate times. We live in a fucked-up racist country—a conservative Christian hellhole of constructed "tradition" and sexism so insidious and vehement, it's impossible to look toward that slippery brick without fear of getting bashed in the face. Who's watching anymore, anyway?

Everywhere I look there's a whole bunch of white people failing to recognize that nearly everyone else in the room is also white. Just because race is a devilish phantom does not mean that we aren't all too often reaping the repercussions of its ever-convincing guise.

———————

It's March 2011 and just this past week, I performed with the Black Took Collective at the California Institute of the Arts near Los Angeles. After the performance, we led the students in a workshop in which together we created lexicon around race that wanted to act against what we already know. We asked students to consider racial trauma and the problems of representing such trauma in ordinary language. The temperature outside was 80 degrees and sun-bright. On the other side of the world, part of Japan got eaten by the earth in one of the most powerful earthquakes ever recorded. Already the discursive machines are at work making it difficult, for those of us watching, for the horror to set in, the body to feel it, the imagination to conjure.

Jeremiah Barber, **Tomoko as Octopus**, 2008

Performance artist Jeremiah Barber gathered his colleagues for an investigation of metamorphosis—inhabitation as self-effacement. Here, his colleague Tomoko, chose an octopus as her spirit animal. Barber, in constructing the costumes, avoided the cloying kinderschema of Disney characters. Instead, he allowed his performers to un-humanize and inhabit the lovability-impaired, the fundraising also-rans, who illustrate the reality of most of us. MKC

WRITERS' BIOGRAPHIES

Beth Loffreda is the author of *Losing Matt Shepard: Life and Politics in the Aftermath of Anti-Gay Murder* (Columbia University Press, 2000). She teaches creative writing and American Studies at the University of Wyoming, where she directed the MFA program for six years. She grew up in Audubon, Pennsylvania, and attended the University of Virginia and Rutgers.

Claudia Rankine is the author of five collections of poetry, including *Citizen* and *Don't Let Me Be Lonely*, and the plays, *Provenance of Beauty: A South Bronx Travelogue*, commissioned by the Foundry Theatre and *Existing Conditions* (co-authored with Casey Llewellyn). Rankine is co-editor of *American Women Poets in the Twenty-First Century* series with Wesleyan University Press. A recipient of awards and fellowships from The Academy of American Poets, The American Academy of Arts and Letters, The Lannan Foundation, Poets and Writers and the National Endowments for the Arts, she teaches at Pomona College and is a Chancellor of the Academy of American Poets.

Max King Cap, former firefighter and copywriter, is an artist whose work in various media has been seen in numerous galleries and museums in the US and Europe; he is also an educator who has, in twenty years in academia, taught most recently at Pitzer College. After earning his MFA from the University of Chicago he taught in the architecture department of the Illinois Institute of Technology and was an artist-in-residence at the Kunst Akademie Karlsruhe in Germany. He is currently a doctoral candidate at the University of Southern California.

Maryam Afaq is a poet and artist who has called many cities home, including Islamabad, Kuala Lumpur, Brooklyn, and San Jose. She has an MFA in Poetry and works a corporate job in the Silicon Valley, where she lives with her husband and daughter.

A native of San Francisco, **Francisco Aragón** is the author of *Glow of Our Sweat* (Scapegoat Press) and *Puerta del Sol* (Bilingual Press), as well as the editor of *The Wind Shifts: New Latino Poetry* (University of Arizona Press). His poems and translations have appeared in *Chain, Crab Orchard Review, Chelsea, PALABRA, Pilgrimage, Mandorla,* and *Jacket,* among others. A former board member of the AWP, he is a faculty member at the Institute for Latino Studies at the University of Notre Dame where he directs their literary initiative, Letras Latinas.

Hossannah Asuncion grew up near the 710 freeway in Los Angeles and currently lives near an F/G stop in Brooklyn. She is a Kundiman fellow and a graduate of the Sarah Lawrence College writing program. Her work has been published by the Poetry Society of America, *Tuesday, An Art Project, The Collagist, Anti-,* and other fine places.

Ari Banias is the author of a chapbook, *What's Personal Is Being Here With All of You*

(Portable Press @ Yo-Yo Labs). The recipient of fellowships from the New York Foundation for the Arts, Djerassi, Headlands Center for the Arts, and the Wisconsin Institute for Creative Writing, he was a second-year writing fellow in 2013–14 at the Fine Arts Work Center in Provincetown. His work has appeared or is forthcoming in *Guernica, Gulf Coast,* the *Feminist Wire, Transom, The Volta,* and elsewhere. He lives and works with used books in Brooklyn, New York.

Dan Beachy-Quick is the author of five books of poetry, *Circle's Apprentice, North True South Bright, Spell, Mulberry,* and *This Nest, Swift Passerine;* five chapbooks, *Apology for the Book of Creatures, Overtakelesness, Heroisms, Canto,* and *Mobius Crowns* (the latter two both written in collaboration with the poet Srikanth Reddy); a book of essays on *Moby-Dick, A Whaler's Dictionary;* and a hybrid collection, *Wonderful Investigations.* He is a contributing editor for *A Public Space* and others, and is currently a Monfort Professor at Colorado State University for 2013–2015.

Charles Bernstein is an American poet, essayist, editor, and literary scholar. Bernstein holds the Donald T. Regan Chair in the Department of English at the University of Pennsylvania.

Reginald Dwayne Betts is a poet, essayist, and national spokesperson for the Campaign for Youth Justice. Betts writes and lectures about the impact of mass incarceration on American society, and in April 2012, President Obama appointed Betts to the Coordinating Council on Juvenile Justice and Delinquency Prevention. He is author of the memoir *A Question of Freedom* (Avery/Penguin), for which he was awarded the NAACP Image Award, and the poetry collection *Shahid Reads His Own Palm* (Alice James Books).

Tamiko Beyer is the author of *We Come Elemental* (Alice James Books), winner of the 2011 Kinereth Gensler Award, and *bough breaks* (Meritage Press). Her poems have recently appeared or are forthcoming in *The Volta, Octopus, Quarterly West*, and elsewhere. She is the Senior Writer at Corporate Accountability International and lives in Cambridge, Massachusetts. Find her online at tamikobeyer.com.

Jericho Brown is the recipient of the Whiting Writers' Award and fellowships from the Radcliffe Institute for Advanced Study at Harvard University and the National Endowment for the Arts. His poems have appeared in *The Best American Poetry 2013, The Best American Poetry 2014, The New Republic*, and *The New Yorker*. His first book, *Please*, won the American Book Award, and his most recent book, *The New Testament*, will be published in the fall of 2014. Brown is currently assistant professor at Emory University.

Jennifer Chang is the author of *The History of Anonymity*. She co-chairs the advisory board of Kundiman and is an assistant professor of English at George Washington University in Washington, DC.

r. erica doyle was born in Brooklyn to Trinidadian immigrant parents. Her work has appeared in *Best American Poetry, Our Caribbean, Ploughshares, Callaloo*, and *Bloom*, among others. Her articles and reviews have appeared in *Ms. Magazine, Black Issues Book Review*, and on the *Best American Poetry* and *Futurepoem* blogs. She lives in New York City, where she is an administrator in the NYC public schools and facilitates Tongues Afire: A Free Creative Writing Workshop for queer women and trans and gender non-conforming people of color.

Diane Exavier writes, makes, thinks a lot, and laughs even more. She hails from Brooklyn by way of her family's journey from Haiti and uses the Caribbean space as inspiration for creating theatrical worlds that reflect her Haitian American heritage. Diane has studied theater at Amherst and Smith Colleges. In her artistic practice is an earnest and constant attempt to escape from the traps of genre, form, language, and time.

Her work has been presented at the Brick Theater, Dixon Place, Independent Curators International, PS122, and more.

Arielle Greenberg is co-author of *Home/Birth: A Poemic*; author of *My Kafka Century* and *Given*; and co-editor of three anthologies, including *Gurlesque*. She lives in Maine and teaches in the Oregon State University–Cascades low-residency MFA program and in the community in Maine, and writes a column on contemporary poetics for the *American Poetry Review*.

James Allen Hall's first book of poems, *Now You're the Enemy*, won awards from the Lambda Literary Foundation, the Fellowship of Southern Writers, and the Texas Institute of Letters. He has received fellowships from the National Endowment of the Arts and the New York Foundation for the Arts. He lives on the eastern shore of Maryland and teaches creative writing and literature at Washington College.

Kasey Johnson received her BA in English from Reed College. She holds an MA from the University of New Mexico in English Language and Literature. She is interested in postcolonial feminisms, indigenous epistemologies, and Native/American literature. Her MA thesis, "Beyond Postcolonialisms: Native and Queer Studies in Native/American Literature," focused on indigenous feminism, Native literary studies, and queer theory in two American novels. She currently lives in Portland, Oregon.

Lacy M. Johnson is the author of *[the two directions of a door]* (Tin House Books) and *Trespasses: A Memoir* (University of Iowa Press), and she is co-artistic director of the multimedia project *[the invisible city]*. She worked as a cashier at Walmart, sold steaks door to door, and was a traveling puppeteer before earning a PhD in Creative Writing from University of Houston. She is currently Director of Academic Initiatives at the Cynthia Woods Mitchell Center for the Arts, where she teaches in the Interdisciplinary Arts Program. www.lacymjohnson.com

A. Van Jordan's collections of poetry include *Rise* (which won a PEN/Oakland Josephine Miles Award), *M-A-C-N-O-L-I-A*, and *Quantum Lyrics*. The poems in *M-A-C-N-O-L-I-A* concern the life of MacNolia Cox, the first African American finalist in the National Spelling Competition in 1936. *Quantum Lyrics* delves into physics, racism, history, and Albert Einstein's work for human rights. Jordan has taught at a number of graduate writing programs, among them the University of Texas at Austin, Warren Wilson College, and the University of Michigan.

Bettina Judd is an artist and poet. She is currently Visiting Assistant Professor in Gender Studies and Africana Studies at Mount Holyoke College. Her book *Patient* won the Hudson Book Prize from Black Lawrence Press and will be published in the fall of 2014. For more information go to www.bettinajudd.com.

Bhanu Kapil lives in Colorado, where she teaches for The Jack Kerouac School of Disembodied Poetics. She is the author of five books, most recently *BAN*, a novel of the race riot, forthcoming from Nightboat Books in 2014.

Helen Klonaris lives, writes, and teaches between the Bay Area and Nassau, Bahamas. Helen is the co-founder and co-director of the *Bahamas Writers Summer Institute,* and the creator of the Gaulin Project, a migratory creative inquiry program in the service of social transformation. Her work has appeared in *Calyx, So to Speak, Proud Flesh,* the *Caribbean Writer, Poui, Small Axe Salon,* and *Anthurium,* among others, and several anthologies. She is co-editing the anthology *Writing the Walls Down* with Amir Rabiyah, forthcoming in the fall through Trans-Genre Press.

Jane Lazarre is the author of many novels, including *Some Place Quite Unknown* and *Inheritance,* as well as the memoirs *The Mother Knot, Wet Earth and Dreams,* and *Beyond the White-* *ness of Whiteness: Memoir of a White Mother of Black Sons.* She directed the undergraduate writing program at Eugene Lang College at the New School for many years, where she taught creative writing and African American literature. She now teaches privately and is engaged in two works in progress, a novel and a collection of poems. Full bio can be found at www.janelazarre.com.

Sandra Lim is the author of *The Wilderness* (W. W. Norton), selected by Louise Glück for the 2013 Barnard Women Poets Prize, and *Loveliest Grotesque* (Kore Press). She is an assistant professor of English at the University of Massachusetts, Lowell.

Casey Llewellyn's work interrogates identity, collectivity, and form. Works for theater include: *The Mechanical Opera Company Presents Zaide!: A Desperate Stab, The Body which is the Town ... , Existing Conditions* (co-written with Claudia Rankine), and *I Love Dick,* an adaptation of the book by Chris Kraus, among others. She's currently working on the novella *Freeing Our Natural Voices / Freeing This Voice / Talking* and a play commissioned by the Foundry Theatre to premier in 2014. Casey studies writing for performance at Brown University with Erik Ehn.

Dawn Lundy Martin is the author of *A Gathering of Matter / A Matter of Gathering,* winner of the Cave Canem Prize; *DISCIPLINE,* which was selected for the Nightbook Books Poetry Prize; *Candy,* a letterpress chapbook from Albion Books; and *The Morning Hour,* selected for the 2003 Poetry Society of America's National Chapbook Fellowship. Her forthcoming collections include *The Main Cause of the Exodus* (O'clock Press) and *Life in a Box is a Pretty Life* (Nightboat Books). She teaches in the Writing Program at the University of Pittsburgh.

Jill Magi works in text, image, and textile, and is the author of *LABOR* (from Nightboat), *SLOT* (Ugly Duckling Presse), *Cadastral Map* (Shearsman), *Torchwood* (Shearsman), *Threads* (Futurepoem), and *Shroud,* a collaboratively written/stitched work with Jen Hofer. She has been a Lower Manhattan Cultural Council resident writer and a resident artist at the Textile Arts Center, Brooklyn. Jill has taught for the MFA programs at Columbia College, the School of the Art Institute of Chicago, and New York University Abu Dhabi.

Soraya Menbrano works for *Poets & Writers,* following a career in arts administration with Cave Canem and LouderARTS. A member of the Williams College class of 2012, she graduated with honors in English for her undergraduate thesis creating a critical framework for the spectrum of performance in American poetry. Originally from the sunniest of states, Soraya now lives in Brooklyn, where she can be found wandering around the park waiting for summer.

Caitie Moore is a poet, curator, and educator living in Brooklyn. She has a forthcoming chapbook from Argos Books. Other poems can be found in *Handsome, MuthaFucka,* and *Strange Machine.*

Tracie Morris is a poet who has worked extensively as a sound poet, bandleader, actor, and multimedia performer. Her sound installations have been presented at the Whitney Biennial, MoMA, Ronald Feldman Gallery, the Silent Barn, and other galleries. Her most recent poetry collection, *Rhyme Scheme,* includes a sound poetry CD. She is currently working on two books, one about the philosopher J. L. Austin and Black vernacular, and a creative project on Ira Aldridge. She is Professor and Coordinator of Performance + Performance Studies at Pratt Institute in Brooklyn.

Isaac Myers, III studied creative writing at The New School, and is originally from Indianapolis, Indiana. His poems have been published in *The Barrow Street Review* and *The Best American Poetry Blog.* He currently lives in New York City, works as an attorney, and aims to publish his first collection of poems and prose pauses, *The Maturation of the Romantic Heart & Mind,* in 2015.

Danielle Pafunda's books include *Natural History Rape Museum* (Bloof Books), *Manhater* (Dusie Press Books), *Iatrogenic: Their Testimonies* (Noemi Press), and *My Zorba* (Bloof Books). She teaches at the University of Wyoming.

Kristin Palm's writing has appeared in *LVNG, Bird Dog, Boog City, Chain, There, Dusie* and the anthology *Bay Poetics* (Faux Press), as well as numerous magazines and newspapers, including *Metropolis, Planning*, and the *Detroit Metro Times*. Her book *The Straits* (two long poems about Detroit, her former hometown) was published in 2008. Kristin currently resides in San Francisco, California.

Jess Row is the author of two collections of short stories, *The Train to Lo Wu* and *Nobody Ever Gets Lost*, and the novel *Your Face in Mine,* which concerns race and plastic surgery. His fiction has appeared three times in *The Best American Short Stories*. His essays and criticism appear often in the *New York Times Book Review, Bookforum, Boston Review, Threepenny Review,* and other venues. He teaches at the College of New Jersey, Vermont College of Fine Arts, and the City University of Hong Kong.

Ira Sadoff's latest book of poems is *True Faith* (BOA Editions). His critical book on poetics and politics is *History Matters*, published in 2009 by the University of Iowa Press.

Evie Shockley is the author of the poetry collections *the new black* and *a half-red sea*, and a critical study, *Renegade Poetics: Black Aesthetics and Formal Innovation in African American Poetry*. Her work has been recognized and supported by Princeton's Holmes National Poetry Prize, the Hurston/Wright Legacy Award in Poetry; fellowships from the ACLS and the Schomburg Center for Research in Black Culture; and residencies from MacDowell and the Millay Colony for the Arts. She teaches English at Rutgers University–New Brunswick.

Tess Taylor grew up in El Cerrito, California. She's the author of *The Forage House* (Red Hen Press). Her chapbook of poems, *The Misremembered World*, was selected by Eavan Boland for the Poetry Society of America. Her work has appeared in *Atlantic Monthly*, the *Boston Review*, the *Times Literary Supplement, Memorious*, and *The New Yorker*. She was the 2010–2011 Amy Clampitt Resident in Lenox, Massachusetts. After seventeen years away, she once again lives in El Cerrito.

Joshua Weiner is the author of three books of poetry, most recently *The Figure of a Man Being*

Swallowed by a Fish (Chicago). He is also the editor of *At the Barriers: On the Poetry of Thom Gunn,* and the poetry editor of *Tikkun* magazine. He is the recipient of a Whiting Writers' Award, the Rome Prize from the American Academy of Arts and Letters, and a fellowship from the Guggenheim Foundation, among others. A professor of English at the University of Maryland, he lives with his family in Washington, DC.

Simone White is the author of the full-length collection *House Envy of All the World* (Factory School, 2010) and the chapbooks *Unrest* (Ugly Duckling Presse/Dossier Series, 2013) and *Dolly* (Q Ave Press, 2008 with the paintings of Kim Thomas). White is a Cave Canem fellow and in 2103 was named as a New American Poet for the Poetry Society of America. She is completing a PhD in English at CUNY Graduate Center and lives in Brooklyn, New York.

Ronaldo V. Wilson, PhD, is the author of *Narrative of the Life of the Brown Boy and the White Man* (University of Pittsburgh), winner of the Cave Canem Poetry Prize, and *Poems of the Black Object* (Futurepoem Books), winner of the Thom Gunn Award and the Asian American Literary Award in Poetry. Co-founder of the Black Took Collective, Wilson is also an assistant professor of Literature at the University of California, Santa Cruz. Forthcoming books include *Farther*

Traveler: Poetry, Prose, Other from Counterpath Press and *Lucy 72* from 1913 Press.

Rachel Zucker is the author of nine books, most recently a memoir, *MOTHERS,* and a double collection of poetry and prose, *The Pedestrians.* Her book *Museum of Accidents* was a finalist for the National Book Critics Circle Award. Zucker lives in New York with her husband and their three sons. She teaches at New York University and is a National Endowment for the Arts fellow.

ARTISTS' BIOGRAPHIES

Jeremiah Barber is a performance and media artist whose work has been featured at the JACK arts space in Brooklyn, The Headlands Center for the Arts, and the Museum of Contemporary Art Chicago. His work attempts to find transcendence through humor, absurdity, and drama by tackling the impractical task, and shouldering the weariness of time. He has received numerous award and residencies and earned his MFA from Stanford University.

Liz Cohen's work has been shown extensively throughout the United States and Europe. In addition to solo exhibitions in New York, Paris, and Stockholm, Ms. Cohen's performance art/photography has been featured at Museum Tinguely in Basel, Switzerland and at Ballroom Marfa, in Marfa, Texas. Ms. Cohen is represented by Salon 94, Galerie Laurent Godin, and David Klein Gallery. She is currently an Artist-In-Residence at the Cranbrook Academy of Art.

Edgar Endress teaches new media and public art at George Mason University. Born in Chile, he has exhibited extensively throughout the Americas, most recently in Medellín, Colombia. His work focuses on syncretism in the Andes, displacement in the Caribbean, and mobile art making practices. In association with Provisions Library (for art and social change), he initiated the Floating Lab Collective that deploys interdisciplinary artists in collaboration with urban communities. He received his MFA in Video Art from Syracuse University. He has received numerous grants and fellowships, including from the Virginia Museum of Fine Arts and the Creative Capital Fund.

Wendy Ewald has for over forty years collaborated in art projects with children, families, women, and teachers in Labrador, Colombia, India, South Africa, Saudi Arabia, Holland, Mexico, and the United States. Starting as documentary investigations of places and communities, Ewald's projects probe questions of identity and cultural differences. In her work with children she encourages them to use cameras to record themselves, their families, and their communities, and to articulate their fantasies and dreams. Ewald herself often makes photographs within the communities she works with and has the children mark or write on her negatives, thereby challenging the concept of who actually makes an image, who is the photographer, who the subject, who is the observer and who the observed. In blurring the distinction of individual authorship and throwing into doubt the artist's intentions, power, and identity, Ewald creates opportunities to look at the meaning and use of photographic images in our lives with fresh perceptions.

Wendy Ewald has received many honors, including a MacArthur Fellowship and grants from the National Endowment for the Arts, The Andy Warhol Foundation, and the Fulbright Commission. She was also a senior fellow at the Vera List Center for Art and Politics at the New School from 2000-2002. She has had solo exhibitions at the International Center of Photography in New York, the Center for Creative Photography in Tucson, the George Eastman House in Rochester, Nederlands Foto Institute in Rotterdam, the Fotomuseum in Wintherthur, Switzerland, and the Corcoran Gallery of American Art among others. Her work was included in the 1997 Whitney Biennial. She has published twelve books, her fifth, a retrospective documenting her projects entitled "Secret Games," was published by Scalo in 2000. "To The Promised land," was published in 2006 to accompany an outdoor installation in Margate, England commissioned by ArtAngel. She is currently an artist in residence at Amherst College where she has taught the class "Collaborative Art: The practice and theory of working with communities" since 2005. "This is Where I Live" (Israel and the West Bank) will be published by MackBooks in 2015.

EJ Hill is a performance artist who continually struggles with the complexity of the body's cultural and historical inheritances and implications. A native of South Central Los Angeles, Mr. Hill's work has been exhibited in Los Angeles, Chicago, New York, Buenos Aires, Salzburg, Berlin, and Tokyo. He received his MFA from the University of California, Los Angeles.

William Pope.L is the recipient of a Guggenheim Fellowship, NEA fellowships, and the USA Fellowship in Visual Arts, among many other awards. He was included in the 2002 Whitney Biennial and is known for his provocative performances, such as his ATM Piece, and his decades-long series of crawls across New York City, commemorated in eRacism, a retrospective which showed at several prominent museums and galleries. The Black Factory, his most recent project, toured the East Coast and the Midwest. He teaches at the University of Chicago.

John Jota Leaños is a social art practitioner who utilizes a range of new media, photography, public art, installation, and performance focusing on the convergence of memory, social space and decolonization. His work has been shown at the Sundance 2010 Film Festival, Cannes Short Corner 07, the 2002 Whitney Biennial, the San Francisco Museum of Modern Art, and the Museum of Contemporary Art, Chicago. Leaños is a Creative Capital Grantee and a Guggenheim Fellow (2013) who has been an artist in residence at the University of California, Santa Barbara in the Center for Chicano Studies (2005), Carnegie Mellon University in the Center for Arts in Society (2003), and the Headlands Center for the Arts (2007). Mr. Leaños is an Associate Professor of Social Documentation at the University of California, Santa Cruz.

Nery Gabriel Lemus was born in Los Angeles, in 1977. His work addresses issues of stereotype and immigration, the intersection of racial and dissociative racism; and the poverty, abuse, and neglect that can lead to the failure of families. Mr. Lemus received his BFA at Art Center College of Design in Pasadena, and his MFA at the California Institute of the Arts, and also attended the Skowhegan School of Painting and Sculpture in Maine. He is a recipient of a COLA Fellowship Grant from the Department of Cultural Affairs, Los Angeles, and the Rema Hort Mann Foundation Fellowship Award. He is represented by Charlie James Gallery in Los Angeles.

Charles McGill is a multidisciplinary artist whose work has been exhibited in group and solo exhibitions in museums and galleries in the United States and Europe, been reviewed in the *New York Times*, the *Village Voice*, and *Art in America*, as well as being included in numerous public and private collections. A recipient of an Art Matters and New York Foundation for the Arts grant, as well as fellowships from the Ford Foundation and the Virginia Center for the Creative Arts, he is also a former artist-in-residence at the Museum of Arts and Design in NYC. Mr. McGill received an MFA from the Maryland Institute College of Art and is a professor of drawing and painting at colleges in New York and Connecticut; he is represented by the Pavel Zoubok Gallery in Manhattan.

Amitis Motevalli was born in Iran and moved to the US in 1977, prior to the revolution. She explores the cultural resistance and survival of people living in poverty, conflict, and war. Her working-class immigrant background drives her art, which contests stereotypical beliefs about people living in diaspora and criticizes the violence of dominance and occupation, while invoking the significance of secular grass roots struggle. Through various media and collaborative public art, Motevalli works with transnational Muslims, across economic and political borders, to create an active and resistant cultural discourse. She currently lives and works in Los Angeles.

Dread Scott makes revolutionary art to propel history forward. In 1989, the entire US Senate denounced his artwork and President Bush declared it "disgraceful" because of its use of the American flag. His work is exhibited internationally, including in the Whitney Museum, MoMA/PS1, Pori Art Museum (Finland), BAM Fisher, and galleries and street corners across the country. He is a recipient of a Creative Capital Grant and his work is included in the collection of the Whitney Museum.

Alice Shaw is an artist and educator based in San Francisco. Her photographs have been shown internationally; locally, she is represented by Gallery 16 in San Francisco. A graduate of the San Francisco Art Institute and a recipient of a 2002 Art Council Award, Ms. Shaw often infuses personal/reflexive documentation with humor and poignancy. Her work is included in the San Francisco Museum of Modern Art and other collections. She has practiced photography for over 25 years and she has been a visiting lecturer at UC Davis, UC Santa Cruz, UC Berkeley, San Francisco State University, The California College of Art, and the San Francisco Art Institute. Her book, *People Who Look Like Me*, was published in April of 2006.

Kyungmi Shin, a sculptor and installation artist, received an MFA from UC Berkeley. Her works have been exhibited at Berkeley Art Museum, Sonje Art Museum (Korea), Japanese American National Museum, and the Torrance Art Museum. She has received grants from the California Community Foundation, Durfee Grant, Pasadena City Individual Artist Fellowship, and LA Cultural Affairs Artist in Residence program. Since 2004, she has created numerous public art projects across the nation, including Los Angeles, Winston-Salem, Chicago, and Norfolk.

Ian Weaver is a Chicago-based visual artist and Instructor at the School of the Art Institute of Chicago. He received his MFA in Visual Art from Washington University in St. Louis, and his work has been seen at the South Bend Museum of Art, the Saint Louis Art Museum, Illinois State Museum, and the Kemper Art Museum. He has been a recipient of numerous residencies, including Yaddo and the Millay Colony, and his awards include grants from Artadia and the Joan Mitchell foundations.

Jay Wolke is an artist and educator living in Chicago, Illinois. He has authored three photographic monographs: *All Around the House: Photographs of American-Jewish Communal Life* (Art Institute of Chicago, 1998), *Along the Divide: Photographs of the Dan Ryan Expressway* (Center for American Places, 2004), and *Architecture of Resignation: Photographs from the Mezzogiorno* (Center for American Places—Columbia College Press, 2011). Mr. Wolke attended Washington University, St. Louis (BFA) and the Institute of Design, IIT (MS). His photographs are in the permanent collections of the New York MOMA, the Art Institute of Chicago, and the San Francisco MOMA, among others. He is currently a Professor and Chair of the Art and Design Department, Columbia College Chicago.

ACKNOWLEDGMENTS

Claudia thanks Allison Coudert and John Lucas.

Max thanks the laborer in the white boiler suit.

Beth thanks Rattawut Lapcharoensap and Adrian Shirk. Adrian's work on the manuscript was a model of care and intelligence. Thanks also to Caldera Arts and the Ucross Foundation for time and space to work on the collection.

Deepest gratitude to Rebecca Wolff and Douglas Kearney.

All artwork has been provided courtesy of the artist(s); except William Pope.L's *White People Are A Desalination Plant in Puerto Rico*, courtesy of the artist and Mitchell-Innes & Nash, NY.

FENCE BOOKS

OTTOLINE Prize
Inter Arma   Lauren Shufran

Motherwell & Alberta Prize
Negro League Baseball   Harmony Holiday
living must bury   Josie Sigler
Aim Straight at the Fountain and Press Vaporize   Elizabeth Marie Young
Unspoiled Air   Kaisa Ullsvik Miller
The Cow   Ariana Reines
Practice, Restraint   Laura Sims
A Magic Book   Sasha Steensen
Sky Girl   Rosemary Griggs
The Real Moon of Poetry and Other Poems   Tina Brown Celona
Zirconia   Chelsey Minnis

Fence Modern Poets Series
In the Laurels, Caught   Lee Ann Brown
Eyelid Lick   Donald Dunbar
Nick Demske   Nick Demske
Duties of an English Foreign Secretary   Macgregor Card
Star in the Eye   James Shea
Structure of the Embryonic Rat Brain   Christopher Janke
The Stupefying Flashbulbs   Daniel Brenner
Povel   Geraldine Kim
The Opening Question   Prageeta Sharma
Apprehend   Elizabeth Robinson
The Red Bird   Joyelle McSweeney

National Poetry Series
Your Invitation to a Modest Breakfast   Hannah Gamble
A Map Predetermined and Chance   Laura Wetherington
The Network   Jena Osman
The Black Automaton   Douglas Kearney
Collapsible Poetics Theater   Rodrigo Toscano

Anthologies & Critical Works

Not for Mothers Only: Contemporary Poets on Child-Getting & Child-Rearing	Catherine Wagner & Rebecca Wolff, editors
A Best of Fence: The First Nine Years, Volumes 1 & 2	Rebecca Wolff and Fence Editors, editors

Poetry

A Book Beginning What and Ending Away	Clark Coolidge
88 Sonnets	Clark Coolidge
Mellow Actions	Brandon Downing
Percussion Grenade	Joyelle McSweeney
Coeur de Lion	Ariana Reines
June	Daniel Brenner
English Fragments A Brief History of the Soul	Martin Corless-Smith
The Sore Throat & Other Poems	Aaron Kunin
Dead Ahead	Ben Doller
My New Job	Catherine Wagner
Stranger	Laura Sims
The Method	Sasha Steensen
The Orphan & Its Relations	Elizabeth Robinson
Site Acquisition	Brian Young
Rogue Hemlocks	Carl Martin
19 Names for Our Band	Jibade-Khalil Huffman
Infamous Landscapes	Prageeta Sharma
Bad Bad	Chelsey Minnis
Snip Snip!	Tina Brown Celona
Yes, Master	Michael Earl Craig
Swallows	Martin Corless-Smith
Folding Ruler Star	Aaron Kunin
The Commandrine & Other Poems	Joyelle McSweeney
Macular Hole	Catherine Wagner
Nota	Martin Corless-Smith
Father of Noise	Anthony McCann
Can You Relax in My House	Michael Earl Craig
Miss America	Catherine Wagner

Fiction

Prayer and Parable: Stories	Paul Maliszewski
Flet: A Novel	Joyelle McSweeney
The Mandarin	Aaron Kunin

Fence is a biannual journal of art, poetry, fiction, and Other, in continuous publication since 1998. In 2001 Fence Books launched and has published six to eight titles per year. Fence runs three book prizes: The Ottoline Prize, for a book of poems by a woman who has previously published a book of poems; The Fence Modern Poets Series, for a poet writing in English; and the Fence Modern Prize in Prose. Fence is a participating publisher in the National Poetry Series. Fence also publishes The Constant Critic, an online journal for poetry criticism, and La Presse, a book-series of contemporary French poetry in translation. For more about our authors, titles, and activities visit fenceportal.org.